Susan Joyce

THE LAND OF LOST CONTENT

Into my heart an air that kills
From yon far country blows:
What are those blue remembered hills,
What spires, what farms are those?
That is the land of lost content,
I see it shining plain,
The happy highways where I went,
And cannot come again.

A.E. Housman

1

Erin opened her eyes, stretched, yawned, raised both hands to her wild flame red hair and ruffled the sleep out of her head and the lingering echoes of the cock crow from her ears.

"I hear you . . . I hear you," she murmured as she yawned again, slid her legs out from under the rough woollen blanket and placed her bare feet gingerly onto the cold bare stone floor. Shivering slightly she pulled the thin cotton night shift tightly around her breasts and made her way over to a large chipped enamel ewer and bowl that sat on a rough wooden table. She lifted the ewer and tipped out a stream of crystal clear water into the bowl, then, after a long moment's delicious hesitation, dipped both her hands in, leaned forward and splashed the water over her face and neck.

Minutes later, her early morning ablutions complete and dressed in a rough calico dress, hose and sturdy shoes she made her way to the rustic kitchen and began to prepare the morning meal for her employer, William Gaunt, his wife and their seven sons.

As she busied herself with the preparations for breakfast she hummed a little tune to herself. It was one that her father, who had been widowed when she was not yet three, had often sang her to sleep with. The melody, as it often did on quiet mornings with the rest of the household still in their beds, brought back memories of her 'other' life; a life far away from crack of dawn risings and seemingly endless rounds of near drudgery.

Her father, Dermot O'Conner had been a fairly prominent 17th Century Cork businessman with a respectable property portfolio and her early years had been spent in relative comfort. Dermot was a doting father to his only child. He was, unfortunately, also a heavy drinker – a slowly snowballing habit brought on by his wife's early death that would, in time, turn into full blown alcoholism.

As his addiction grew Dermot's business acumen began to

melt away. He made a number of risky decisions that left him badly out of pocket. Then, in an attempt at a quick fix solution, he turned his increasingly unsteady hand to gambling. Disaster: disaster that was soon to mushroom into total calamity. His property lawyer, Walter Coppinger, rode to his rescue. Walter offered a hefty loan secured against Dermot's remaining property portfolio. Dermot, befuddled with drink gratefully and with effusive thanks, accepted. The problem, as Dermot was soon to discover, was that the loan agreement document was in fact a convoluted bill of sale for all his property. Walter wasted no time in collecting.

Erin, now a budding 17, was ignorant of the calamity that had landed on her poor father's shoulders. For Dermot's part, his shame at throwing away his only child's inheritance became unbearable. Within three months he drank himself into mental and physical oblivion.

At her father's funeral, Walter offered his humble and sincere commiserations on her untimely loss. He also proposed marriage. Erin was appalled. Whenever Walter had visited her father on business, his openly lustful looks had left her repulsed. When he proposed marriage she had craned her head back, looked up into his sallow gaunt face and given him a straight answer. She would rather marry the devil himself than the man, who she suspected, had cheated her dear father out of his property.

Walter's face had betrayed no emotion. He had inclined his head turned on his heel and left. Three days later bailiffs arrived with a court order and threw her out onto the street.

Destitute and penniless, Erin, for the first time in her young life, was faced with the harsh realities of existence. She had no roof over her head and no learned skills to which she could turn in order to make some sort of living. In desperation she approached a number of her late father's old business associates for help. Unfortunately Dermot's long-term alcoholism and the way it had affected his personality had led most of these God fearing men to turn their backs on him.

One man alone had shown some pity by offering temporary shelter as she sought some kind of employment. He had also gone a little out of his way to contact a friend who was a leading citizen in the little coastal town of Baltimore, some fifty or so miles to the south, to ask if perhaps there might be some sort of menial opening for a young orphaned girl from a good background. Two weeks later a letter had arrived offering a position of maid to an English settler family who lived and worked in a small well-established fishing community that operated from Baltimore's cove.

"They are English settlers and Protestants," her benefactor had said. "But they are decent hard working people and I think you should accept." What he hadn't added was that a distance of fifty miles would remove her far enough from sight and mind that he and the rest of her late father's business associates would not need to feel any sense of guilt if confronted by her plight.

William Gaunt was a decent man. He, his wife and their seven young sons lived in one of the 26 thatched cottages that ringed the cove. The work was hard and especially so for a young woman who had never had to get her hands dirty before. She cooked and cleaned for the family and gradually, over a period of several weeks, she grew to accept that her old life was gone. She also met the man who would steal her heart.

James Pallow was an orphaned 20-year-old fisherman born to English settlers. He and his younger brother, Thomas, were part of the small Baltimore fishing fleet, the men of which earned their living catching pilchards around the waters of Inisherkin Island, Clear Island and Roaringwater Bay.

She had seen him from a distance going about some business or other several times over the last few weeks, but had never been close enough to get a really good look at him. What she had seen though certainly caught her attention. He carried his tallish, stocky, broad-shouldered frame with an air of confidence, that to her innocent mind, bordered on the sin of arrogance – an impression fuelled further by the way his fair haired head and strong chin seemed to go before him as he strode about his business.

All this from afar; and then it happened. She had just left the little bakery shop that nestled beneath the walls of the 16th Century castle Du'n na Se'ad – *The Fort Of The Jewels* – a squat tower house that looked down on the little cove, its clutch of cottages and the moored fishing fleet, and had made to turn a corner when he literally bumped into her. She had blushed to the roots of her flaming red hair when their bodies collided and two strong calloused hands had lightly grasped her bare upper arms. She had stammered some sort of apology and in reply he had actually introduced himself and then asked her name! She was momentarily lost for words and his wide-set light blue eyes had twinkled in his weather-tanned face as he saw the reaction his question had caused.

"Erin O'Connor," she had finally replied as her heart skipped a beat.

"Ah. You are Irish then." She quickly gained composure.

"Yes;" she shot back, "and you are an English land grabber then." His lips folded back to show two even rows of teeth that gleamed brightly against the brown skin of his face. He smiled a genuine smile as he looked deeply into her emerald green eyes.

"And an Irish girl with a flaming nature as well as a flaming head." It was now her turn to smile; then she ducked by him and had to stop herself several times from glancing back, as she almost skipped all the way back to the Gaunt's cottage.

They had bumped into each other several times over the next two weeks and with each *accidental* meeting she warmed more to his ready smile and gently teasing way with words.

He was English and a heretic, a combination which, before she had met him, would certainly have meant that she would never have even dreamed of even speaking to him.

But then again, she thought, he wasn't really English because he had been born in Ireland, so he couldn't really be all bad, could he? *But*, said a little voice in her head, *what about him being a Protestant then; that wasn't a little thing was it?* She had shrugged her slim shoulders and whispered: "So, it's not as if I'm in love with him or anything . . . is it?" But then, almost before the words had faded on the air a blush to rival the one when they had first met laid the lie – and was immediately followed by a soft breathy and startled: "Oh gentle Jesus, Mary and Joseph . . ."

Under the oil lamp's dancing flame the ruby ring shed a warm, but deceptive glow – for in truth it was as cold as the heart of its wearer.

Lawyer, magistrate and wealthy property owner Walter Coppinger's thin lips twisted into a tight rictus of a smile as the goose quill pen scratched its way across the coarse vellum paper. Finished, he then added the date *21s May in the year of Our Lord 1631,* placed the pen on the desk in front of him, straightened the ring on his left hand third finger and studied the result of his handiwork. "Perfect," he muttered. And the thin smile widened.

In the morning he would take the document to the authorities in Cork and lodge it as evidence in his counter action against his orphaned niece, Jeanette Grant, who was claiming that he had cheated her out of her inheritance. She was right of course; but to Walter's mind that was totally irrelevant. He had taken a great deal of time and trouble to plan and execute the clever deception and he was immovably determined that that time and trouble would not be wasted.

Three years earlier, when she was 14, he had given her in marriage to a wealthy 80 year old client. Eighteen months into the grotesque union the girl's husband had died and magistrate, lawyer and moneylender, Walter, who had graciously agreed to manage the estate for his young unworldly niece, had succeeded in diverting much of it into his own coffers.

He rolled the vellum into a neat tube, tied it with a length of blue ribbon and pushing his chair back eased his lanky frame to its feet. Yes, he had had to wait for the old fool to die; but with a few judicious strokes of the pen, he had managed to relieve his poor widowed niece of the full burden of inherited wealth.

And yes, he thought to himself, *she will pay dearly for putting me to the inconvenience of a court case. When I win I'll make sure that the dear girl will soon find herself back before the magistrates on a serious criminal charge.* And he would win, of that there was no doubt, for Walter Coppinger was a man of great influence in his home county of Cork, where nobbled juries, forged documents and trumped up charges were his stock in trade.

Then, once he had removed this particular minor irritant, he would be able to concentrate all his attention on the one major irritant that had cast a long and dark shadow over almost half his 50 years of life.

From his seat in the little hookers gunwale James glanced up at the sound of the sea gull's lonely cry. He watched with an almost detached air, as with blood red wings it slit the early summer evening sunset sky. He watched and smiled thinly. Tomorrow the pilchards would run and this solitary bird would be joined by a hundred of its kind – a squawking tumult of grey and white diving bodies and gaping beaks.

He leaned forward and with practised ease coiled the rope on top of his portion of the tarred hemp net that lay in the hooker's beached stern. Finished he lingered for a few minutes savouring the solitude and the way the lowering sun turned the water in the bay to copper tinged molten gold. And the colour reminded him of flaming red hair. She was in his thoughts a hundred times each day and every night he dropped off to sleep with her lovely innocent face with its entrancing emerald eyes and perfect little snub nose banded with freckles, indelibly imprinted on his mind's eye.

There were a few other girls from the cove and in the village above that looked down on the fishers' little cottages, but none were anything like her. She was fiery, yet vulnerable; educated yet oddly unsophisticated. So very different from how he pictured girls from the big cities of Dublin or Cork would look and act; girls who would almost certainly look upon a common fisherman with nought but haughty disdain. He sat and quietly marvelled at the turn of fate or chance that had led to their paths crossing - and smiled again.

As they bobbed gently on the evening tide the other four hookers - three with their own portions of the net and without the weight of his body - rose and fell in gentle unison, and with each fall their keels grated softly on the small cove's shingle beach. As the sound slowly seeped into his head he reluctantly turned his thoughts back to practical matters and softly muttered:

"Patience ladies, the morrow will soon be come." He smiled once more and patted his hooker's gunwale, before climbing out, turning on his heel and striding off towards the little necklace of rough cottages that ringed the Cove.

2

Walter Coppinger almost always dressed head to toe in black. It lent him, he knew, an air of dark menace that marked him out from among the *ordinary* rabble. His only concession to the appearance of wealth was the ruby ring, which, it was whispered, got its colour from the condensed blood of all the unfortunates he had squeezed the life out of in court. Walter had picked up on this story and was quietly pleased as fear was a good emotion to plant into the minds of those who thought they might oppose him. His troublesome niece was one such. She had been served with legal papers demanding that she attend court to answer charges he had brought against her and now she had the temerity to pay him a visit at his Bandon house that very morning.

In the privacy of his study she had been in the process of reviling him for a blackguard and a thief, when he had smiled, raised a huge knobbly right fist and smashed her full in the mouth, sending her tumbling backwards and down, where her head came into thumping contact against the leg of his desk.

He had smiled again as he looked down at the unconscious form with the bloodied mouth and shattered teeth. Smiled, straightened his ruby ring and raised a long nailed finger to score a long scratch down his right cheek.

"Oh my," he had muttered, "attacked by a mad woman in my own home." Then: "It was all I could do to save myself from serious injury," he had added, as he rehearsed his reasons for defending himself before she was inevitably found guilty of assault and thrown into prison.

Satisfied with the rehearsal he had taken a linen handkerchief from a pocket then, in order to make the injury seem more serious, he had smeared the drops of blood that had formed on his cheek before throwing the semi conscious girl out into the cobbled street and making his way to the sheriff's office to lay his wholly justified complaint.

Now, in the early afternoon, he approached a rough tavern

that sat in a small mean back street just off Kinsale harbour. He pushed open the door, stooped and made his way through into a smoke hazed, low ceilinged room that was filled with a dozen or so shabbily dressed chattering men.

As a strong smell of stale sweat assailed his nostrils he wrinkled his nose and allowed a look of disdain to cloud his hawkish features. The babble of voices suddenly stilled. Stood in a little island of space in the middle of the room, his height, his dress and the look on his face as he surveyed the dregs before him had an impact. The drinkers, to a man, recognized the entrance of a personage of substance and one rarely to be found in such mean surroundings. This, they sensed, was someone who was obviously intent on carrying out a mission of some delicacy.

Walter, ignoring the stares, glanced slowly around the dingy room until his dark eyes fastened onto the object of his secret visit. The man, who was sat on his own at a table in a shadowy corner, returned the eye contact and nodded.

"Mister Coppinger," said the man with a note of respect in his voice as Walter strode over, inclined his head and slowly folded himself onto a rough chair opposite the slight, middle aged weasel eyed and raggedly dressed man.

"Looking as prosperous as ever was sir," the other said, taking in Walter's rich clothing. Walter didn't waste a smile.

"And you William Cleary," he replied casually, "are looking the same slit purse gutter rat that last I saw cowering before the magistrates in Cork a year past." Cleary's narrow set eyes hardened at the cold words, but his mouth split into a black-toothed, gap-toothed smile. Walter Coppinger was not a man that you lightly took offence to. He was a man, William knew, with dark connections and a history of calling on the services of all manner of murderous thugs when trumped up lawsuits failed to achieve his aims. He was also known to take a great and perverse delight in handing out beatings personally – particularly against women. Cleary knew of an instance involving a young Cork woman, Ellen ni' Driscoll, who had sought legal advice from Walter Coppinger after coming into a considerable inheritance. Walter, true to form, altered the deeds to her estate by simply removing her name and replacing it with his own.

Ellen had complained, but to no avail. His power with juries was just too great and she had lost her case against him. At one stage, heavily pregnant and virtually penniless, she had begged Walter for some money to tide her over. His response was immediate and horrific – he battered her senseless and had her thrown over a cliff. By some miracle Ellen survived but her baby did not.

No, Cleary decided; Walter Coppinger was not a man to trifle with.

"As you say sir," William said meekly. "And how may I be of service?" Walter came straight to the point.

"You have dealings with the provisioning of privateers; men who rove the seas in search of plunder. I need to meet with one such." William's face took on a puzzled look.

"Privateers you say? Not I sir, you are surely mistaken. Dealing with such as those can be a hanging offence!" Walter leaned forward and spoke coldly and slowly.

"And refusing to deal with me will lead to hanging being a merciful release from this vale of tears." Cleary swallowed hard and cleared his throat.

"There is sir," he said, "so I am told, two such vessels anchored off Rosscarbery Bay by Glandore." Walter nodded.

"And who captains these vessels?"

"A renegade born of Scotland and plying his pirate trade out of Algiers – so I am told."

"And this villain's name?"

"Robert Fleck – so I am told. Although, again – so tis said – having renounced Christianity and turned Turk, he now uses the name Morat Rais." Walter nodded.

"Good. Get word to this captain Fleck or Morat Rais and tell him that there is a gentleman of means who wishes to engage his services in a venture that will gain him handsome profit."

William Cleary ran his tongue over suddenly dry lips and tried hard not to let his unease show as the hulking black bearded figure sat opposite him all but blocked out the fading early evening light that dripped into the vessel's tiny cabin. He tried hard; but was unable to dampen a nervous facial tic. Nor could he erase the scene from his mind that had turned his blood cold when he had come aboard the pirate ship. Right there in front of him he had seen them, practising their infernal fighting moves. They wore baggy cotton trousers, shirts, sleeveless waistcoats and bright red caftans. Folded around their waists was a long red scarf that held their weapons, prime among which was a vicious razor sharp yatagan, a short deadly blade shaped in an exotic double curve. He knew who they were. They were the most feared fighting force in the world . . . . The legendary Turkish Janissaries.

The image in Cleary's head suddenly hazed then disappeared as the other occupant of the cabin demanded: "And who is this gentleman of means?"

Cleary was always on the lookout for a quick profit, be it from a snatched purse or a sudden cudgel rap to the back of an unsuspecting head. Surprise was his stock in trade; but now, face to face with this huge bearded questioner, his coward's heart quailed.

"His name is Walter Coppinger sir. He is a man of high standing throughout the whole county."

"Standing how?" Cleary swallowed nervously. The promised five pounds that awaited his return with news of a mission accomplished, seemed suddenly very far away. His apparent ignorance of Fleck had been a blind to cover his own tracks. He knew of Fleck all right and knew of his current occupation. And it was this that was worrying him. Supposing he himself ended up in some filthy slave market!

"He is a lawyer, magistrate and wealthy property owner sir." Fleck raised a huge ring bedecked right hand and absently scratched his bearded chin. He had made many enemies over the years and there were any number of people who would cheer to see him dancing on the end of a rope. Caution was called for.

"A lawyer, magistrate and wealthy property owner you say?"

"Aye sir, the very same sir." Fleck's dark eyes narrowed.

"And what, pray tell, would a man of the law be wanting from the likes of Morat Rais?" William shrugged.

"That I can't say sir, only that I am charged to relate that your meeting with him could lead to a substantial profit for yourself sir." Fleck was intrigued. In his occupation the words 'substantial profit' were words that demanded earnest attention. His two vessels were almost provisioned and within a day or two he would be catching an early morning tide and be off about his business. Until then, he decided, it would do no harm to listen to what this man of 'high standing' had to say. But first he needed some reassurance. He raised his right hand again and with a crooked forefinger beckoned the other. Eager to please, the small man obeyed but as he leaned forward the huge hand opened and thick corded fingers clamped around his throat.

"I could," said Fleck casually, "snap your scrawny neck." Cleary's rheumy eyes bulged and opened wide with panic and the increasing pressure of the pirate's iron grip. "Indeed," added Fleck in a soft almost disinterested voice, "I *will* snap your filthy neck if you tell me false; if you seek to lead me into a trap." William tried to garble a reply. Fleck cocked his huge head to one side

"What? What say you?" The pressure eased and the big man's hand opened.

"Not I sir, not I!" croaked the other, as with a grimy, black finger nailed hand he rubbed his throat. "I tell you true sir, as I knows it."

"True you say?"

"Aye, Gospel truth sir!" Fleck nodded. He knew Cleary's kind. The man would sell his mother into a poxy whorehouse for the price of a flagon of ale, but he had a *reputation* to maintain. His chosen *career* would suffer should the word get about that he could not be trusted as an *honest* criminal. That, Fleck knew – and the fact that the man was a snivelling coward. The privateer nodded slowly.

"So be it then. Bring this gentleman of high standing here to me at 10 of the clock on the morrow."

3

As she forced the brush through her rebellious hair Erin wrinkled her nose in annoyance at her mane's contrary nature. No matter what she tried to do to tame it, it always seemed to win. She sighed lightly in front of the little cracked mirror then put thoughts of savage scissor cuts away for another day. Instead, she thought *He will be here within the hour;* and as she thought it, a little flutter of anticipation in the pit of her stomach launched a roseate flush up and into her cheeks.

The elder of the boys, George and Jonathan, had been baiting her mercilessly at the table for the past two days about her new beau. "He smells of dead fish!" said George.

"Yes, dead fish," chipped in Jonathan, the younger at twelve to his brother's thirteen, "fish that has been dead for twenty seven years!" And each time that they tried to embarrass her Helen Gaunt, with the memory of first love still fresh in her mind even after almost fifteen years of marriage, rode to Erin's rescue and chided them into obedient silence. She would then lower her knitting, nod gently in Erin's direction and the smitten girl would blush, smile shyly, lower her eyes.

In the mirror, her mouth formed a little moue of annoyance with the result of her brushing. She sighed lightly again, then turning from the glass, sat quietly for a while and reflected on the way their budding relationship was developing. At first she had been confused by the tumbling emotions that threatened to overwhelm her young head. He was a Protestant, a heretic. He was almost English, the offspring of land grabbing newcomers; newcomers that had stolen the very birthright of her fellow Irishmen and women. These were truisms that she had heard repeated many times as she grew up in an exclusive Irish environment. But were they truths?

On their now regular walks she had listened to him as he casually spoke of the history of the 'newcomers'. How his late parents, along with others of their generation had been all but thrown out of England due to their fierce radical Calvinist views which were totally at odds with the political and religious establishment of the day. Their leader, the late Reverend Thomas

Crooke, in an effort to secure a place where his followers could practice their religion without fear of persecution, had paid a substantial sum of money some 20 years earlier to a local impoverished Gaelic chieftain, Fineen O'Driscoll, to secure a long term lease which gave them tenancy of the area around *The Fort of The Jewels* and the Cove that led out to Inisherkin island, Clear island and Roaringwater Bay.

Crooke had then brought in English West Country fishermen who could use their advanced Cornish processing techniques to turn the settlement into a thriving base for the capture and ultimate distribution of the fruits of the sea.

It was these legitimate settlers James explained who had begun fishing and built and manned the plant that processed the catches from the vast shoals of pilchards that regularly ran along the coast. She had found out from him that the work was hard and dirty and most of the men and a number of the woman in the little village put in a full six day shift, either in netting or processing the catches.

At the plant, known as the fish palace, where the catches were salted ready for shipment some workers were employed to chip large blocks of salt with pickaxes, while others washed the preserving salt from the last month's catch. When ready for packing the fish were crammed into huge casks and false lids – slightly smaller than the mouth of the casks – were forced down by weights until the valuable lamp oil was squeezed out. Once the oil had been harvested the pilchards were then re-packed ready for shipment to far off – and to the villager's uneducated minds – such exotic places, as France, Italy and indeed, the New World!

James himself, along with his brother and several of the village men, spent their long working week at the oars of their small boats where they strained every muscle and sinew in pursuit of the flashing silver shoals.

No, she decided, these people were not land grabbers; not 'usurpers'. True they were heretics; but there were worse things in life than these honest toilers. Many worse things and many worse people – much worse people. This last thought brought on a little shiver of revulsion as she ran through her mind the casual way in which James had mentioned *that* man's name.

They had been sitting on a rough bench outside the little bakery where they had first bumped into each other and he had been telling her more about the little community's history. The day was pleasantly warm and sat next to him, eyes lightly closed and face tilted towards the welcome sun, she was not really listening to what he was saying, but rather to the deep masculine timbre of his voice – when her eyes snapped open in sudden shock. "Walter Coppinger," he had said.

"Who!" She had gasped as the detested name swiftly reined in her drifting mind. Taken slightly aback by the tone of her voice he had frowned and said "Walter Coppinger, he is the one who has tried for years to oust our people and take the village and the refinery for himself." The blood had drained from her face. Alarmed, he had reached out and placed an arm around her shoulders.

"You know this man?" he had asked. She told him everything and his face had hardened.

"He will not harm you here." A cast iron statement delivered with a slight pause for emphasis between each word. She had leaned closer to him and allowed his muscular arm to draw her even closer still. "No," she had replied softly, "I know he can not."

Her reverie was suddenly halted by a bold knock on the door to her little room.

"Come Jonathan," she said with a mock serious edge to her voice, for she knew the knock and was ready for his teasing. The door opened and a pale, gap-toothed freckled face grinned at her round the door jamb.

"He is here, your smelly fisherman," he chimed. Erin growled and made as if to grab the boy, who shrieked in mock terror and leapt back from the door frame to lapse into a little fit of giggles.

"Beast!" she roared as she stalked after him.

"Jonathan!" William Gaunt's stern voice brought his young son to an instant skidding stop as followed by Erin, the boy burst into a sitting room that because of the number of bodies in it seemed tiny and cramped.

"Behave boy, we have a visitor!"

"Yes father, sorry." William allowed the ghost of a smile to crinkle the sides of his mouth. Of all his sons, pale, sickly Jonathan was his favourite.

From her seat at the rough table Helen also smiled and then beckoned the boy to an empty chair by her side.

James, with his face freshly scrubbed and unruly hair partially trained into place, stood loosely to attention with his large hands, fingers interlaced, held awkwardly in front of him. He had never been 'a-courting' before and in the crowded room with so many eyes on him he felt a little ill at ease.

It wasn't as though he was totally inexperienced. With no-one to answer to he had, on three occasions, along with Thomas, visited some of the less godly establishments that were to be found around Glandore harbour.

They had imbibed a little and even, on one occasion, engaged the services of two ladies of ill repute. Thomas had crowed about it for weeks; while more reserved James had prayed for forgiveness and privately agonized lest his 'equipment' might fester and fall off as some of the older fishermen had, with deadly serious faces, told him it might.

Erin, who was not much more than a child herself smiled inwardly as she took in his childlike stance and obvious unease. Outside, when they were alone, he was totally in charge; here though, in unfamiliar surroundings and in an unfamiliar situation it was a very different matter. Helen too noticed his discomfort and with a mature woman's understanding of such matters, she moved to put him more at ease.

"So, mister Pallow, tell me, will they run tomorrow?" James nodded.

"Yes mam, they will – and early too, if I am not mistaken."

"Early, you say?" James nodded again.

"Yes, very early mam." Helen's face took on a mock serious look and she added a hard edge to her voice.

"Ah, well then young man, you best be sure to have our charge back well before the cock's first crow!" James, relieved at the gentle joshing, grinned.

"I will mam, on that you may rely."

Outside, Erin slipped her hand above his crooked elbow and laid it lightly on his muscled forearm. It was perhaps a forward thing to do, but then, they were walking out.

She glanced shyly up into his profile. He glanced down and smiled.

"And so, Miss O'Conner, would it be dancing you're after on this foine night?" She laughed gaily at his clumsy attempt at an Irish accent.

"Perhaps," she said glancing down, "if it would be wise to chance those great clodding feet treading on my own!" He grinned.

"Certainly unwise, I think," he said lightly, stopping for a moment and raising his right foot for critical inspection. He had never in his young life attempted to dance to any music and let alone with a girl in his arms.

Her tinkling laughter sent a little thrill racing along his spine and as they resumed their leisurely stroll up towards the village proper and the little cluster of stalls that were nestling beneath the walls of the *Fort Of The Jewels*, he leaned a little closer to her in order to breathe in the scent of her freshly washed hair

In a few days time it would be the Feast of Saint John, Midsummer's Day and Fair Day, the one day of the year when the villagers down at the cove were able to put aside briefly their lives of grinding toil. The one day when they could start to look forward to the true beginning of summer; when the days were longer, the nights shorter and after a dark bleak winter spirits gently soared like released doves into a sparkling blue sky. On that day, June 24th, the stalls ranged around the walls of the Fort would be decked with bunting and the air would be alive with the shouts of hucksters, showmen, musicians and the heady strains of music.

And later, as the sun went down, all the young people of the village proper and those from down by the cove would gather round lit bonfires and take turns in leaping over the dying flames in a ritual that ensured good fortune and kept evil spirits at bay.

As they drew abreast of the cluster of stalls Erin sensed a slight but definite tremor of tension enter the forearm beneath her fingers. She glanced up and saw that his eyes were not focused ahead, but to the right, towards the nearby steeple of Tullagh Parish Church with its odd weathervane in the shape of an open-mouthed fish.

"James?" she asked softly. He turned his head back towards her and a sad little smile blossomed on his lips.

"The church," he said simply.

"The church?"

"My mother and father are buried in the graveyard there." She nodded. He had told her about his mother's tragic early death due to complications that had set in after she had delivered his brother, Thomas, and of their father's drowning some two year's ago in a sudden squall out in Roaring Water Bay.

"Will you take me to see them?" she asked. He nodded.

Set on the brow of a hill facing the ocean, the tiny graveyard was protected from the relentless battering of Atlantic winds by the encircling arms of a rough hewn stone wall; and although built high enough to protect the 30 or so simple gravestones from the wind, the wall offered no real protection to the living.

As they stood in solemn silence in front of the final resting place of James' parents – which were placed close to the wall and overlooking the bay below – a strong breeze played around their bare heads causing their hair to dance like fronds of red and gold kelp caressed by the restless sea. And with the breeze there also came into this place of life lost a reminder of organic life in the form of the salty tang of rotting seaweed, the odour of livestock and above all, the fishy stench that was wafted up from the fish processing plant.

"Do you miss them greatly?" Erin said quietly as she looked down at the flat gravestones with their brief, compact summaries of life. James nodded.

"My father, yes, he was a good man."

"And your mother?" he nodded again.

"Of course, even though I don't remember her, I was very young when she died." Now it was her turn to nod.

"Yes, we have both suffered greatly. My mother and father are gone and your own also." At her side, James reached out and without raising his eyes from the twin graves, enfolded her tiny hand in his.

After some thirty seconds he lifted his eyes from the graves and to catch her attention, swung their enclosed hands back and forth. She smiled softly and sensing that he wished to return to the land of the living, she led him gently back they way they had come.

As they passed in front of the church door, she reflected briefly on her own situation. She was a catholic and all here in the village were not. A short time ago she would have looked upon this place of worship with cool detachment. Now, she accepted it and the right of those who passed through its door to proclaim their faith in the manner of their own upbringing. Even so, because church attendance was a legal and moral duty she still felt a slight unease as she sat in the pew alongside the Gaunt's on Sunday mornings; but she told herself, we are all Christians who honour the one true God and does it really matter that we do so in slightly different ways?

Back beneath the walls of the *Fort Of The Jewels* she suddenly realized they were still holding hands and the realization caused a soft blush to blossom on her cheeks. She was about to slip her fingers from his, but chanced a quick glance up into his profile and saw that he did not seem to have noticed their compromising situation, or if he did, it did not give him any cause for embarrassment. She smiled shyly and let things stand.

With a still warm low westering sun on their faces they passed the little bakery shop where they had first met and climbed towards the village proper with its little collection of shops, businesses and the 40-odd houses; all of which were larger and more substantial than the 26 simple thatched roof stone cottages that housed the small fishing community down at the cove.

The melancholy mood brought on by pain from the past had slipped from James' shoulders. Now, in the vibrant present all he felt was the living heat of her hand and the promise that lay behind her beautiful green eyes. *She is THE One* he thought and squeezed her hand gently. Erin smiled and returned the pressure.

"Ale," he said gaily.

"Ale?" she replied. He grinned and wet his lips.

"Aye, wench; ale and mayhap a little roast mutton and bread. The climb has wetted my appetite." She laughed and her laughter sent another little shiver dancing along his spine.

"But sir," she murmured demurely, "surely imbibing of ale is not something that a chaste young maiden should partake of."

"Fear not," he said gallantly as they approached the little rough stone fronted inn, "your honour is safe – at least for as long as you so will it!" She squealed in mock outrage.

"Beast thy name is Man!" she chided.

"Aye, but man can also aspire to the honourable," he said softly as he gave her hand another little squeeze. She looked up into his weather-beaten face and nodded. "Indeed," she said simply as he led her to a rough wooden bench and table that sat outside the inn entrance.

The ale, served in pewter mugs, was not very much to her liking, as she found it a little rough on the palate. *Tis a man's drink,* she thought, and very different from the occasional glass of wine she had had in her father's house. *But*, she added mentally, *those days are now gone and with them the coddled child that I was.*

4

He reached the brow of the hill and looked out at the sky and the sea. He saw a sky, without a single speck of cloud that shed a benign blanket of unstained light; a pure light that dripped down upon an oily languid sea to spread a soft luminescence over the water's surface. He casually studied the low waves that rolled in slowly to break gently upon the little strand and his fisherman's mind dwelt on the timeless nature of that sea. *It is always the same . . . even when it changes,* he thought. It was ever deep, fathomless, aloof, inscrutable and utterly remote and unconnected from the moods and affairs of man.

As he looked almost directly down onto the little pebble beach and the moored hookers, Samuel Carter placed both hands on his hips, leaned slightly forward and for a few seconds breathed in short rapid pants. The climb although not particularly steep had taxed his lungs and brought a ruddy glow to his cheeks and for the thousandth time he thought bitterly on the cruel way that fate had treated him.

Although in age, admittedly a little past his prime, he had retained a sturdy body honed by hard work at the oar. Work that until fairly recently had seen him match any other man in the chase for the sea's bounty.

Now, at almost forty years of age the creeping shortness of breath and the almost constant dull ache in his chest had led to him having to abandon the oar and with his physical strength slowly waning, Samuel was now left with only one prime faculty – the sharpness of his eyes. It was this faculty that had led to him taking on the position of official 'huer'. His job it was to take up station on the hill overlooking the cove and signal to the fisherman waiting patiently in their rowing boats below as soon as he spotted a mercurial silver and green cloud racing just beneath the dark water in their direction. This morning he did not have long to wait.

"They come!" he shouted to the men below, raising both arms above his head and swinging them in a northerly direction. On the small strand below the waiting men exploded into action. The keels of the five little hookers grated on shingle as they were thrust out into the gently lapping waves and their eager rowers leapt agilely aboard to snatch up their oars. Side by side and stroke for stroke they raced into the surf and with their backs to the open water, they looked up every thirty seconds or so towards the hill where Samuel directed them with extravagant arm gestures towards their lightening quick quarry.

Ten minutes of maximum muscle straining back breaking effort passed before on the hill, Samuel made a quick repeated encircling motion with his arms. It was the signal the rowers had waited for. At one end of the line of hookers, with James at the oars and Thomas at the stern beginning to lay out the tarred hemp net, they peeled off and began the circling move, while at the other end of the line the fifth hooker that was net free, with John Davis and Robert Harris at the oars, sped ahead. The fourth boat then mirrored James' move and the others now peeled off from line to lay net and begin the circling manoeuvre.

Now, from their position at the mouth of the rapidly closing net, James and Thomas could see clearly the dense serpentine line of fish arrowing towards them. Seconds later the darting run entered the net and within a handful of seconds turned into a silver and green roiling cloud of confusion as frantic trapped bodies turned back against the incoming surging tide.

At the still open mouth of the net the fifth hooker raced into position and John Davis and Robert Harris shipped their oars and snatched up broad bladed bats to thrash the water and cause fleeing fish to turn back in panic into the purse of the net. As the mouth of the net closed the dark cloud of bodies thickened and the first fish jumped. Its leap almost took it into James' boat. So close was it that he could clearly see the dark lateral lines along its flank and its colour, ethereal green above the line and sparkling silver below. As its leap lost momentum and it plopped back into the water more and more of the little fish, each no larger than a man's hand leaped.

Within seconds the surface seethed with flashing bodies; bodies with tiny scales that beneath the rapidly rising sun sparkled with soft tints of rose and silver and gold. From above now squadrons of noisily squawking sea birds dived into the purse of the net to snatch up and gorge on fish, then with crops full wheel away in lumbering flight.

The net was now fully closed and in practised unison James and Thomas' hooker along with the fourth, which was manned by John Cartwright and Stephen Ryder, secured the lead lines of the net to their sterns, turned and began to make their slow, muscle straining way back towards the shore where the little line of women, older men and boys patiently waited with their woven baskets to ferry the catch back to the fish palace.

"A good catch!" James shouted to the little crowd waiting patiently on the strand as he and Thomas leapt from their hooker and joined in with the other men to haul the bulging net out of the water and up onto the little shingle beach. As soon as the net was pulled clear of the water the waiting crowd strode forward and began to fill raffia baskets with the precious catch and load these onto a pony-drawn cart, which soon full and with its little retinue of attendants for company set off on the short journey back to the fish palace.

After six more launches into the surf and four backbreaking, muscle torturing hours of toil Samuel Carter, from his high vantage point, gave the extended arms crossed signal that the run was over and the little fishing fleet brought home their final catch of the day. Once the pony cart was loaded and set off on its final journey back to the fish palace the empty net was then inspected for tears and some minor repairs carried out, before being carefully rolled and re-stowed in the sterns of the little fleet of hookers ready for a return to the chase, hopefully at first light in the morning.

Later, in the tiny cottage that he shared with Thomas, James, stripped to the waist, carefully lifted the huge black-leaded kettle from its tripod over the peat fire that burned in the hearth and emptied its steaming contents into the large tin bath that was part filled with cold water.

"Scrub well brother," Thomas said lightly. "And when you have shed the stink of fish from your manly arms and chest, do you the same for that rarely used part which you hope to introduce to your little Irish catholic maid." James growled. He had been the butt of Thomas' crude humour for days now and it was beginning to irk him.

"Her name is Erin," he muttered darkly. "And she is a girl of virtue." Thomas laughed.

"Aye, and you brother, are you also a man of virtue? If so be aware, for virtue demands a harsh and thorny road!" James muttered something under his breath before stepping out of his rough leather breeches and woollen underclothes and easing himself into the gently steaming tub.

Thomas' teasing had begun to strike home. His younger brother had always been the worldly wise one. It was he that had initiated their earlier forays into Glandore and that – to James' more innocent mind – shameful act of lust that even now, months later, still brought a blush to his cheeks whenever it wormed its way back into his mind.

After he had washed away the clinging odour of fish and donned his Sunday best clothes James made his way up from the cluster of thatched cottages towards their meeting place outside the little bakery. She was there waiting and her beautiful beaming smile gave his clumsy feet wings as he almost floated up the last thirty feet.

She noticed his clothing. "Master Pallow," she chided gently, "Sunday best, and tis no more than a Friday..." A little self conscious smile played across his mouth and he nervously ran his tongue over his lips. "Aye," he said a little gruffly, "Sunday best to mark a very special moment Miss O'Connor." Erin frowned lightly, his odd manner puzzling her slightly. "James?" she managed, as he reached out, took her hand in his then dropped to one knee. Her eyes opened wide and a little rosy bloom spread over her cheeks. "James?" she managed again, before he blurted out: "Erin O'Connor...would you do me the great honour of becoming my wife!"

5

Robert Fleck studied the tall gaunt man closely. He took in the sombre black clothing and the contrasting blood red ruby ring that graced a bony finger. He, Fleck, could read men and after two minutes in this man's company he knew he was sitting opposite a ruthless piece of work. *As ruthless as me – almost*, he thought, allowing a faint smile to crease the corners of his mouth. Walter Coppinger was also studying the other occupant of the tiny cabin. He noticed Fleck's smile and to combat it creased his own brow into a frown. Was this Fleck, or Morat Rais, a man to be trusted with a sensitive venture which, if it failed could lead to extremely dire consequences and perhaps even the gallows?

"I know of your business and I am taking a dire risk in coming here," Walter said gravely. Fleck nodded lightly.

"And yet you come. Your business then must be of much importance, if you, a man of great wealth risk being stolen away for ransom." Walter smiled thinly.

"Ransoms are paid by loving families and friends – I have neither . . . and no need of such." Fleck nodded slowly and then in a bright businesslike voice said:

"Well then Mister Coppinger what service is it that you would have of me?" Walter, who in his business dealings always operated under the maxim that men of little substance always puff themselves up with words, said without preamble: "I want you, two days hence, to steal a village."

Back in his Bandon home Walter eased him self into the comfortable horse hair stuffed leather chair and with hands together in parody of prayer, reflected on the turn of events. *This man, Fleck, or Morat Rais,* he thought, *is a scoundrel of the first order…a man,* he added mentally with a thin smile, *after my own heart*. Was he to be trusted? No, certainly not; but needs must. "Do I fear him?" Walter mused to himself "No;" he answered flatly, "if there is fear, it is he who should fear me. For when did a dragon ever die from the poison of a snake?" The words were a spoken affirmation of another of Walter's personal maxims, that 'he is most powerful who has power over himself'.

Walter's power was indeed far reaching. In the case of Baltimore's fishermen however, that power had come up against a number of so far, insurmountable obstacles. All attempts to oust the heretic usurpers and replace them with catholic Irish had failed dismally.

Over the years he had tried recourse to the law several times, but in each case the lease supplied by that now dead old rogue Fineen O' Driscoll had held true. Even now, when the term of tenure was formally up he had not been able to shift the cursed English Protestants, as the courts found that long continued tenancy and the amount of development and work put into the area by the settlers entitled them to stay in perpetuity.

Desperate times now called for desperate measures. There was risk but "He will be true to his grasping nature," Walter muttered with an accompanying nod of the head as he pictured the bearded ruffian's face when the rich shower of gold coins were trickled onto the cabin's rough cedar wood table. The coin was a sign of his intent, and, yes the rogue could take it and run for deep water; but the prospect of huge further profit in the slave markets of Algiers would be too hard to let pass by.

Fleck had raised initial concerns. He did not know the waters around Roaring Water Bay and there were dangerous shallows where the risks of running aground were great. Walter had met that concern by saying that he had access to the kind of men who, for a consideration – which he, through a third party, was prepared to advance – did know them and would pilot him in. "Naval vessels," Fleck had countered. "There must be naval vessels in these waters."

"No," he had responded. "The only naval gunship is *The Fifth Whelp* and she is berthed at Kinsale fifty miles north, where her master is at odds with Sir Thomas Button the Admiral of the King's Ships regarding payment for provisioning and crew wages." Fleck had asked how he, a lawyer, magistrate and businessman, was privy to such information. "I make it my business," Walter had replied coldly, "to know everything of import that plays out in these parts." Satisfied, Fleck had nodded and the deal was done.

Now all that remained of the planning stage was for William Cleary – who had been warned on pain of death not to mention the name of Walter Coppinger – to approach carefully one of the dockside dregs who had knowledge of the local waters and pay him to act as pilot for the venture. Then once that had been done and the raid successfully carried out Cleary, the last loose end that could be traced back to him, would meet a sudden and mysterious bloody end.

James Hackett handed the reins to William Cleary, climbed down from the little pony cart and looked out to sea where, beneath a sky the colour of smoke, the two three-masted vessels a musket shot from shore, bobbed gently in a soft swell. "Xebecs," he mouthed quietly as he took in their distinctive shapes with pronounced overhanging bows and sterns and narrow floor but considerable beam, which allowed for an extensive sail plan. They would usually be square-rigged on the foremast and lateen-rigged on the main and mizzen.

When they needed to sail close-rigged, or close to the wind, they would show a full lateen rig. "Built for speed," he muttered. He knew vessels such as these and knew who in the main, made brilliant use of them. From his seat in the little cart Cleary looked down and grinned. "Aye, they are that...speed and with the means to strike fear into the hearts of any prey."

Hackett was an experienced sailor, having even at one time been a master himself. But that was in better times; now times were hard and the promise of, to him, a small fortune for what was no more than a day's work was too much to pass up.

As Cleary turned the cart around and set off on the long trek back to Kinsale, Hackett narrowed his eyes and stared after it for a minute. He didn't trust the man; no-one trusted Cleary; but the comforting chink of heavy coin in the little leather drawstring purse and the promise of more when the job was done, nudged any nagging doubt to the back of his mind.

Earlier, as they sat in a quiet corner of a rough tavern in Kinsale, Cleary had not gone into details. He would not be drawn on the name of the benefactor and had merely said that he, Hackett, was to guide these vessels safely into Baltimore harbour at dead of night. "And what is the purpose of this night time excursion?" he had asked. Cleary had shaken his head.

"You will know when the time comes; but be content to know now that Ireland will benefit."

James Hackett was no fool and as he looked out at the two vessels riding at anchor he knew what they were here for. Gun ports for twelve cannon on each side and when rigged for speed – and almost certainly with their hulls thickly greased with tallow to allow them to virtually glide through the water like hunting sharks – they would present a vision from hell for cursed English prey.

Hackett eased the pistol from the waistband of his breeches, cocked the hammer and aiming in the general direction of the moored vessels sent a shot out across the water. Minutes later in answer to his signal, a small ship's boat manned by two rowers was lowered and struck out towards the shore.

6

"**S**o child," Helen said softly from her seat at the rough table, "does it go well with you and your young man?" Sat opposite, Erin lowered her eyes slightly and nodded.

"Yes, it goes well."

Helen put down her knitting and smiled. "Good, I am very pleased for you he is a young man of open and generous nature." Now it was Erin's turn to smile, as with a sparkle in her green eyes she answered: "Oh yes mam, he is, he truly is! And I have just consented to be his wife!" A warm, genuine smile crossed Helen's face . . . before practical matters intruded.

"I am truly happy for you child . . . but you must know that there are problems though . . . problems of religion . . . Erin nodded slowly.

"Yes, but it is not a problem between us."

"No, but a problem to others perhaps, as I have heard talk . . . Erin's face hardened slightly and her back stiffened. *Ah, there is fire in there and not just in the flame on her head!* Helen mused to herself.

"I know mam that there are some girls who harbour hopes towards him and that they may start tongues wagging. I also know that there are others who do not approve; but are we not all Christians? Do we not all worship the same god?" Helen nodded.

"We do child, but there are strains that conspire to keep us apart." Erin in spite of her youth and previous sheltered life knew what Helen was referring to. That very spring 16 nuns had been evicted from their convent in Dublin's College Green; while in Cork, communities of friars had been rooted out and expelled. Now, scant months later, there was a brooding air of bitterness abroad, with rising Catholic anger caused by feelings of betrayal and Protestants beginning to feel besieged.

"Yes mam," Erin said, "I know of this; but we are but two young people who," she paused for a heartbeat or two, "are . . . in love." Helen allowed a sad little smile to crease the corners of her mouth.

"Yes child and I know that in your heart love must conquer all . . . let us hope that in time it will be so." Erin's firm nod said that *yes it would be so*. The older woman then took up her knitting, signalling that the heart to heart was at an end. She knew that the young girl sat opposite had suffered turbulent times in her short life; knew that it must have been hard for her to adjust to the dramatic changes that had been forced upon her. She, herself, had never known the *other life* – one of relative comfort. By the age of sixteen she had met and married her husband in the little fishing village of Newlyn in Mount's Bay, Cornwall.

William, a staunch Calvinist, was nine years older than her and earned a meagre living as a crab fisherman. He was a regular churchgoer where he wholeheartedly embraced Calvinist ideals. Ideals, that differed radically from high-church Anglicanism's reliance on heavy ritual and the elite hierarchy of Bishops. He, like his fellow believers wanted a much simpler structure where every man 'is his own priest'.

Six months after they had married in 1618 and heavily pregnant she had agreed to his firm proposal to move to Baltimore in County Cork. Word had come back to him of an established settlement of English fishermen and their families from Devon and Cornwall, who under the leadership of a prominent Calvinist minister, Thomas Crooke, were making a living for themselves free of the shackles of religious persecution.

The early years had been hard. William toiled with other men at the oars while she, when not heavily pregnant, worked in the fish palace processing and packaging pilchards. Payment from the co-operative venture was meagre, but it was enough to put food on the table in their soon overcrowded cottage, with a little left over.

William, who was a man of foresight, saved up enough money to buy a rooster and some chickens and later a sow and a boar and began a second livelihood producing table fowl and piglets. This extra money eventually allowed him to make a grand gesture towards his overworked wife – he surprised her by employing a maid. Helen was almost dumbstruck. She herself was not too different to a 'serving maid'…and now she had become an 'employer'.

The maid, Joan, a local girl, cooked and cleaned and looked after the younger children for almost a year, before falling pregnant to one of the village boys and taking her leave. Now, here Helen sat with Joan's replacement; a young girl that she had taken an immediate liking to and now almost regarded as the daughter she had never been blessed with.

Erin had never known her mother. Never really had any

female friends with whom she could share the joys and pains of growing up. She had never attended a regular school, her father insisting – up until the time when his addiction to gambling left him almost penniless – that his position in Cork society called for a private male tutor for the girl.

Now as she looked across the table at the serene woman with the work reddened rough hands and the first threads of grey in her dark hair she felt a warm feeling in the pit of her stomach. Life here, so far away in distance and in comfort from her earlier existence would, three short months ago, have been unthinkable; but now she felt that the daily round of hard work and the company of decent honest people had combined to release a hidden inner 'person' in her; a person who had a role in a life that offered so much more than the desperation she had left behind.

I am blessed, she thought. *Blessed with a new life and with the love of a good man.*

7

From his poop deck Morat Rais stood alongside his second in command and captain of his other vessel, Jan van Reebek, and looked down at the assembled crews of white renegadoes, Janissaries, their chaouch's (sergeants) and their overall commander, the agha-bachi, Ali Ben Afara.

"Sons of Islam," Morat shouted down to them in Sabir the lingua-franca of the North-African pirate enclave, "you have ventured far from the land of the Prophet, *Glory to his name*, now we will strike the infidel in his very heart!" The assembled men cheered for they knew that rich pickings were now surely not far away. Every man among them, from the lowest deckhand to the most exalted aboard stood to profit from each infidel delivered safely to the slave market in Algiers.

"Whet your yatagans, prime your muskets and trim your arrows," he told the Janissaries, "for tomorrow, *praise Allah*, you will taste sweet victory!" Four hundred iron-heeled shoes beat out a thunderous staccato on the wooden decking and two hundred voices in return shouted "Allah Akbar!"

As midnight approached Morat gave the order to make

ready to set sail and within an hour both vessels shipped anchor and with no running lights showing, quietly eased out into deeper water where there was less chance of being spotted from shore and also less risk of running aground on a shallow sand bank.

Hackett knew these waters well. He knew how treacherous they could be for those who were not regular sailors. Roaringwater Bay in particular had led many a vessel to grief when the *Wind Dog* rose. "When the bay is as flat and as smooth as a slab of grey marble that is the time to beware," he told the captain. "For then the Wind Dog is soon to be unleashed and all must take note of the horizon. Should there be seen a shimmering half-rainbow dancing just above the water then a tempest may soon be loosed." Morat had nodded. He had a very limited knowledge of the waters around Inisherkin and Clear Islands which stood at the mouth of Roaringwater Bay and they would have to skirt the edges of the bay when, with their precious white Christian cargo, they flew south with hopefully no pursuers on their tail. "Good," he had muttered. And Hackett's chest had swelled with self importance.

In the damp and cramped area between decks in both vessels the Janissaries readied themselves. Each odjak of 20 men, with a chaouch in charge, inspected weaponry and the mood was one of ultra professionalism gained from years of rigorous training where they were forced to undergo many severe hardships. Originally an order of celibate monkish warriors the Janissary militia was formed in Constantinople as a kind of foreign legion to maintain the Sultan's hold over his provinces and they had grown to such numbers that their level of power in Algiers now rivalled that of the Sultan himself who was forced to tolerate their growing influence.

Ali Ben-Afara carried his tall angular honed body with a casual grace that was at odds with the tiger within that was released in battle. "Assalamu alaikum," the tall man said softly, lowering his eyes slightly and bowing lightly as he entered the captain's cabin. Morat returned the greeting with the same level of deference. He knew that the agha-bachi was a man who demanded and got total obedience from his men. Morat also knew that he held most white renegadoes in contempt for their lack of discipline and morals.

"We are to enter into a dangerous quest that will, if Allah, *praise be to his name*, grants it, secure a rich prize of infidel bodies," Morat said. The agha-bachi inclined his shaven head the merest fraction as the captain continued. "We must strike swiftly and be gone before any infidel ship can cause us grief." The agha-bachi nodded again. He understood Morat's meaning. This time there would be no time for dallying, no time for the renegadoes to take their perverted pleasures with captured women.

"You will instruct your men that no harm must be offered unless it can not be avoided. Healthy bodies mean a good bounty for us all." The agha-bachi nodded again even though he didn't need Morat's instructions. All prisoners were official state property and he would make sure that property was looked after.

"It will be so," was the quiet reply from Ali Ben Afara as he bowed and left.

Sat alone in his cabin Morat reached for the decanter of brandy on the table, poured out a generous serving into a crystal goblet and eased a chair out from the table with a foot. He put both feet up on the chair, reached into a tunic pocket and took out a clay pipe and leather tobacco pouch and placed them on the table. This was the time he relished; the quiet time before his nerves were stretched taut as humming bow strings and his thumping heart sent blood roaring through his veins in a red tide that threatened to feed muscles and mind to bursting point.

He had experienced the raw primitive thrill of battle many times; but as he took a sip of brandy from the crystal goblet and rolled the liquor over his tongue in appreciation of its bouquet he reflected that those battles were mostly in the distant past. They had mainly come in the days before he had sailed into Algiers; the days when his intended victims were rich fleeing merchantmen not sleeping country bumpkins.

He took another sip of the brandy and sighed lightly. *I have become fat and lazy and content with amassed wealth*, he thought. *Perhaps the time nears when I should retire to my palace and the arms of my many comely female slaves. Or, perhaps even seek amnesty and return with my wealth to Scotland?* The thought nibbled at the edges of his mind for a minute before he pushed it aside. Retirement was surely followed closely by death and when that spectre approached him he would much prefer to face it sword in hand *and not* he thought ruefully, *with a glass of brandy in hand, or lay between the legs of some empty headed ninny of a woman.*

He nodded slowly and drained the brandy in a single gulp without savouring its bouquet and took up his pipe. The time now was not right for thoughts of retirement, nor was it right for thoughts of past glorious battles and victories. Now there was a job in hand and although that job promised to be straight forward, there was always the risk of the unexpected.

Later, as he went up on deck and took his place alongside the helmsman, the craggy silhouette of Inisherkin Island appeared out of the gloom on the bowsprit and Hackett joined them to take control of the navigation. "We now lie close the very mouth of Baltimore harbour," he said to Morat who was stood at his side.

"And where will our anchorage lie?" Hackett nodded ahead.

"There is a safe position at the entrance of the Eastern Hole east of Whale Rock. There we will be hidden from view by a rocky outcrop."

"And how far will we stand from the harbour?"

"Tis then but a good ten minute row to our destination." Satisfied, Morat left Hackett to guide the vessels to their mooring place and gathered his crew of renegadoes and Janissaries for a final briefing.

"The hour approaches," he said calmly. "I will go ashore with ten musketeers and a guide to seek the lay of the land. If all is well when I return we will wait till the night is far advanced."

An hour later with the oars wrapped in a caulking material to deaden any noise, Hackett guided one of the ships' four longboats into Baltimore harbour where it was quietly moored alongside the line of hookers.

Morat stationed his musketeers alongside the little vessels and left whispered instructions to keep their ears open for any shouted signs of discovery, then with Hackett by his side and his

Moorish clothes covered by a long cloak, he boldly strode out into the sleeping village.

They studied the lie of the semi circle of 26 thatched cottages and then casually walked up to and around the fish palace. When he was satisfied that there should be no obstruction to his plans and that there was a clear line of retreat Morat then had Hackett lead the way up into the village proper and the more substantial houses and little businesses that slept in the shadow of the squat tower house that was *The Fort Of The Jewels.* There Hackett pointed out the homes of the village's more prominent citizens . . . citizens who might bring in substantial ransom money.

His job complete, Hackett wished Morat Rais good luck and not wanting to risk joining the other captives in chains, begged leave to go. At the pirate captain's nod he quickly slipped away under a star sprinkled dark sky, with the delicious thought of a heavy purse to come adding lightness to his feet. Satisfied with the reconnaissance Morat retraced his steps and was back aboard his flagship within an hour of landing.

"The way is clear," he told his renegadoes, the agha-bachi and assembled chaouch's. "Soon we will strike a blow that will turn the infidel's heart to ashes in his throat. Soon you will all glory in Islam's victory and your purses will be swollen with gold!" The attack was set for three o'clock, the time when the sleeping body is at its lowest ebb and buoyed by his words the Janissaries made ready for the appointed hour.

As the hour arrived Morat Rais cursed softly to him self as he looked up into the bright face of a gibbous moon. He had hoped for the cover of deep darkness in order to create maximum confusion among his intended victims when his men and Ali Ben-Afara's Janissaries were let loose to create their own unique brand of havoc. A little perturbed at the lack of greater darkness he nevertheless consoled himself with the certain knowledge that these simple early to retire and early rising God fearing Christians, would be tucked up in their beds at such an ungodly hour.

Down on the main deck his dogs of war, faces lit with the joy of impending action, eagerly awaited his command while the four large ship's boats gently strained against their tethers in impatience for the off.

He took a deep breath and savoured the moment before raising and dropping his right arm. The response was immediate as almost two hundred heavily armed men swarmed over the side and in almost silent practised unison took up their positions in the boats below.

Morat nodded in satisfaction at the professional actions of his raiders and with only skeleton crews left behind on the two xebecs, and primed to take up position at the mouth of Baltimore harbour within minutes of the raiding party's departure, he climbed over the side.

Like shadows gliding across the face of the dark water the four boats homed in on the harbour. Within scant minutes the first boat's bottom grated softly on the little shingle beach and four dozen wraith-like forms detached themselves and formed a tight knit square on the strand. Minutes later the fourth square with Morat Rais at its head had joined the others. Each chaouch, each odjak and every single unit of each odjak knew exactly what to do. They were well schooled in the art of swift and deadly surprise attack.

With their men close behind them Morat and Ali Ben-Afara strode out towards the centre of the necklace of sleeping cottages. Twenty yards from the first cottage Morat raised an arm in a signal to stop. Seconds later the aga-bachi with his back to his men raised his right arm high and pointed it to his right. Instantly, twenty Janissaries carrying unlit torches fanned out in a line in that direction. Ali Ben-Afara repeated the signal with his left arm and twenty more torch bearers strode silently to his left. As soon as all were in position the agha-bachi raised an arm again and a Janissary torch-bearer at the end of the left hand line produced tinder and a flint, struck up a little spluttering flame and applied it to his pitch soaked torch.

The instant the flame took firm hold he raced along the line and within half a minute forty torches flared into life. Ali Ben-Afara raised both arms above his head then brought them swiftly down and the two lines of men raced forward to launch their burning brands onto the tinder dry thatched roofs.

As the thatch burst into crackling flame the agha bachi raised a whistle to his lips and blew a long single note . . . a note that released the brake that was holding his men in check. Suddenly the still night air was rent with yells, screams and profane curses as the attackers with their gleaming yatagan blades lit by dancing motes of reflected fire, surged forward. Doors that were never locked were smashed down and a surging tide of berserker humanity poured through the openings.

Inside many of the cottages pandemonium hardly had chance to take hold. Confused, sleep addled occupants were dragged from their beds and frog marched out into the cold night air. Children were snatched up and carried roughly over shoulders, while those that wriggled in terror, were clasped firmly in bare muscular brown arms.

In the Gaunt's cottage light sleeper William had been woken by an odd noise, a kind of crackling that seemed to come from outside on the roof. He carefully eased himself out of bed so as not to disturb his sleeping wife. As he stood with head cocked beside the bed the odd noise suddenly took on stunning significance in his still sleep fogged brain . . . he smelt it . . . Fire! He raced through to the little parlour, reached out for the door latch and then was stopped in his tracks by a terrifying wall of screams and shouts from outside that seemed to emanate from a thousand throats. He stood stunned for a few seconds then as he tried to gather his senses the door burst in off its hinges.

As the leading Janissary raced through the gap William instinctively thrust out his arms in an attempt to ward off collision. The Janissary merely reversed his yatagan and delivered a crushing blow to the infidel's temple with the brass hilt of his weapon. William slumped forward onto the attacker's chest and was thrust to one side to fall behind the door which was hanging lopsidedly on its bottom hinge. Seconds later Erin, Helen and the boys were dragged through and out of the gaping doorway and into a scene from hell.

The night was awash with noise, with shouted curses, children's cries, women's wailing and the crackling roar of flame. And through it all there was the leaping, whirling madness of hundreds of demons in strange garb with teeth flashing in brown alien faces.

Within seconds Helen, Erin and the boys were driven down to the strand where the raiders were busy segregating the stunned captives into two groups, men in one and women and young children in the other. George and Jonathan were roughly dragged from Helen's side and placed with the men who were herded into a tight closely guarded circle and made to lie face down while Helen, along with other women and the village's younger children were forced into the boats and quickly ferried out to the pirate's closely moored vessels; leaving behind a little beach almost choked with more stricken-faced men, women and children.

Minutes more and these prisoners too had been segregated and the returning ship's boats were soon filled and struck out again towards the waiting xebecs.

Thomas was awoken from a dreamless sleep by loud shouting coming from somewhere outside. He threw back the thick woollen blanket, glanced across at his still sleeping brother and made his way over to the cottage door. He opened it and was staggered by the sight. The whole village was ablaze.

There were figures, many, many, figures, leaping about in the firelight. Women and children were screaming, men were shouting, screaming in a strange unknown tongue.

Suddenly, out of the melee two figures, one carrying a lighted torch, detached them selves and began to run in his direction. They were men in bizarre alien clothing, men waving large gleaming knives and they were almost on him. As the leading figure launched his blazing torch onto the cottage roof Thomas turned swiftly on the doorstep and reached for the ancient harpoon that his father, a one time whaler had hung on a wall. He snatched the heavy oak shafted weapon down but before he could bring it round to bear they were bursting through the open doorway.

Spotting the weapon in his hand the first man raised his blade high and charged. Thomas thrust the oak shaft upwards and grunted as it smashed against the man's jaw. The attacker dropped to his hands and knees and Thomas strode over him and brought the harpoon round to meet the second attacker. Suddenly facing the wicked barb, the man skidded to a halt. Thomas smiled grimly and made a swift jabbing movement. The man backed off a pace but as he made to step forward to press his advantage, Thomas felt a sudden red hot searing pain in his lower legs. Behind him the first attacker still on the floor had brought his razor sharp blade around and drawn it cruelly across the back of his knees.

The yatagan bit deeply, severing the tendons, Thomas' legs folded underneath him and the harpoon's barbed head dipped sharply. Seizing his chance, the second attacker leapt forward and his teeth flashed as he whipped his deadly blade across the infidel's unprotected throat.

As the life blood spurted out drenching his hands the killer heard a bellowing pain filled roar from inside the cottage and in the gloom saw a white faced devil charging towards him. James, his eyes blazing and face contorted in rage leapt over the prone attacker and snatched up the harpoon from his dead brother's hands.

Thomas' killer backed off sharply whipping his yatagan back and forth at arm's length. James, savagely intent, kept his eyes riveted on the slashing blade. He took a swift pace forward and then his head exploded and a dizzying array of scintillating light motes flashed behind his eyes.

The first attacker stood unsteadily on his feet and lowered his yatagan. The heavy brass hilt had done its job and the berserker infidel was unconscious at his feet. He could very easily have run the dog through from behind, but his agha-bachi's orders to protect the Pasha's property whenever possible had held firm.

8

On the deck of Morat's xebec Erin and the three boatloads of women and children huddled together in the pre dawn gloom as a band of moonlit grinning savages surrounded them with a circle of steel. Like the others she was in a state of shock. A scant hour ago they had all been snuggled up in warm beds with only their normal daily duties stretching out in front of them. Now they dared not even think what might lie ahead.

"Prisoners below!" The shouted order was followed by a closing in of the ring of steel and the women and children were forced towards an open hatchway that had a steeply angled ladder attached to it. The light that filtered down from the open hatch revealed a large hold and as they were herded down the ladder they saw that the decking below was strewn with damp smelling straw and the bare planking walls were slick with a thin film of moisture. The only furnishing visible was four large empty wooden buckets and a small barrel that contained what appeared to be drinking water and had a pewter ladle attached to it by a length of coarse twine.

As the last of the women and children stepped off the bottom rung of the ladder it was hauled up and disappeared over the lip of the open hatch leaving them trapped and totally at the mercy of the whim of their captors. Somewhere in the semi darkness a child began to cry.

The two Janissaries callously shoved Thomas' body clear of the doorway and between them slowly half dragged half carried their unconscious victim back towards the strand, where they dumped him into the bottom of one of the waiting boats containing a number of other men from the village. As the boat with its heavily armed guard pulled out into the surf and made its way towards Morat's second xebec the captain smiled. The raid had been carried out with military precision.

There were over a hundred prizes now on board the two vessels and as he turned to face the higher ground where the *Fort Of The Jewels* and the village proper lay, there would soon be more. And these prisoners, if Hackett was to be believed, would, unlike the peasants down at the cove bring rich ransom money. But it was not to be.

Richard Hardman muttered a light curse to himself as he was dragged out of his warm bed by his complaining bladder. As he made to move over to the chamber pot that sat in front of a window he stopped, blinked and then his jaw dropped open. It was night, but the night sky down by the cove was ablaze with orange light.

He rubbed his eyes and then saw where the strange light was coming from. The necklace of cottages was ablaze! A second after this realisation his ears tuned in and the faint sounds of yelling and screaming drifted up to him. It was an attack! He ran from the bedroom and snatched down a long barrelled musket from its hooks on the wall, dragged open a drawer in a dresser, pulled out a battered powder horn and a musket ball, charged the ancient weapon and raced over to the door.

Outside, he shuddered in the cold night air, aimed in the general direction of the cove and fired. As soon as the echoes of the shot died he ran back inside and took up an old military drum and a pair of drumsticks and almost before he got back out through the door began a furious rat-a-tat-tat of warning.

With a hundred men at his back Morat had begun to make his way up towards the *Fort Of The Jewels* when a single musket shot rang out from that direction and was followed by an urgent drum tattoo. Startled, the captain called a halt and after a few seconds of deliberation ordered a quick retreat. He was a seasoned campaigner and although it chaffed him greatly to leave behind a good potential profit, it was not worth the risk of running into stubborn defence. He would have to take what he had.

Back down on the shingle beach he ordered his men into the ship's boats and gave the command to cast off and heave on the oars.

Once aboard his vessel, Morat gave the order to get under way and within minutes both vessels had moved out into deeper water and turned their bows to the south.

On the rough decking James slowly opened his eyes to a dull throbbing ache in the back of his head. He groaned and then the sound was cut off as a devastating realisation flooded into his brain. Thomas! The slashing blade! The spurting crimson fountain! He tried to roll onto his side but a strangely shaped boot with an upturned steel tipped toe forced him back. He shook his head to clear his vision and looked upwards. The boot became a leg that was clad in baggy white cotton trousers, then a baggy white cotton shirt, a sleeveless red waistcoat and finally, a moustachioed brown face that looked down on him with casual disdain swam into view. He tried to push the boot away but rough hands latched onto his arms, dragged him to his feet.

With both arms pinned he was dragged over to the other prisoners who were surrounded by at least 40 knife wielding guards and thrust into the circle of stunned ashen faced Baltimore men. Still unsteady on his feet he staggered forward and was saved from pitching onto his face by the steadying arms of John Carter and Samuel Davis. James took a deep breath, shook his head again to clear his mind and swallowed hard.

"Thomas," he said hoarsely. "They have slain my brother." Samuel Davis looked deeply into James' tear filled eyes.

"Are you sure James, could he not be sorely wounded?" James shook his head again.

"Slain," he said simply; then with an up-welling of emotion: "I saw his life blood gush from his severed throat!" As he spoke a sob was forced from his lips and Samuel reached out both arms and pulled the young man's head down onto his shoulder.

"Then he is with God now James," he murmured. "God will look after him."

The other men feeling James' pain closed in around him and muttered quiet words of sympathy. They all, to a man, had liked James' bright eyed life loving younger brother, had all at one time or another shared in or been the butt of his harmless juvenile japes. They were all rugged god fearing men, not given to outward shows of deep feelings; but more than one of them had to swallow hard to keep from letting slip a life time of checked emotion. James, feeling their sympathy, lifted his head off Samuel's shoulder and ran the back of a hand across his eyes to clear away the tears.

"Thank you Samuel, for those kind words," he said softly. "Yes Thomas is in God's hands now. And we, it seems are in the hands of the Devil's henchmen." No sooner had he spoken that they were herded like cattle towards the stern where three white turbaned Negroes dressed in loose flowing white cotton robes were stood next to a pile of thick iron chain linked manacles.

One by one they were pulled forward and the manacles were fitted to their ankles allowing them to take paces of no more than 18 inches – and at the same time remove from their minds any ideas of leaping overboard in an attempt to swim to freedom.

When they had all been dealt with they were driven towards an open hatchway and made to climb down a ladder into a small hold. The ladder was then taken away and they were left alone in the gloom to discus their situation. Samuel Davis was the first to speak.

"How many are we?" he said. A quick count told them that there were 24 men and two boys, George and Jonathan Gaunt.

"Who; other than Thomas," he added quietly, "is not here?" White faced Jonathan answered.

"Our father is not here," he said softly. "We saw him senseless on the floor when we were taken."

"Then God willing he is saved with nought worse than a wounded head," Richard Evans said kindly looking at the boys.

"And Ould Osburne also is not with us," Bob Courtney said.

"He was left behind on the strand when we were taken," William Fletcher said, before adding with a grim sardonic smile: "His crippled hands that were no use in slavery were no doubt his salvation."

Their numbers counted and the missing named, they then turned to the subject that ripped at the heartstrings of every man and boy – the women and children. Here, due to the mad confusion of milling bodies, the moon shadowed darkness and the fact that they were segregated and made to lay face down surrounded by a ring of flashing yatagans meant that the men had no definite knowledge of their loved ones situation.

Agonising images of their women and children's possible fate weighed heavily on their minds and filled their mouths with clogging ashes that stilled their tongues. Soon each man among them found a small space on the bare plank decking and lay down with only his tortured thoughts for grim company.

Erin placed a protective arm around five-year old Stephen's

shoulders and whispered soft words of comfort to Helen's youngest son who's lips were trembling with a mixture of fear and confusion.

"We will be fine Stephen, God will be our protector," she murmured. The child looked up into her calm face and as she nodded firmly he made an effort to still the trembling.

"Good boy," she said as she bent down and kissed his cheek.

Helen, who was surrounded by her other boys caught Erin's eye, smiled wanly and mouthed the words *thank you*. The mother of seven sons who had no daughter felt a lump rise in her throat and felt her heart lurch as she looked across at the young woman who she had grown so fond of. *We are in great moral peril*, she thought. *But you and other young maidens among us are in much greater peril.*

Erin saw the troubled look in Helen's eyes and flashed back a warm smile that was meant to signal *don't worry we will prevail.* The older woman nodded lightly and turned her attention back to her other boys.

Throughout the cramped hold the other mothers were doing their best to calm worries among their young sons and daughters and soon an air of quiet resignation took hold and the words of comfort died off to leave a heavy silence in their wake, broken only by the occasional baby's cry followed by a mother's soft shushing.

Several hours dragged by before a dark face appeared over the lip of the hold and a large basket filled with loaves of black bread was lowered down for Helen and some of the other women to break and distribute as evenly as they could. They had to moisten the brick hard bread with water from the barrel before the younger children could eat it and Helen said that although she would not even feed it to her pigs they should stay firm in their faith because they were almost certain to see no better fare for some time. She had no sooner spoken than the empty basket was drawn up, the ladder was removed and the hatch cover was slammed into place leaving them in total cloying darkness.

On deck Morat had noticed a sudden darkening of the sky. He turned his gaze to the near horizon where the sea and sky appeared welded together without joint. And yes, it was there, a shimmering half rainbow dancing above suddenly flattened waves. Hackett's words of warning came back to him. It was the *Wind Dog.*

As he watched the placid water took on ripples that grew into slowly dancing white horses. A scant minute more and the horses morphed into a thousand saw toothed jagged shards that picked up pace and came racing eagerly towards him. From above a shrill piping caused him to glance upwards. The square-rigged foremast sail had begun to buck and dance as the rising wind plucked at it.

He swore a savage oath. Should he try to outrun it, or should he shout for the sails to be reefed and try to ride it out? He would run. Above the rising wind he bellowed for a full lateen rig and then swore again as the scurrying renegadoes and deckhands were not as quick about it as he demanded.

"Batten down the hatches!" he roared a minute before the squall hit them and the sea rose as though pushed up from the deeps by a rising leviathan. The vessel climbed up a huge wave and at the crest he looked down into a boiling black trough laced with white needles – a wolf's open jaws lined with grinning white teeth. The vessel shuddered, slid over the edge, raced down, hit the bottom of the trough and shuddered again as its bow dipped into angry white water then clawed its way back up the steep incline.

In the darkness below deck women and children screamed in terror as the vessel's bow dipped alarmingly and they were sent skittering across the greasy wooden planking to end up in bruised tangled heaps of flailing arms and legs.

Before they had chance to gather their thoughts they were then sent careening backwards as the bow rose at an almost impossible angle. For the next agonisingly long hour they were sent tumbling forward then backwards before the bucking vessel settled onto a more or less even keel and the hatch cover was removed to reveal stricken white faces and a decking that swam with vomit flecked water from the upturned water barrel. With trembling hands Helen drew her wet shift tightly across her breasts.

"Are there any serious hurts?" she asked through chattering teeth. Her question was answered by a dreadful wail.

"My baby! My baby!" All eyes turned towards a stricken Besse Turner who held a small limp swaddled form in front of her at arms length. Helen looked into the other woman's pleading eyes; eyes that begged for a comforting answer; an answer that could never come. The baby's face was blue-black, its mouth and chin were smeared with bright red bubbles of blood.

"She is gone Besse, your dear Mary is gone," Helen murmured softly. "She is with God now." Besse shook her head. "My fault," she said slowly. "My fault," she repeated. "I fell on her as I clutched her to my breast." Helen held her arms out to the stricken woman who almost collapsed into her embrace and buried her face into a comforting shoulder.

"No Besse, it was not your fault, you are not to blame. It was a terrible accident," she said softly as the young mother's body was racked with sobs.

Some of the other women came forward to try to console Besse but Helen, over the stricken mother's shoulder, shook her head sadly and mouthed a silent 'no'. She knew that there was nothing that could be said, no depth of expressed sorrow that could be offered, which would in any way ease the pain of a mother's deepest loss.

A nautical mile astern the men's plight during the storm was as nothing compared to that of their womenfolk and the children. They were all, to a man, familiar with the moods of the sea. Also, the smaller hold that was their temporary prison was partly filled with spare sails and rigging, all of which provided welcome buffers against the buffeting.

Once the tempest had blown itself out and the hatch cover, which had been battened down at the storm's approach had been removed, the men lapsed again into a mood of melancholy.

James alone among them was plagued with horrific flash backs of glittering blades and spurting fountains of bright red blood. He sat with his back propped against a bulkhead and stared blindly ahead clenching and unclenching his fists as conflicting emotions battled for control of his mind. The guilt that came from his being asleep when he should have been at his brother's side; the pain of loss and the small but smouldering spark of rage that threatened to ignite into a wild in-quenchable blaze, ate into him.

He clenched his teeth tightly together until his jaw ached. He had to isolate the feelings. The guilt would never leave him, but he must put it away for now, for in the situation that he was faced with guilt could only eat away at resolve. Loss too would have to find a little corner of his mind where it could sit quietly awaiting the right time to summon forth. For now all that mattered was the spark of rage. He would not let it get out of control; for that way lay brooding madness. No, he would place that spark in a tightly lidded mental tinder box, kept dry, ready to be opened to receive a breath that would bring it to roaring life.

On the crowded deck Helen placed a supporting arm around Besse's waist as the young woman, with trembling hands reluctantly held out the tiny body stitched into its canvas shroud. The stony faced Janissary nodded lightly, took hold of the little bundle with exaggerated care and moved slowly over to the vessel's rail where he waited for the captain's signal. Morat held an arm up palm out towards the Janissary then spoke to Helen and Besse. "You wish to offer any words?" Helen looked briefly into Besse's ashen face and saw that the young woman was struck dumb.

"Yes," she said quietly, and then in a clear loud voice: "Dear Lord, accept into your safekeeping the soul of this innocent child stolen from its home and now taken from the loving arms of its heart sick mother. May she rest eternally in your loving care . . . amen." With her final word Morat lowered his arm and Besse let out a low agonised moan of loss as the Janissary gently released the weighted bundle, which with hardly any splash sank quickly beneath the cold grey waves.

With the smell of smoke heavy in their nostrils and the

bitter taste of ashes on their tongues the stunned people from the upper village wandered among the still smouldering ruins. The younger children, who appeared not to be touched by the tragedy, raced gleefully among the burnt out cottages chasing a half dozen squealing piglets and flapping chickens; stopping only briefly to look at the butchered bodies of a large boar and a sow.

At the end cottage furthest away from the cove a silent group of adults loaded a blanket covered body onto the little pony cart used to transfer the seas bounty to the fish palace and solemnly set off on the short journey to the parish church.

Three days later with the sun low in the sky, a tall, gaunt figure dressed head to toe in sober black stood among the ruins. He nodded and a thin smile formed on his lips. He was pleased, even though it was a great pity that the village had been razed. It would cost him a pretty penny to rebuild. But, then again, the prime aim had been achieved - the Protestant usurpers had been spirited away and now all he had to do was to approach the courts in Cork with his rescue plan for the village. As a good citizen he would offer to rebuild and re-settle with Irish workers at his own great expense. And there would not be any dissenters to his plans as there was no-one left to raise objections.

Satisfied, he turned on his heel, climbed back into his carriage and set off back to his Bandon home. There he would arrange a meeting with one of the shadowy men who he had occasion to call upon to carry out some delicate task. William Cleary had served his purpose and as the only participant in the affair that could be traced back to him, that link would be permanently severed.

Once the last dark smudge of land had been left in their wake, removing any thoughts of going over the side in an attempt to swim to freedom, the men's shackles were taken off and they were allowed up on deck for a few hours a day. It was a welcome temporary release from their stinking quarters where it was too easy to let dark thoughts creep in upon them. They were even employed about ship's duties, helping to trim sails, clean out latrine buckets and scrub decks. James in particular welcomed the work, which proved a temporary balm to his tortured mind.

The days stretched into weeks and although mentally far from happy with their lot the welcome hours of activity at least kept the prisoners in the toned physical shape fashioned by their previous toil back in Baltimore; all that is, except for young Jonathan. William Gaunt's favourite son had never in all his short life been in rude health. Now that health began to fail and he spent less and less time up on deck, preferring instead to lie below.

His pallid complexion took on a sickly yellow cast and his eyes seemed to lose their focus and sink deeper into his face. James, who had taken it upon himself to care for the youngster made an effort to get him to come back up on deck to take the air, but after two or three unsuccessful attempts he let the boy be.

"It is as though he is giving up on life," James said to Samuel Carter, who shook his head sadly.

"The boy has always been of ill health James. There have been times indeed when his poor father and mother had almost given him up for lost."

One other on board had noticed Jonathan's increasingly frequent absences up on deck. The scar faced Armenian renegado had been watching the young fair haired boy closely and had often run his tongue over his lips as the slim, blue eyed pale faced infidel had passed close by.

Now the Armenian looked slyly around the deck. Most of the prisoners were occupied with ship's tasks, while a little group of six were sitting together over by the starboard rail.

None of them were looking in his direction so he casually sauntered over to the open hatch, thrust a leg over the lip and quickly climbed down the ladder.

It took several seconds for his eyes to adjust to the dim light and to find his target. Jonathan, with eyes closed, was stretched out on the bare decking with his head resting on a coil of rope. The renegado grinned, turned quickly to glance up at the open hatch, then silently crept over to the boy's side, stooped, flipped him over onto his stomach and clamped a hand over his victim's mouth.

Minutes later he climbed to his feet and quickly made his

way back up on deck, where he casually mingled with some of the other renegadoes.

Over at the starboard rail James climbed nimbly to his feet, stretched and began to move towards the open hatch only to be stopped by Samuel Carter.

"Perhaps tis best to leave the boy to sleep," Samuel said. James nodded.

"You may be right Samuel. I will leave him for another hour then see if there is anything we can do to make him more comfortable.

As the sun sank lower and the prisoners' time on deck neared its end James climbed down the ladder into the hold. "Jonathan?" he said softly; then a little louder, "Are you awake boy?" There was no answer. He squinted slightly in the gloom then made out a still shape lying at the far side of the hold. "Come boy," he said adding a note of playful rebuke, "You will be sleeping the blessed day and night away!" The shape didn't move. A sudden ripple of foreboding made James stride over to the still figure. "Jonathan are..." The question died on his lips.

The boy was laid on his stomach. His nightgown was drawn up around his waist. There was a bright smear of blood on his exposed buttocks...and a loop of the rope that he had been using as a pillow was wrapped around his neck.

James' mind reeled and he gasped and shook his head as if in an attempt to dislodge the terrible scene that was before his eyes. He knelt quickly at the boy's side removed the rope from around his neck and gently turned him onto his back. "My God, no!" he cried as he placed his hand on Jonathan's cold chest and tried to find a heart beat. There was none. He climbed shakily to his feet, then raced over to and up the ladder and exploded onto the deck. "Murder!" he roared. "The boy has been ravaged and murdered!" The prisoners leapt to their feet and rushed over to James' side while the deckhands stopped what they were doing and turned to look at the scene.

"Murdered!" James repeated as with a snarl he pushed aside the press of prisoners and charged over to and up the five steps leading to the poop deck. At the top of the steps he almost cannoned into the captain who was in the act of leaving his cabin. Jan van Reebek, seeing the look on James' face let loose a Dutch curse and snatched a pistol from his belt and levelled it at James' head.

His would be attacker glared down the barrel of the pistol. "Sir," James said through gritted teeth, "I come not to offer you harm, but to report a grievous wrong!" Van Reebek lowered his weapon slightly but kept it aimed at the prisoner's heart.

"A wrong you say? You are my prisoner," he answered in heavily accented English, "and prisoners are wronged, and that is the end of it!" James shook his head. "You are not a heathen sir, so answer me this, do you condone rape and murder of one of your prisoners…a mere boy!"

The captain lowered his pistol as two of his crew raced up the steps and took hold of James' arms from behind. James made no attempt to shake them off, instead his eyes narrowed and he said simply: "Answer me sir." Van Reebek nodded.

"Show me," he said and signalled to his crewmen to release their grip on James.

Back down in the hold with the Baltimore men standing at a respectful distance, George was knelt cradling the lifeless body of his brother as James and the captain with three armed Janissaries at his back, descended the ladder. Van Reebek approached the still form and glanced down casually. "The boy has been sick," he said matter-of-factly. "And the illness has been the death of him."

"And this!" James shouted, gently turning the body over and pointing to the blood stained nightgown. Van Reebek shrugged.

"There are maladies that show such signs." James' eyes blazed with anger.

"And this!" he shouted again as he pointed to the raw red marks around the boy's throat; then indicated the coil of rope. "That was about his neck!" The captain looked from the rope then back into James' eyes.

"The boy convulsed and the rope became entangled around his neck." James took in the bland look on the captain's face, snarled and lunged forward. Van Reebek moved smartly backwards and two of the Janissaries stepped forward with their yatagans raised. James froze his attack but his eyes blazed and his jaw muscles tensed and bunched as he fought the emotions that had come close to causing him to lose control.

"You are a true heathen," he said icily through clenched teeth, "and your prophet will be proud of you." A thin smile creased the corners of van Reebek's mouth.

"And you my friend will have a lifetime to learn how a slave must conduct himself," the captain said softly before he gave his Janissaries a barked command. The guards whirled their blades around their heads and advanced on the prisoners, who were forced to retreat to the far side of the hold. Van Reebek gave another short order and one of the Janissaries bent down, lifted Jonathan's body, slung it over his shoulder and stepped over to the ladder. Samuel Carter took a step forward.

"Where do you take him?" he demanded. Van Reebek smiled again.

"You would prefer I leave him here for the rats to gnaw on?" Samuel lowered his eyes. James then spoke out.

"The boy must have a Christian burial," he said firmly looking at the captain. Van Reebek returned James' look and nodded. "Of course," he said smoothly before turning and with his guards at his back mounted the ladder which was quickly snatched upwards.

Back up on deck the captain's face hardened. The boy would have fetched a good price at auction where young fair skinned blue eyed boys were much prized. He shrugged and nodded to the guard who had the body slung over his shoulder, then tilted his head towards the vessel's rail. In the immediate silence that followed the captain's exit the prisoners below heard the splash.

9

As they had done for the past seemingly endless weeks, the women and children made their way gratefully up on deck to savour the sweet fresh air on their faces and the few hours' daily respite from their cramped filthy quarters with its overpowering stench from the communal waste buckets. Helen and her boys, blinking against the morning sunlight led the way and were followed by Erin, Ould Osburne's young maid, Anna Thompson, Joane Broadbrook, Bessie Flood and the rest of the bedraggled party.

Together they made their way over to the stern quarterdeck and the curtained off area which offered them a little privacy and the chance to, at least temporarily, delouse themselves and the children. They had only been there a very short time when Helen, who had been absently taking in the general activity, noted something different in the air.

"There is a change," she said as she looked out from their curtained off section. Whereas before the vessel's crew had gone about their business in a casual unhurried manner, now the men on deck moved more quickly and there was a level of alertness about them, that and a certain jauntiness in those movements that she had not seen before.

"There is a change of mood," she said. Erin, who had been drinking in the sweet air and the delicious way the stiff breeze played through her tangled hair, opened her eyes and lowered her head.

"Mood?" She said softly. Helen nodded.

"Look at them." Erin looked and saw what Helen meant. She turned towards the older woman and her mouth opened to comment, but then was frozen into an 'O' as over Helen's shoulder she saw it. There, on the horizon, a long dark, blue/black smudge that split the pale blue sky from the endless rolling waves.

"Land," she said calmly as the realization dawned that the desperate voyage would soon be at an end.

Two hours later the vessel had come close enough to shore for them to make out some features. They saw wooded hills and rocky escarpments and as they stood watching these slip slowly by their thoughts were plagued with mixed emotions. Land held out an offer of welcome release from their miserable ship bound existence; but that very land with its insipidly innocent visage could perhaps, behind a cunning cloak of welcome, reveal a startling savagery that would forever blight the rest of their lives.

Two hours more and as they rounded a headland, the

women and children on deck whose world had consisted for so many desperate days and weeks of stinking bilges, fleas, cockroaches and rats, were struck almost dumb by the sight that lay before them.

They had entered the cobalt blue waters of a beautiful horseshoe shaped bay that was protected from the ravages of storms by a long stone built semi-circular breakwater or mole. Slightly inland, under the dazzling mid-day sun, like a sparkling diamond on a green velvet cushion, a huge pyramid shape of blindingly white stone lay against a backdrop of verdant hills. As they drew nearer the shore the triangle revealed itself to be a walled ancient city. Closer still and they could make out individual structures, flat-roofed buildings, octagonal minarets, mosques and squat forts bristling with the black mouths of dozens of canons ready to repel any attack from the sea.

Erin's heart sank within her breast. Surely no rescuers could possibly find a way through such defence! Dispirited she turned to Helen, who stood by her side gazing with awe at the sight of a city that dwarfed anything she had ever seen before.

"We can not hope for rescue from the sea," Erin said pointing to the fortresses. Helen tore her eyes away from the dazzling sight and followed Erin's gaze and murmured: "We must not lose hope child. We must trust in God. There must be a path to salvation . . ."

"All prisoners below!" The barked demand from the foredeck cut off any further discussion as a group of half a dozen Janissaries emerged to shepherd the captive women and children back down to their stinking quarters.

"At least we are soon to be set ashore," Helen said with a slight note of optimism in her voice. Erin nodded. "Yes, but ashore to what?"

James' eyes shot open as the unmistakable sound of distant canon fire echoed off the dripping mould covered walls.

"We are pursued!" John Ryder yelled. "Salvation may be to hand!" James scrambled to his feet just as the whole vessel shook to a deafening salvo of returning fire. Now all the men were on their feet and excitedly babbling.

Long minutes agonizingly ticked by as the men strained their ears to hear. Nothing; nothing but the soft creaking of timbers as the ship sailed serenely on. Puzzled, they looked from one to the other. Why no more fire? James shook his head and was about to say something when another sound seeped through the timbers. It was cheering; cheering and bizarre alien music in the form of clashing cymbals, drums and reedy pipes. "We are not pursued, the canon fire was a greeting," James said flatly. "We have arrived."

Sat behind his desk, Consul, John Frizell, ran his forefinger round the collar of his tight fitting tunic. He was hot – and far from a happy man. For six years now he had served as English consul in the hell hole that was Algiers; six years of banging his head against English and Algerian walls.

London refused to pay prisoner ransoms on the assumption that it would only lead to more raids and kidnappings. The Algerians predictably reacted by increasing their raids.

Now another two vessels had berthed with their white cargo. He would, naturally, protest to the authorities in the strongest terms and seek to get the captives released on some obscure technicality of law. He would of course, without any shadow of doubt, be wasting his time.

Frizell sighed. His own lot was not much better than that of the poor wretches he was about to confront down at the harbour. As English consul he had assumed he would be offered at least some level of respect when he arrived all those years ago, but unfortunately that fanciful notion had died a quick death within weeks of his arrival when his house was ransacked and his meagre possessions stolen.

Complaining to the authorities proved fruitless and actually led to him being physically beaten at the whim of the then Pasha. Now, in a state of almost chronic depression, his only fervent wish was to be relieved of his post and to return home to spend his last years in quiet contentment freed of the daily rounds of mind numbing futility that were his present lot.

He sighed again, gathered up a leather bound ledger, carefully placed a stoppered bottle of black ink and a pen in his jacket pocket, opened the door and set off to the harbour.

He had not gone more than a hundred yards when the streets – always alive during daylight hours with the cries of Biskra water sellers in their colourful costumes and with large copper tanks strapped to their backs; with Moorish craftsmen in white burnoose cloaks and richly embroidered caps; with Jewish brokers in their coloured shoes; with wealthy Turkish merchants twirling luxuriant moustachios and with jet black porters from the Sahara leading heavily laden donkeys and camels – became packed with a scurrying tide of chattering humanity all bent it seemed on beating him down to the harbour and to the rich spectacle that would there unfold. He shook his head slowly and resigned himself to the onrushing crush.

As he neared the harbour he saw that the vultures were already massed in front of the returning vessels. The city's white robed slave traders were out in force. He elbowed his way through until he reached the front rank and could clearly see the appalled and terrified features of the women captives on the deck of Morat's vessel and his heart went out to the dozens of babes and wide eyed children clinging desperately to their mother's dresses.

On the other, smaller vessel, he saw, in the midst of a Janissary guard a group of men, some obviously cowed, while others stood stiff-backed with traces of defiance etched into their grimy features.

Both moored vessels had lowered gangplanks and a fat richly dressed Moor with a jewel encrusted turban began to waddle his way up onto the deck of Morat's vessel. Frizell nodded to himself; the Pasha's eunuch emissary would get first pick, before the rest were left to the tender mercies of the slave traders.

"Assalamu alaikum, peace be to you," Morat bowed slightly as the fat man, a good head shorter than him self approached. "Assalamu alaikum," the shorter man replied. "Allah has granted you good fortune?" Morat nodded.

"The infidel has been sorely wounded…come," he

motioned the other forward, "come and inspect the fruits of our voyage." From the deck where they had been hurriedly lined up the women and children looked on with a mixture of fear and dismay as the most exquisitely dressed and bejewelled man they could ever in their simple lives have imagined approached languidly and ran a disdainful eye over them.

Zahid Ali had been charged by the Pasha to select only the most striking virgin women who would be sent as tribute to the Sultan in Constantinople. Fair skinned and fair haired was what Sultan Murad IV took particular pleasure in acquiring and as the Pasha's trusted chief eunuch Zahid Ali had a practised eye for securing fresh tender meat to add to the royal harem.

From her position half way down the line Erin's attention was distracted away from the approaching Moor as, on the deck of Morat's other vessel she noticed a ragged group of prisoners. Her heart leapt up into her throat, was James one of them? Had he been captured or…and the thought, took the strength out of her legs…had he been killed during the attack? Desperately she scanned the sorry group but the distance between the vessels and the crush of bodies surrounded by Janissaries was too much. She was still searching for sight of James when she was dragged back to her own situation. The Pasha's emissary had stopped directly in front of her.

"This one," the emissary said casually in Sabir to Morat who was by his side, "is a virgin?" Erin not knowing what was said looked blankly from one to the other. Morat shrugged at the fat man's question and beckoned one of the Janissaries forward. The Janissary stepped up, pulled Erin out of the line and stood by her side at the ship's rail.

As Zahid Ali moved down the line he stopped in front of Alice Head. The eunuch stroked his chin and looked the girl up and down. She was tall, full bodied with dark eyes and long chestnut hair. There were many more like her in the Pasha's and the Sultan's harem, but her skin was milky white and therefore much to be admired. If she was intact, then she would do.

He asked the same question of Morat and Alice was pulled out of line. A little further down the line he stopped in front of Anna Thompson. *This one*, Zahid Ali thought, *is much more interesting*. The girl was almost elfin of body but with full breasts. Her shoulder length hair was crocus flower yellow and her eyes the blue of lapis lazuli. The question was repeated and the girl was brought over to the ship's rail and stood next to Erin and Alice.

"What can they want of us?" Anna asked timidly. Alice put on a brave face to try and re-assure the girl.

"Be of good heart," she replied, "for the worst is surely over." Her words were firm but in her own mind she knew that there could be much worse to come. Like many women of her time she had heard tales . . . horrible tales, of what happened to women who fell into the hands of savage Christian hating Moors. Erin reached out and took Anna's hand in hers and squeezed it lightly.

"Be brave Anna," she said quietly. "We are together and together we must show that Christian women will not be cowed." Anna smiled weakly and nodded.

Within a few minutes the inspection was over and two more young women; Elizabeth Parker and Mary Williams, were taken from the line to join the others at the ship's rail.

"Prisoners ashore!" Startled by the barked order from one of the Janissary chaouch's the long line of women and children milled around in confusion. The air was suddenly filled with wails of despair and the pitiful crying of the younger children and babes in arms. A month or more at sea had dulled the edge of terror. They had fallen into a routine, even though it was one of deep hardship and deprivation. Now they were to be plunged into a new pit of despair in an exotic land far away from their own fondly remembered shores.

From their position at the ship's rail Erin and the four other young women watched as the ragged line of prisoners were herded towards and down the gangplank and swallowed up by a seething mass of cheering, jeering brown faces.

As Helen and her boys drew level, Erin lunged forward and threw her arms around five-year old Stephen. "Be a brave little soldier," she said her eyes welling with tears as he briefly clung to her before being dragged away by one of the Janissaries while another pushed her roughly back against the ship's rail.

Over the Janissary's shoulder she managed to make fleeting eye contact with Helen before the mother she had never had and her five boys were whisked away and down into the maelstrom of alien bodies where they were instantly surrounded by white robed and turbaned men who pressed forward to get a better look at the merchandise.

Within brief minutes the last of the women and children had disembarked and Erin and her companions stood huddled together at the ship's rail trying to follow the captives' slow progress through the densely packed dockside crowd.

"Prisoners come!" The barked order from an approaching chaouch snapped the women's attention away from the dockside melee. With a guard of two Janissaries they were then herded up to Morat's cabin and ushered in to face the pirate captain and the fat exotically dressed Moor.

"You are chosen," Morat said smoothly in English. "But first it is necessary to judge your full worth."

The young women exchanged puzzled glances before the captain nodded towards the two Janissaries who had brought them into the tiny cabin. The men stepped forward and each took one of Anna's arms and dragged her forward towards a low table.

Morat nodded again and the girl's captors forced her down onto her back on the rough table. With a sallow smile Zahid Ali then stepped forward and pulled Anna's nightgown up and over her waist before dragging her cotton pantaloons down. Anna gasped with shock and humiliation as the two Janissaries strode forward and taking a leg each forced her knees up and widely apart.

The Moor squatted down between the trembling girl's thighs and slowly inserted a fat ring be-decked forefinger into her. He nodded lightly, removed his finger and signalled to the Janissaries to release the girl's legs.

"This one is a maiden," he said to Morat. Mortified, Anna scrambled to her feet and gathered up her pantaloons before rushing back to the sides of the other young women.

The scene was repeated again with Elizabeth, Mary and Alice. With Elizabeth and Mary the Moor shook his head briefly. With Alice, he nodded. "A maiden," he confirmed.

Erin had been left to the last as the Pasha's emissary had been greatly taken by her green eyes, pale flawless skin and her lush tangle of red hair and was prolonging the pleasure that he would get from violating her. But before he could signal for her to be brought forward she stepped up boldly with just a roseate blush on her cheeks and throat to betray her discomfort.

"You heathens will not lay your unclean hands on me!" She said coldly to the two Janissaries as she strode over to the table, lay down on her back, raised her skirts and eased her pantaloons down.

Morat smiled and nodded lightly. *A girl of heart*, he thought, *but one who will in time be broken*, he added mentally.

The fat Moor, with a heavy frown clouding his greasy features was not quite so gentle or so swift with his examination this time. Unlike with the others he made a point of studying the girl's face as he prolonged her ordeal. Each time she winced and as the blush spread wider and deeper he got a little more pleasure. It was not pleasure that could release itself in the normal way of a man – a sharp castrating knife in his youth had removed that means of delivery – but it was never the less one that was left to him and fellow eunuchs in the Pasha's palace; the pleasure that could be gained from having some control over those who were not able to resist.

Finally done with his probing he grunted something and eased himself to his feet. "This one," he said to Morat, "will give the Sultan much pleasure."

The pirate captain knew just what the eunuch meant. The Sultan's reputation for cruelty was legendary; and in many cases women were the victims of that cruelty. He had heard that Murad took particular delight in using women as targets in archery practice which he carried out from the walls of the palace. He had also ordered his gunners to open fire on a boatload of women who, in his opinion came too near the walls of his harem; the boat was sunk and all the women drowned.

Yes, Morat thought, *this one's mettle would very soon be put to the test*.

Down on the dockside John Frizell cast his eyes over the bedraggled group of women and children. He sighed lightly and then stepped forward to the little table and rough chair that had been placed there for him to fulfil his consular duties by logging the names of the prisoners. Helen was the first to see his approach and relief flared on her face. It was a white man in an official uniform!

"You are English?" she asked in hope. Frizell nodded.

"Indeed madam. I am his majesty's consul," he replied without enthusiasm.

"God be praised! Can you help us sir!" The consul knew he could not offer any real encouragement, but his caring nature demanded that he say something that might ease the despair of these poor unfortunates.

"I will make strong protestations madam . . . strong protestations . . ." Helen looked deeply into Frizell's eyes and saw the truth reflected . . . those protestations would be pointless.

"We thank you sir!" she said loudly with forced feeling for the benefit of the frightened women and children – and a ripple of hope sped down the line of prisoners.

Within the hour Frizell had taken the details of all 84 women and children. Now there were only the details of the men to log. He looked over the heads of the dockside crowd towards the second vessel and saw movement.

James shuffled forward towards the gangplank, the thick chained leg shackles causing him to take small hesitant steps. He was followed by George and the other men all of whom were also shackled.

Flanked by half a dozen armed Janissaries, they made their cautious way down the gangplank and onto the dockside to be met by a sudden forward press of bodies. Then from the crowd a double handful of swarthy men wearing white cotton robes and plain white turbans emerged and strode purposely towards them. The two leading robed men stopped at James' side, reached out and grabbed his arms and felt his biceps then turned his hands over to check the palms. One pulled at his chin and demanded something in Sabir. James flinched and twisted his head to one side to avoid the touch then one of the Janissaries stepped smartly forward and delivered a stinging blow to his jaw.

"Open!" he shouted. James gritted his teeth for a moment and then as the futility of his action sank in he opened his mouth and like a horse, had his teeth and gums examined. Satisfied, the men moved on to the next in line and were replaced by others.

Frizell watched as the prisoners were in turn examined by the traders. Experience told him that the strongest would probably end up at the oars of a slave galley or in the backbreaking task of maintaining the breakwater, while any who had some sort of trade would be bought for their skills. He also noticed that there was a young fair-haired boy. He shook his head sadly. If things ran true to form this mere child would very likely end up like others of his age and indeed younger, as a plaything of a rich merchant or renegado.

Examinations over, a narrow passageway opened up among the dockside crowd and the prisoners were shepherded through. With every shuffling step they took they were jeered and spat at and to howls of laughter from the crowd were buffeted with fists and slaps from narrow slats of wood.

Bruised and lightly bloodied, the men and the young boy neared the line of women and children all of whom at the sound of jeering and laughter had turned to face the way they had come.

"George, Jonathan!" Helen screamed as she spotted George's fair head. "Praise be to God," she whispered. "They are safe and well!" Her relief was then suddenly tempered. Yes George was there . . . but where was Jonathan?

She anxiously scanned the group of prisoners, but there was no sign of her beloved son. Where was he? *Perhaps he somehow avoided capture*, the thought blossomed in her head. "Yes," she whispered, "that's it, he has escaped! Thank the Lord! His dear father will have some solace..." Her last words were drowned out as the rest of the women and most of the men began shouting tearful greetings across the fifty yards that separated them from their loved ones.

James, one of the few unattached men, alone, stood searching in vain for a flash of red hair. "Erin!" He shouted her name repeatedly, but to no avail.

"James!" He heard his name called and searched the crowd for the caller. He saw her. Helen raised and waved an arm to catch his attention. "She is aboard the vessel and is well," she shouted back across the divide. James acknowledged her words with a return wave, but before he could ask anything else the Janissary guards forced the two groups forward away from the docks and towards the massive city walls where a huge gate swung open to admit them into the city itself.

Overawed by the sheer size of the city – and the exotic sight of two and three storey snow white lime washed buildings, their walls festooned with fragrant scrambling jasmine and oleander; with minarets from which chillingly alien voices of muezzins called the faithful to prayer; with huge grumbling alien humped beasts loaded with goods; with the cries of vendors and, for the women and children, the terror inspired by the sight of silent coal black giants with sweat glistening skins – the stunned prisoners were driven deeper into a foreign world a universe away from their previous simple village lives.

Soon the broad streets gave way to what were more like alleyways, where it was difficult for two people to pass in opposite directions and the crowds of jeering, shouting bystanders thinned and fell back behind them. Now there was in contrast an eerie silence, broken only by the clank of chains from around the men's ankles and the occasional sound of a baby's cries and a mother's calming response.

In the gloomy silence, made deeper by the dark shadows cast by the crowded overhanging buildings, James, for the first time since they had left the harbour, gathered his thoughts. *She is captured; but at least she is unharmed. But why is she not with the women and children? Why? And what cruel fate awaits her in this heathen land?* Aware of being totally powerless he bunched his fists until the knuckles cracked and showed creamy white through his tanned skin. *I will not abandon hope*, he promised her, *not as long as there is breath in my body.*

10

Erin grasped Anna's trembling hand as the wagon's steel rimmed wheels clattered over the rough stone approach to the City gate. Her own heart was racing but she could see that the other girl was in great need of comfort.

Anna forced a wan smile and with a weak grip gratefully returned the hand pressure. *She is in much distress* Erin mused to herself as she glanced across at the other captives, none of whom she had really had any dealings with until they were thrust headlong into their terrible dilemma. Yes, they had exchanged brief greetings when their paths had crossed but she had known very little about any of them; now, suddenly, as the gate swung open like a giant maw about to swallow them, they were sisters in desperate peril.

Once the shaven headed driver had urged the donkey through the gate they were almost struck dumb by the sights, sounds and the sheer mass of humanity that sent their senses reeling. Erin was affected less than the others who had known nothing but village life, but even she had never seen anything like this in Cork.

"It is a vision from hell!" Anna gasped and then recoiled in terror as a heavily laden passing camel thrust its spittle flecked huge gaping yellow toothed mouth into the cart and spat at her.

The little donkey cart made its way along narrow streets where leering men pressed close, made obscene gestures and shouted crude remarks in a strange language, while from curtained off windows the veiled faces of dark eyed women peered out at them in silence. Minutes later they left the narrow streets behind and turned onto a wider road that rose sharply, causing the driver to lay a whip across the wheezing donkey's back to urge it on upwards.

In the back of the cart and clinging to each other for mutual comfort the young wide-eyed women looked on as they approached a huge snow white walled crenellated palace with an enormous bronze double door the height of three men that glittered in the lowering sun. At a shout from their driver the doors swung ponderously open and the cart trundled through into a courtyard the walls of which were covered with a dizzying chiaroscuro of cobalt blue and white mosaic tiles. The floor was paved with slabs of pale pink marble and in the centre a perfumed fountain filled the air with the heady scent of jasmine.

Almost before the cart had come to a stop two huge coal black shaven headed men dressed in red waistcoats and baggy white pants strode out of the shadows and with imperious gestures ordered the women to dismount.

Pale with fear, the young women climbed unsteadily down from the wagon and were ushered towards and through an open doorway at the far side of the courtyard that led into a large vaulted blue domed cupola supported by eight tall red porphyry columns that glittered with embedded white crystals. The walls in between the columns were pale pink Moorish stucco carved into an intricate honeycomb pattern that bled myriad shafts of golden sunlight onto the cool white marble floor and, as they were led across it, dappled their pale faces, arms and bare feet with a warm saffron glow.

At the far side of the cupola they were brought to a stop in front of a heavy oaken door. One of their guards strode forward and from a pocket in his waistcoat produced a thick iron key which he inserted into a lock. On the other side of the door the guard used the key again to lock the door behind them and the prisoners were led down a long narrow corridor the walls of which were covered in a riotous array of crimson, gold, green and indigo hanging silks.

Another heavy door now barred the way and the guard used the key again to usher them through into a large room. A room that contained a dozen exotically dressed and gossamer-veiled young women all of whom lounged on huge plump, coloured cushions arranged around the feet of a bearded middle-aged Moor.

His Excellency, Pasha Hussain, was partly reclined on a low gilt framed red cushioned Ottoman. As the prisoners approached they were, in spite of their distress, struck by the sheer opulence of his dress. His feet were encased within white buskins bound to his legs and secured with diamond buttons in loops of pearl; his upper body was clothed in a three-quarter length loose fitting long sleeved dark blue garment that glittered with precious stones and was secured around his waist by a red silk sash that was studded with rubies and emeralds. On his head, a plain snow white turban, at first sight seemed oddly out of place, until the prisoners noticed that the wrapping was pinned by a huge glittering diamond crescent brooch.

At his side perched on a lower stool the fat eunuch who had recently caused them such acute embarrassment sat with hands crossed between his flabby breasts.

The bearded Moor made a languid beckoning sign and one of the black guards prodded the captives forward and made them stand in a line in front of the Ottoman.

"Which are intact?" The seated man said casually. The fat eunuch jumped up from his stool and stuck out the same pudgy finger that he had used in his examination and indicated Erin, Anna and Alice, all of whom looked blankly on.

"Take the other two to the women's quarters," the bearded Moor said casually with a dismissive wave of his hand. "The intact gifts for the Sultan are to sail on the first tide tomorrow."

James had no sooner made the vow that the sad procession turned a corner and found itself entering a large sun blasted palm fringed square. Squinting in the brightness, he made out some twenty white robed and turbaned Moors, some of whom he recognized from the earlier dockside examination who had obviously come by a shorter route than that taken by the captives.

One of the unrecognised Moors, an older white bearded man with a huge white moustache strode forward and addressed the Janissary chaouch, who turned to his men and gave a short barked order. Within seconds the Janissaries had herded the women and children into the centre of the square and the men, accompanied by cries from the women, were force marched towards and down a narrow side street where they disappeared from view.

Within minutes the square was full of stragglers from the docks and the women and children became the centre of attention of Moorish merchants, slave traders, renegadoes and a rag bag army of the city's citizens who, it seemed, were along merely for the pleasure of baiting the infidel captives. Terrified by the noise, the totally alien environment and the swarthy features of the crowd, the women and children huddled closely together.

"Behold!" The white bearded Moor demanded loudly and the crowd was suddenly silenced. "Behold," he repeated. "See what jewels we have for you to examine. See their alabaster faces and pale limbs; see their fair hair and blue eyes. See the sturdy boys and budding girls who will provide a lifetime of service in the kitchen . . . or in the bed chamber," he added loudly to ribald laughter.

As soon as the laughter died one of the Janissary guards stepped forward and roughly pulled three of the younger women from the line. The bearded Moor then had them paraded around the square, all the time keeping up a commentary of the prisoners' merits. "See," he said, "this one has fine full breasts; she has been fed on rice and beef and creamy butter. Who will bid . . . who will bid?" A slave trader and a merchant stepped forward. "Yes, come," the bearded Moor beckoned. "Feel her breasts, check her teeth, is she not worth a king's ransom!"

And so it went on. The women without children were paraded first and each one of them was taken to a separate curtained off area and examined in very intimate detail to see if they might be worth the extra price of a virgin.

As each was sold the white bearded Moor logged the price into a ledger and the newly purchased slave was lightly manacled and with tearful backward pleading looks was led away to disappear through the crowd. Then it was the turn of the women with children.

Pregnant Bessie Thomas was paraded with her two young daughters clinging to her shift. "See her swollen belly," the slave master shouted. "I offer two for a single price!" Three merchants bid and a final offer was accepted from a Jewish trader. "And for the young females . . . what offers?" The winning merchant shook his head leaving two more new merchants to enter their opening bids.

While the slave master's banter and the bids were progressing Bessie had stood with her arms around her girls' shoulders with a look of total shock on her face. She had watched the single women being sold one by one and now the realization that her girls were to be torn from her side and spirited away into a hellish heathen life that offered God only knew what kind of suffering and depravity was too much to bear.

"No!" she screamed, "You will not steal my babies from me!" Bereft, she clung desperately to the weeping daughters and two Janissaries strode forward and ripped the girls from her arms. Devastated she watched as the bidding progressed and within two minutes ended with both girls sold to a grinning fat middle aged merchant.

As her girls were marched off Bessie, overcome with emotion, slumped to the ground and was then roughly hauled to her feet by a janissary guard and delivered to the Jewish trader, where she too was lightly manacled and then led off to her lonely fate in an alien city hundreds of times larger than anything she had ever known before.

As Bessie and her girls disappeared from sight through the crowd the other women knowing what awaited them began to weep and wail. Seeing their mothers' distress the children too began to cry and soon the square was awash with tears.

It made no difference; the sales continued. Joane King and her eldest daughter, Joyce were sold together, but her seven year old twins Thomas and Edward were bought by a grinning scar faced Armenian renegado who made a point of running his hands lingeringly over their young bodies before his final winning offer.

Helen and her five boys were brought out next. Five-year old Stephen was pried from her side and tearfully paraded while his mother imploringly held her arms out in his direction in a futile attempt to comfort him. Next came seven year old Robert, then eight year old Timothy; followed by 10 year old twins, Richard and Adam – and with each individual sale a dagger thrust deeper into her mother's heart.

When her turn came she was led around the square drained of emotion, her legs numb and her mind incapable of grasping the enormity of her loss. She was bought by a Lascar merchant and blank eyed, led away.

Within the hour the last of the prisoners were sold and the square emptied, leaving behind no trace of what had taken place. It was now just another pleasant, quiet, palm fringed square sat beneath a pale blue cloudless evening sky.

At the end of a long narrow street the men were brought to a stop at the entrance to a huge courtyard thronged with a bewildering mix of chattering men of, it appeared, a wide assortment of nationalities. Their skins ranged from blackest ebony to off white. Many were dressed in what seemed to the captives, finery; some wore plain white burnoose cloaks with richly embroidered caps on their heads; others were obviously European renegadoes sporting their tattooed arms and gold ringed ears; while more still wore what appeared to be little more than rags.

Around the perimeter of the courtyard there were a number of stalls, some selling a range of breads and other foods, while others displayed canvas clothing, shoes, tobacco and a variety of pots and pans. In between these stalls on one side of the walled courtyard there was a large open recess that housed a dozen rough wooden tables with raffia backed chairs arranged loosely around them – and in the chairs a singing, shouting, swearing mob of renegadoes were drinking rum or rough ale from battered pewter flagons.

On the opposite side of the square another, smaller recess, with a multi-coloured beaded curtained frontage was attracting the attention of two drunken grinning renegadoes. As, with their arms around each other's shoulders they reeled about in front of the curtain it was swept partially aside and a bare pudgy brown arm adorned with a number of silver bracelets emerged and a bright purple nailed hand beckoned them in.

As the prisoners were herded into and through the courtyard a narrow passageway opened up and they were briefly buffeted with slaps from the jeering cheering mob. With their heads down and shoulders hunched against the attacks James and the other men reached the far side of the courtyard and were brought to a halt in front of a barred metal gate built into a wall.

One of the Janissaries strode forward, stuck his face up against the bars and shouted something. Seconds later a huge bare-chested Negro emerged from the gloomy interior with a large rusty key in his hand and unlocked the gate.

"In! In you infidel dogs!" The Janissary chaouch's shouted order galvanized the other guards into action and the prisoners were forced through the doorway with heavy blows and curses. Inside, the Negro locked the gate behind him and the Baltimore men were marched down a dimly lit corridor that contained a number of barred iron doors on either side. They were brought to a halt outside one of these doors and the black guard approached, unlocked the cell and they were herded inside with more blows and curses.

As the cell door clanged shut and the key was turned in the lock the men stood in silence for a few moments as their latest situation slowly sank in. They had spent weeks in damp filthy ship's bilges, plagued by rats and vermin, only to breathe pure air for a brief spell before being plunged into another black hell hole.

In the deep gloom a sudden whimper sent a chill racing along James' spine. He glanced down at the dim pale oval that was a white face, reached out and placed a comforting arm around George's trembling shoulders.

"Courage," he said simply. "We have come this far. We must trust in our Lord to provide us with the strength to overcome." The boy's shoulders stiffened and he drew in a deep shuddering breath. James nodded and a sad little smile creased the corners of his mouth. The boy's world had been turned upside down and he had suffered greater loss in the last few weeks that any man, let alone boy, should have to suffer.

"I will not cry." It was a simple statement spoken quietly by a frightened boy, but one that gave the grown men heart.

11

As he sat opposite the Admiral, Pasha Hussain made a conscious effort to inject the right level of command into his voice. "You have made ready to set sail?" Ali Bichnin, who sat cross-legged on a plump purple cushion, bowed his head lightly.

"Yes your Excellency, my vessel is provisioned, the taxes have been safely stowed and I await your tribute of concubines to the Sultan..."

"Good," the Pasha interrupted. "We must make sure that my nephew the Sultan is pleased with the taxes and our tributes; a pleased Sultan will look elsewhere to slake his thirst for violence against his loyal subjects." Bichnin smiled thinly. He didn't care if the Sultan's evil temper were to be visited upon his Excellency the Pasha. In fact, he couldn't care less if the Pasha's head ended up rolling on the very floor of this audience chamber – he had his own agenda and with any luck he would soon be able to put that agenda into motion.

"As you say Excellency," he said smoothly. "It is best that the Sultan's darker moods are directed towards more worthy targets."

As Admiral of a fleet of corsair ships, Bichnin held a position of power; in fact some even saw him as the real ruler of Algiers – not the Pasha. An Italian corsair he had, years earlier, sailed into Algiers in command of a pirate ship that he had used to ply his trade in the Adriatic. Realising the potential that Algiers could offer to an enterprising man he had quickly accepted the circumcision knife and embraced Islam, changing his name from Piccinio to Ali Bichnin.

Unlike many other corsair captains who were content to operate from one ship he then invested the profits from piracy in the purchase of new vessels and was soon a very rich man. So rich in fact that he owned two palaces in the city, a villa in the suburbs and several thousand slaves. He was known to donate to the city by funding a large sumptuous public baths and more importantly, to cement his conversion to Islam in the eyes of the city's peoples, he had even built a grand mosque.

The Admiral's spectacular rise worried Hussain, he did not trust Bichnin. He suspected that the Admiral had his own designs on power; but then he also knew that his own continued prosperity and indeed, position in Algiers, depended for the time being very much on the powerful pirate Admiral and his fleet of ships. *I must make cunning plans, for when the time is right, then word to the Sultan warning of possible treason should see the matter resolved,* the Pasha thought as he stroked his beard in momentary reflection, before continuing.

"Yes, it seems there are many who try the Sultan's temper Admiral," Hussain replied softly, "for word reaches me that the his moods are ever blacker."

Bichnin nodded. His own sources had relayed information back to him. He knew that the Sultan had imposed the death penalty on anyone caught smoking or drinking coffee or alcohol – even though he drank coffee and alcohol himself. He also knew that Murad had formed a habit of wandering the streets of Constantinople at night carrying out his own inspections. If he caught someone with a pipe in his mouth or drinking alcohol or coffee he used his prodigiously heavy two-handed sword or a huge mace to behead or spill the brains of the unfortunate 'criminal' on the spot.

"As you say Excellency," Bichnin repeated. "Our glorious Sultan is become a man of many worrying moods. Moods that I hope not to encounter…" the Pasha smiled thinly.

"Yes, it would be truly unfortunate Admiral should you arrive at an inopportune moment, such as when his Highness is dressed in yellow…" Bichnin frowned lightly.

"Yellow?" Hussain's smile widened.

"Yes Admiral, yellow. I am told that when he arises from his bed and is seen to dress in yellow then the whole palace walks on tiptoes in fear of a berserker mood that promises instant death to any that incur his displeasure." The Admiral nodded.

"And I see that the thought gives birth to humour in his Excellency," Bichnin said sardonically, noticing how the Pasha's smile had suddenly widened. Hussain shrugged.

"I have great faith in your ability to ride out any storm Admiral, be it at sea or in the Sultan's palace in Constantinople. *And should you perchance succumb . . . well so be it*, he added mentally.

Now it was Bichnin's turn to smile. "Kind words much appreciated Excellency. Now I must conclude plans for sailing." The Pasha's smile faded as the Admiral rose to his feet without permission and bowed lightly before turning on his heels. *Insolence will reap its reward*, Hussain thought, *when the time is right*.

In the palace apartment that the eunuch had led them to Erin and her young companions were stunned again by the opulence. The floor was tiled in pale green marble shot with gold specks and littered with a multitude of plump coloured silk cushions. In amongst these cushions like islands in a tranquil sea were a number of rectangular soft wool fringed *Medallion* and *Hamadan* Persian rugs decorated in blue, gold, ivory and brown. In the centre of the floor there were two low rosewood tables; on the larger of the two there was a large pink glass bowl encased in a golden filigreed basket that was overflowing with a selection of strange exotic fruits. Alongside this there was a large silver salver containing several thin slices of cheese, a small stack of skewered lamb in bit sized chunks, six small flat oval shaped pieces of white bread and some small round honey and nut cakes. On the smaller table three polished obsidian tumblers were arranged around a large silver gold handled pitcher which was giving off a strange heady bouquet.

After weeks of privation and near starvation the women cried out and rushed over to the tables.

"It is manna from heaven!" Alice cried as she fell to her knees in front of the pink bowl. With a trembling hand she picked up a veritable clump soft plump purple berries, sniffed at them then detached a half dozen and crammed the ripe alien fruit into her mouth and moaned with pleasure as the sweet juicy pulp instantly brought back to life taste buds that had been numbed by stale bread, thin gruel and brackish tasting water.

After they had eaten and drank some of the delicious perfumed sherbet the women sat in a little circle on the silk cushions and were about to discuss their situation when the door to the apartment swung open and two women dressed in plain white cotton shifts, with their arms full of clothing in a riot of colours entered and placed the items on the marble floor.

Close behind them four short dark-skinned bald men in baggy white trousers and red beaded waistcoats and carrying huge gently steaming copper vessels marched in and made their way over to a beaded curtain at the far side of the apartment. One of the men swept the curtain aside and the captives glimpsed a large sunken bath that appeared to be partially filled with water. The men in turn emptied their vessels into the bath, then without speaking left the apartment. As the door closed behind them the two women approached and made beckoning signs towards the bath chamber.

"We are to wash away our grime; would that we could also wash away the memory of our past ordeal," Erin said as they were shepherded through the beaded curtain.

Inside the bath chamber the two women indicated that the captives strip off their filthy garments. Anna, blushing turned to Erin.

"It is not becoming..." she whispered. Erin shrugged lightly.

"We have suffered greater moral discomfort Anna," she said softly as she quickly slipped out of her nightclothes. "Remember the examination in the presence of men aboard ship..." Anna's red cheeks burned brighter as that terrible indignity came back to mind.

"You are right, for are we not sisters together in peril," she said as she and Alice stripped off their own clothes and followed Erin into the beautiful decadent luxury that was the pink rose petal strewn perfumed water, while the two servant women gathered up the filthy garments and left.

After they had bathed their grimy bodies and washed the dirt and matted tangles out of their hair they made their way back through the beaded curtain into the apartment, where in the mound of clothing they found soft woollen towels and a tortoiseshell comb. Minutes later and feeling for the first time in many weeks like normal young women, they turned their attention to the clothing.

Anna squealed as she picked up and held out at arms length a long pale blue pair of loose fitting pantaloons that were striped in gold. "Can we really wear such outlandish garments?" she asked with the hint of a laugh. Erin smiled at the wonder in Anna's voice and for the welcome change in her mood.

"We must little sister, or else go naked as new born babes," she said. "Our own beautiful garments are gone," she added with a little laugh.

For the next few minutes the women forgot their predicament and with smiles gasps and giggles sorted through and made their choice of garments from among the pile left by the servant women; and the choices were many.

There were long pantaloons with gold or silver stripes, three-quarter sleeve length tops embroidered with beads and sequins, silk veils studded with crystals and hip scarves with rows of coloured beads and coin fringes. All of these came in a variety of colours – red, pale blue or green, fuchsia, rust and purple. Finally they each tried on and selected a pair of soft beaded ankle length slippers, and revelled in the snug sensuous feeling of being able to wriggle toes that had been for so long bared to the terrain and elements.

Freshly bathed and clothed, the women sat down again in a little circle and began to discuss the latest turn in their situation.

"Why have we been separated form the others?" Anna asked. Erin thought she knew why.

"The pirate captain," she said. "He told us we were chosen, but that our worth must be judged. Elizabeth and Mary failed the test of maidenhood." Alice nodded.

"Yes, so we are chosen over them and they have been taken away to some purpose that we can only guess . . ."

"And what is our purpose?" Anna innocently asked. Erin knew a little more about life than her young fellow prisoner. She had had the benefit of an education in a city environment and matters of the world were not totally unknown to her; never the less she kept her fears to herself.

The small windowless cell was totally bare of any furnishing, apart from a thin layer of mouldy straw that was strewn across the raw earth floor. The walls were of rough undressed stone that felt cold and damp to the touch and the only light seeped in from the dim corridor outside the cell door.

"At least it seems we have no furry fellow prisoners to share our accommodation with," James said in an attempt to lighten the sombre mood.

"No," Tom Edwards added scratching his head, "but I

myself have brought several little guests with me t'would seem." His light hearted comment sent a little ripple of quiet laughter tripping round the cell as James pressed his face against the bars and looked left down the corridor towards the barred gate that opened onto the busy courtyard.

"We surely shall not be kept here over long," he muttered as he turned back towards the others. "The Moors have not brought us to this far strange land to rot in this foul cell."

"No, they have not. They will have some dark purpose in store," Bob Courtney offered. "There are pirate galleys to row and other dire trials that await us." All the men had heard horrific tales of slaves being chained to the oar for years and being forced to suffer cruel physical torment with barely enough food to keep body and soul together. Then when they died at the oar, or went mad or could take no more, being tossed overboard like buckets of human waste.

Bob Courtney's words and the thoughts they gave birth to lay heavy on their minds and within minutes they had all slumped to the floor and their budding sense of oneness had dissolved into twenty-four islands of brooding solitude. Soon even the half light faded and true night crept upon them, causing each to withdraw further into themselves to a place where nothing existed, other than the pounding of hearts in the cathedrals of their chests.

"Up dogs!" The black jailer's barked order bounced off the stone walls and into their sleep dulled ears. "Up! Up!" he repeated. James and the others rose stiff-legged to their feet.

As the key turned in the iron lock James, for a fleeting moment thought of rushing at the man. He smiled and shook his head. *Madness*, he thought, as he saw the squad of armed Janissaries in the corridor and felt the drag of manacles on his feet.

Outside in the early morning empty courtyard they were ordered to line up in single file and a Janissary chaouch gave the order for them to march.

The streets were fairly quiet with only the odd water seller or little donkey train for company as they made their way out into the city proper. Soon they were taken onto a wider road that rose sharply and led them to a great snow white walled palace with a huge bronze door. The Janissary chaouch strode forward and hammered on the door with the brass tipped handle of his yatagan. Seconds later the double doors swung smoothly open and they were herded through. Minutes later the prisoners found themselves in a large richly furnished empty room.

As soon as they were lined up in the centre of the floor the Janissary escorts stood back against the room's walls and took up a stiff-backed arms folded, eyes dead ahead stance. Satisfied with the guards' appearance the chaouch then left through a small side door.

A full hour crawled by before the door opened and a dozen or so richly dressed and obviously important men strolled through and without so much as a glance at the prisoners, arranged themselves on silk cushions in a rough semi circle in front of a low gilt-framed divan. Another minute passed before the door opened again and three male servants entered carrying large silver trays containing drinking glasses, plates of sweetmeats and small silver urns. They placed these down on the floor, bowed deeply and left.

As the prisoners watched the men poured themselves tea from the urns, sampled the sweetmeats and chattered amongst themselves. Suddenly from somewhere outside the room a gong chimed. The seated men climbed swiftly to their feet as the door opened and a middle-aged bearded and turbaned Moor, followed by a scribe carrying paper, pen and a small bottle of ink entered. The Moor made his way over to the divan and with the scribe squatting at his side sat down. He waved a ring-bedecked hand casually and the men sank down to sit cross-legged in front of him.

Morat Rais and the two other pirate captains who were squatted with the city's richest merchants and the Pasha's construction overseers had been through this ritual many times. The Pasha would make small talk and then move on to matters of economic interest, quizzing the captains about their plans for more raids. The merchants, who, along with the Pasha, provided money to fund the attacks for a share of the profits, would then get their chance to ask any questions of the pirate captains before the scribe read out details of profits gained from recent slaving raids.

The stunned prisoners, who were an apparent irrelevance, watched from the sidelines as the business of the day continued towards its lengthy conclusion. Eventually the Pasha clapped his hands and climbed to his feet. At this signal the others also rose and stood respectfully with heads slightly bowed as their ruler left the room. As the door closed behind him the men left behind finally turned to face the prisoners.

"Come," the scribe said as he put down his pen and paper and climbed to his feet. "Come see what is on offer." At his words the Janissary chaouch barked out a command and the guards who had stood completely motionless for hours snapped into action and with curses and slaps forced the weary prisoners to stand at attention. James, who stood at the front of the prisoner line, was the first to be examined.

"This one has strong shoulders built for carrying heavy loads," the scribe pointed out. "And see," he continued, lifting up James' hands and studying the palms. "See the callused skin . . . he is made for heavy work or the oar!" Two of the Moors stepped forward and began to examine James. They checked his arms and chest, felt his thighs and looked inside his mouth to see if his teeth were in good condition.

"See," the scribe said loudly, "is he not a fine specimen; there is many years' heavy work in this one . . . who will bid?" James listened to the scribe's words and although he couldn't work out what was said, he knew their meaning. He was being offered for sale like a beast in the marketplace.

12

Erin, Anna and Alice – clutching the linen bags that held changes of the so recently alien but now admired clothes – crossed the courtyard to the sound of morning songbirds singing in the lemon trees and climbed into the donkey cart.

"We are to travel a distance," Alice said quietly tapping the bag in her lap. Erin nodded.

"Yes and I think we will at least travel in more comfort than that which brought us here."

After a welcome evening meal, a luxurious bath in rose scented water and a reasonable night's sleep stretched out close together on piles of silk cushions, each of them had had time in the early morning to take further stock of their situation. What lay ahead was, they admitted totally unknown and like all things unknown gave cause for concern; but like most young people who lived for today they were able to push the future to the back of their minds and focus on the here and now.

Now the bronze gates swung ponderously open and the driver cracked his whip. *Once again we are set on a course not known* Erin thought, as minutes later the little party turned right off the wide road to make its way back towards the harbour . . . just before a bedraggled line of male prisoners came into sight from the left and approached the bronze gates.

The early morning virtually empty streets journey back to the harbour was almost surreal in its ordinariness. This time there was no bewildering crowds of alien faces, no leering men, no twitching curtains. This time only the occasional foraging dog, the soft rumble of iron rimmed wheels over the stone road and the constant grumbling of the donkey as it hauled its load.

As they neared the harbour Erin glanced across at Anna. She and the other young woman were perhaps only a year or two at the most apart in age, but to Erin's mind Anna was little more than a child. *She was so sorely troubled and afraid yesterday*, Erin thought, *but now she seems to accept our situation . . . and even find some pleasure in it,* she added mentally as Anna felt Erin's gaze on her and turned and smiled.

She was about to say something to Erin when she noticed that the other, with an odd expression on her face, was looking not at her, but straight ahead.

Anna followed Erin's gaze and saw the reason. A hundred yards away a Janissary with a leather whip was beating a man. The man, who was dressed in a filthy cotton shift and a short red waistcoat, was on his knees facing away from his tormentor with his head almost resting on a huge stone. His bare arms were raised with his hands cupped around the back of his neck in an attempt at protection. Around him other prisoners with ankle manacles containing long heavy chains were struggling to carry more huge stones towards the landward edge of the long semi-circular breakwater that protected the harbour from the ravages of the sea.

Closer and the women could hear the crack of the whip, the victim's cries and, could see where his waistcoat had ridden up, the red stripes of blood that decorated his back through the flimsy shift. Anna's hand flew to her mouth to stifle a gasp of horror. She had almost come to accept the fate that lay in store for her but now this act of barbarity brought her situation crashing back to her with brutal bludgeoning force.

"They are monsters!" she moaned as Erin threw a protective arm around her shoulder and drew her close. Within a minute the donkey cart had made its way onto the harbour front where a huge galley almost twice the size of the vessel that had been their prison for long weary weeks lay at anchor thirty yards from shore. It had a raised metal clad prow that carried a large forward facing cannon, two great masts that carried furled lateen sails and two covered decks, a small one at the prow and a larger poop deck, above which Erin could see a platform covered by a red silk canopy from which a profusion of blue, green and red pennants hung rippling gently in the early morning breeze.

From her earlier experience she knew that this was probably the pilot's position and also a vantage point for the captain who would be able to view everything that took place on the vessel's open deck below.

"It seems that this is to be our new accommodation," Alice said as the driver hauled on the reins of the little donkey cart. Erin turned her attention back to her companions.

"Yes Alice, it must be so," she said quietly, "and let us pray that what awaits us at journey's end is not as bad as we might fear." Alice was about to say something, but her reply was cut off by sudden action on the vessel's deck where a worryingly familiar figure accompanied by two Janissaries appeared. The gaudy clothing was different but there was no mistaking the fat waddling figure of the eunuch who had performed the embarrassing personal examinations on board the other vessel that had carried them from their homes.

From their seat in the donkey cart Erin and her companions looked on as the Janissaries lowered a small dinghy over the side, nimbly climbed aboard and struck out towards the shore. As soon as the dinghy landed one of the Janissaries climbed out and marched over to the cart. He barked out a short order and made a sharp 'get down' gesture towards the women.

"Come sisters," Erin said with forced brightness – as much for her own sake as for Anna and Alice's. "The sea beckons once again."

On board the galley the eunuch made no attempt to speak to them other than to utter a short barked order to follow him. He escorted them past rows of rough wooden benches that spanned the width of the long open deck and past piles of stacked oars – that were almost three times the length of a man – and up three wooden steps to a tiny cabin on the prow deck, where he ushered them in and made a show of locking the door behind him as he left.

The cabin was clean and tidy, though sparsely furnished. It contained a rough oblong wooden table with two benches, three thick straw filled mattresses on the floor and a small hanging oil lamp suspended from the ceiling timbers. In one corner there was another smaller wooden table with a pewter pitcher sitting in a large pewter bowl and two rough cotton towels. In another corner a simple wooden bucket completed the furnishings.

"It is a great improvement from our last shipboard lodgings," Erin said. Alice smiled. She knew that Erin's forced good humour was meant to calm all their nerves and especially those of easily frightened Anna.

"Oh yes, my Lord, a great improvement indeed!" Alice answered brightly. "Do you not agree Anna?" The younger woman glanced round the cabin, swallowed, wet her lips and with an effort to control a tremor in her voice agreed that it was.

They had spent almost an hour sat at the table in quiet contemplation when sounds of activity from outside distracted them. They heard barked orders, the staccato beat of many iron shod shoes on deck, more orders and finally after another half hour the creak of the windlass as the anchor was raised.

From his position on the poop deck Ali Bichnin watched as the Janissary odjak with drawn yatagans disappeared below deck like ferrets down a rabbit warren; then a minute later re-appeared behind a clutch of two dozen shaven headed near naked and heavily ankle shackled men.

The men, shielding their eyes against the morning sun were herded towards the rows of wooden benches where they slumped down and sat in cowed submission. The process was repeated a further five times before all the benches were full and four renegado crewmen passed the heavy oars through to the seated slaves. When each oar was taken up by three slaves the Admiral gave a raised arm signal, the 144 rowers dipped their shoulders and 48 broad bladed oars rose and hovered above the waves like gliding falcons' wings poised in flight.

The Admiral's arm descended and the oars as one dipped into the still water. From the deck one of the renegado crewmen looked up towards Ali Bichnin for the signal. The Admiral nodded lightly and at a single word barked command from the slave master renegado, the rowers bent forward and hauled on the oars.

"We are leaving," Erin said softly as a low groan from deep in the galley's timbers filtered up to the cabin and she felt the vessel move forward, at first haltingly and then more smoothly.

James bunched his fists in bitter impotence when the two men turned their backs on him and began a lively conversation with the scribe. After a minute or so, the scribe clapped his hands and one of the Janissary guards strode over, tugged on James' arm and dragged him over to stand against a wall.

The scenario was repeated again and again as the prisoners were paraded in front of and then examined by the potential buyers. Eventually after much bargaining John Davis, Robert Harris, Stephen Ryder and Robert Mould joined James; then after the bidders had taken a brief break for tea and idle chatter, Samuel Carter, William Fletcher, Richard Evans, Adam Thomas and John Cartwright, also joined the others against the wall.

The rest of the men, who were older and less physically well built were then sold in ones and twos to various bidders, while finally an ashen faced young George was taken by one of the European looking renegadoes.

From his position standing against the wall James caught the words "Come boy," spoken in English by the man as he moved towards the side door obviously intent on leaving with his purchase. As they drew close to him James stepped out from the wall. "Sir," he said earnestly, "The boy; you will treat him well?" Morat Rais smiled thinly.

"He is to be a page boy, no more." James nodded.

"I thank you sir, for he has suffered grievously." This time it was Morat Rais who nodded.

"He will be treated fairly – unlike the rest of you men and some of the women who I liberated from Baltimore . . ." The pirate's words, delivered so casually, landed like a hornet's sting.

"You . . . you are the one who . . . " James' stunned reply, aimed at the pirate's retreating back hung in the air as Morat Rais and his new slave boy disappeared through the door and a cascade of tumbling emotions; shock, aching loss and finally, smouldering rage, coursed through James' body. That was the man ultimately responsible for his brother's and Jonathan's deaths and for the bitter loss of the woman he loved; the man who had ripped apart a hard working God fearing community for the sake of devil's gold. He drew in and slowly exhaled a deep breath. *Rage will consume me*, he thought. *I must remain in command of my emotions if I am to stand chance of deliverance from this cruel fate.*

Any further thought was then cut short by a barked command from the Janissary chaouch and the prisoners were quickly force marched out of the palace by the way they had entered. Outside, James and his little group of five were made to stand together as were Samuel Carter and his group while the other manacled men, led by their purchasers and an armed Janissary were marched off in one's and two's.

"Some of us are surely destined for the oar," Robert Harris muttered to James as the last of the older prisoners disappeared from sight. James nodded. He like most people who lived and or made a living close to shore had heard terrible tales of pirate raids and the horrible fates that lay in store for poor captives who were spirited away to lives of misery and fiendish torture in Moorish lands.

"We are it seems soon to find out," James muttered as the Janissary chaouch strode over to the prisoners and gave the order to form a single file and move. Flanked by guards the two little groups of men, separated by several paces, were marched back down towards the city.

We are not to be taken back to the cells, James thought as he realized they were moving in a different direction to when they had approached the palace earlier. Several minutes later the little group were brought to a halt in front of a high arched opening built into high walls, through which they could see part of what was obviously, to their rustic minds, a monstrous dark and forbidding looking building.

As they were marched through into an enormous courtyard at least two hundred yards square, the prisoners were further taken aback by the riot of activity. They had entered a gigantic version of the sights and sounds that had first greeted them when they had been led into that other much smaller courtyard with its stalls, bars and cells.

Here there were, it seemed, dozens of shops, taverns and public cook houses all of which had wooden tables and chairs arranged around them. The taverns were thronged with hundreds of chattering men of what seemed a dozen different nationalities smoking from clay pipes and drinking flagons of wine served by gaunt pallid-faced slaves who blank eyed, wandered wraith-like among the crowds; while from the cook houses the tantalizing aroma of frying meats set the juices in the prisoners' shrunken stomachs gurgling with the memory of distant meals.

As James looked around in awe he noticed that what had first seemed from outside the archway a single building was in fact three separate buildings. To the left and right there were two huge square stone built blocks with barred gate entrances, while in the centre there was a smaller stone building with an open arched wooden door from which he could see sombre robed European chaplains entering or emerging.

We are in a heathen land, James thought, *but it seems we are to have the scant comfort of Christian ministrations.* His thought was immediately followed by an order from the chaouch and they were force marched over to the left hand building where a guard who stood outside the gate produced a key, unlocked and swung the heavy metal grill open.

Inside, the prisoners were marched down a narrow dimly lit corridor and into a small door less anti-room that contained nothing but a single chair and a small rough wooden table on which rested a large wooden bowl of gently steaming water. Stood impassively by the table was an ebony skinned Negro who was holding a wicked looking razor in his right hand.

"You sit!" The chaouch tugged at James' arm and forced him over to the chair. With his eyes fixed on the razor James did as ordered and within two minutes his head, eyebrows and growth of beard were shaved leaving behind a number of angry red marks, some of which wept blood. Finished, he was made to stand aside while the others were also shaved.

When they had all been dealt with they were taken back out into the corridor and to another anti-room. There the shackles and short linking chain which restricted their walking were struck off and a thick metal circlet with two lips at the slightly open end and with an eyelet at the back that held a heavy three foot long chain was prised further open and fitted to their right ankles. A mushroom headed brass rivet was pushed through two holes in the circlet's lips and hammered in to close and secure the anklet firmly in place.

They were then ordered to strip off their soiled nightclothes and were each issued with a grubby woollen blanket and a baggy skirt-like garment drawn in at the knees to form rough trousers. They were also given a floppy wide-necked shirt and a red waist-length sleeveless jacket.

Once they had pulled on the strange garments they were marched back out into and down the corridor, before a sharp left bend led them to a scene from hell.

The huge dimly lit almost airless room that confronted them reeked with the stench of human sweat, urine and excrement and was alive with low moans of pain, despair and angry shouted curses.

As James' eyes adjusted to the fitful light that dripped through small high barred windows he made out a series of long thick metal poles spaced some six feet apart, each of which were bolted to the floor and disappeared upwards into the gloom. At regular intervals of about three feet each pole had metal eyelets through which thick cord was strung supporting canvas hammocks, many of which sagged heavily with bodies.

"Blessed Jesus!" Robert Harris muttered as he took in the scene. "We are come to Lucifer's waiting room." The other captives gathered closely together in a little knot, each equally appalled at the sight, sounds and smells. With an effort James made his voice sound much lighter than his mood.

"Well here we are and we must make the best of it," he said a little louder than he had intended.

"You are English?" The disembodied voice seemed to float down from on high.

"English, yes!" James directed his response in the general direction from which the question seemed to come.

"The ladder, bring it over here." James marked a movement in one of the tiered hammocks and then saw a bare arm emerge and point to a rough wooden ladder propped against one of the upright poles. When he had done as told the owner of the arm climbed down and with James at his side, made his way to the little knot of newcomers.

"Welcome to Bagnio One," he said holding up a hand in mock greeting.

The man was painfully thin. His shaved skull, face and his bare arms were burnt a deep reddish brown colour giving him an appearance of rude health – an appearance that was immediately contradicted by a number of raw weeping lesions that covered the tight skin of his bald pate. "I am John Thompson late of Camborne, Cornwall," he said as the group opened up to admit him. "Where were you taken?"

"From the village of Baltimore in Ireland," James said.

"You are not English then?" said their puzzled new friend.

"English settlers," James replied. The man nodded.

"Ah well, wherever you hail from your mother tongue is

most welcome in this stinking hole of a dozen alien ones," he said lightly raising both skinny arms to encompass their surroundings.

For the next few minutes the new captives asked questions that were answered in a flat emotionless voice. He and five fellow fishermen had been taken in St Ives Bay more than six years ago. *No, the others were not here now – they were all dead*. "Were there any other English or Irish prisoners here?" *No, there are some other English, but they are in Bagnio 2, where with others they are used on public construction and repair works and road maintenance projects*. Had he spent time chained to the oar? *Yes*. For how long had he been chained? *He didn't know for how long; but it must have been for more than four years. Now, while the fittest of Bagnio One worked on the never ending task of maintaining and repairing the harbour mole*, *he with others less fit laboured in the quarry dressing smaller stone into building sized bricks*. "Was the mole repair work odious?" He smiled thinly. Whatever work they had been used to before, he said dryly, *would be as child's play when placed alongside the backbreaking soul destroying slavery that lay ahead in that direction.*

This last statement delivered with toneless, but iron conviction, caused them to pass stricken glances between themselves. James seeing the effect the man's words had on the others, stepped in.

"We must steel ourselves," he said firmly. "We are young and strong and used to hard labour and with the help of God we will prevail." The man smiled thinly at James' words, but offered no more on the subject; instead he said that they should each find an empty hammock and get what sleep they could conjure up before a rude dawn awakening.

13

Erin's face hardened as Zahid Ali entered the tiny cabin. The eunuch smiled. He always enjoyed it when his presence caused a reaction and especially so when that reaction was one of concern or naked fear. This young woman didn't fear him he knew, but she was, at least for a few weeks totally under his control. He may not now hold the power of life or death in his podgy hands but he could make life very uncomfortable and that knowledge caused his smile to widen.

"Your quarters are to your liking?" Erin blinked and her eyes opened wider.

"You speak English!" The eunuch tilted his head and his slack lipped mouth formed itself into a little moue.

"Of course, I am the head eunuch to his highness the Pasha. I speak English, French and Turkish . . . as befits a personage of importance," he added with an edge of pomposity to his tone.

"Where are we being taken?" The eunuch's smile widened.

"You are being taken to someone who, with a simple click of his fingers, has the power to snuff out a thousand lives." Erin swallowed nervously but her voice remained firm.

"And this person, this person of power, what will he want of us?" Zahid Ali laughed, but there was no laughter in his voice when he answered.

"He demands only your bodies and your souls!" Anna's hand flew to her mouth to stifle a cry and Alice moved quickly to her side to place an arm across the girl's shoulder. Erin turned briefly and gave Anna what she hoped was a comforting smile, then turned back to face the eunuch.

"We are women," she said defiantly, "and we may not be able to protect our bodies against violation but no heathen will take our souls!" Zahid Ali scowled and he waved a ring bedecked hand in dismissal.

"Your infidel souls are no concern of mine," he said. "You are peasants and I am here to educate you."

What he did not add however was that his presence on this voyage had been forced upon him by the Pasha who thought it would be to his advantage with the Sultan if the tribute of women arrived schooled in language and manners.

In addition the Pasha also considered it sound sense to have a keen pair of ears and eyes there to keep watch on the Admiral.

Zahid Ali had of course bowed to his Pasha's will, but privately he was far from happy. He suspected there were other reasons for the 'honour' bestowed upon him. He had heard rumours of the Sultan's murderous moods and thought that perhaps his Pasha was keen to distance himself as far as possible from those moods, and particularly so, as it was also rumoured that the Sultan held his uncle, the Pasha, in a very low regard that bordered on contempt.

No wonder then, he thought, *that I am to take his place in the lion's den*.

Another reason for his lack of enthusiasm was that over the four years that he had been at the Pasha's palace he had, through hard work and cunning advanced from the position of a lowly eunuch to one of some power. He had forged a tight grip within the palace, a grip that could be loosened by lengthy absence and the thought made him resolve that these infidel women would learn to regret their part in taking him away from his rightful place as head of the Pasha's household.

Erin bridled at the eunuch's dismissive words.

"I am no peasant!" she spat back. The eunuch smiled, turned on his heel and without another word left the cabin. As the key turned in the lock Alice took her arm off Anna's shoulder and moved to Erin's side.

"Sister," she said quietly, "that man has an evil nature; it is perhaps best that you do not give him excuse to vent it on us." Erin's cheeks coloured and she lowered her head a little in acceptance.

"You are right sister," she replied softly. "My tongue sometimes overrules my head." Alice was about to say something else but was stopped by Anna's agonised cry.

"Oh what is to become of us! We are in mortal danger of losing our very souls!" Erin quickly strode to the younger girl's side and took up her hands in her own.

"Sister, we must remain firm in our shared faith. Mine may differ a little from yours and Alice's but we all must trust in the One True God." Anna took a deep breath and nodded.

"Yes sister," she said quietly. "You are right; I promise to be of stronger heart." Erin smiled and placed a kiss on the young girl's cheek.

The day dragged on with only the appearance of a Janissary carrying a tray containing food, a pitcher of water and three glasses to break the monotony.

After they had eaten and slaked their thirsts they sat at the rough table. Their conversation was stilted and contained long silences where each of them turned their thoughts inwards.

Erin agonised over the fate of Helen her surrogate mother and the boys. But most of all, as she had earlier on their arrival, she agonised over the fate of James. *He is so bold and brash* she thought. *What if he had put up valiant resistance? What if . . . God please let it not be . . . . What if he had been cut down by those screaming devils? No,* she assured herself, *he is safe, I feel it in my heart.* And just to reinforce the feeling she folded a hand into a small fist and beat her breast three times; wherein a sudden, deep, aching, yearning void blossomed . . . a void that longed with every fibre of her being to be filled.

Alice had no close family ties. Like Erin she was an orphan who served as maid to an elderly aunt and her husband who owned the little haberdashery and sail making store that nestled under the walls of the *Fort Of The Jewels.* She had been staying over night at the cottage of Richard Evans and his wife Cora down at the cove where her close friend Emily Smythe served as maid. *One night* she thought, *I was there for a single night . . . a night that has turned my life upside down.*

Anna was also a maid. She cooked and cleaned for the Fish Palace manager, Ould Osburne, who was almost crippled with swelling of the joints in his hands. Her parents and two younger brothers had left the Cove a year earlier when she was fourteen due to her father falling foul of the community's strict moral code by entering into a relationship with a married woman – who was also forced to leave. Young unworldly Anna was appalled by her father's behaviour and for almost a year suffered agonies of embarrassment from constantly being reminded of his infidelity by several of the village girls; most of whom were only too pleased to make fun of the not too bright pretty little blond haired girl.

My sisters will take care of me she thought. *They are my family now.* And she carried the thought in her head as they all retired to their mattresses for the night.

"Up!" Zahid Ali demanded as soon as he entered the cabin. The captives, who had spent a restless night plagued with terrible thoughts and dreadful dreams struggled to their feet.

"Your education begins!" The eunuch sneered. Erin rubbed the sleep from her eyes and faced their tormentor.

"What education?" she demanded.

"You are to learn how to speak, behave and perform in the presence of your superiors." Erin's fiery nature bubbled to the surface, but with a conscious effort she damped it down.

"We are in no position to argue," she said with forced meekness. The eunuch nodded.

"Good, then we begin. When in the presence of your superiors in the Sultan's palace you will never speak without first being spoken to. When you do speak you do so with eyes turned down and with head bowed." Erin's lips tightened but she made a determined effort to remain silent.

"When spoken to with words that require an answer you always reply with humility and end your reply with Highness, My Lord or My Lady." Erin's nature flared again.

"We have but one Lord and will answer to no other!" The eunuch glared, turned on his heel and strode over to the cabin door.

"Today you will have no food or drink. Tomorrow we will try again."

As he left and turned the key Erin stared at the locked door and bit her lip.

Outside, Zahid Ali smiled thinly and mentally patted himself on the back. It was clever of him he thought to demand that a Christian must address a Moslem with the term 'My Lord'. "Yes," he muttered to himself, "the tedious voyage will provide me with entertainment in making the fiery headed one bend to my will."

Inside, Alice saw that Erin was embarrassed again by her actions. "You spoke true, sister," she said kindly. "But perhaps the time is not right to champion our faith." Erin, a little shame-faced nodded.

"Would that I had your tight control over emotions sister," she murmured. Alice shook her head.

"Your temperament is what makes you what you are sister. Do not change, except to perhaps learn to count to five before attacking!" Erin forced a smile. She had come to greatly admire Alice's steady nature and the way she was able to confront situations with a clear head and a circumspect tongue.

From the back of the cabin, Anna, who had not really been paying attention to the brief conversation said: "I am hungry!"

"Up infidels!" The black guard roared and cracked his whip. All around the still dark room hammocks swayed as the lash's sharp voice cut through the foetid air. Within ten minutes the hammocks were empty and their occupants had lined up. James and the others stood immediately behind John Thompson in a ragged rank that contained at least 80 to 90 souls.

"Where do we go now?" James whispered to Thompson. The man turned his head slightly and muttered: "We go to dine my friend." Any further words were cut off by a barked single word order from the guard and the line began to move slowly forward.

Within another five minutes the prisoners were ranged outside and shivering in the early morning chilly air where, in spite of the hour, the courtyard was busy with the setting up of dozens of stalls and the comings and goings of traders and a large number of unchained general slaves who were bringing in all manner of goods and foodstuffs.

An odjak of Janissaries with a chaouch at their head which had been standing to attention outside the outer gate to the bagnio chivvied them back into a neat line and moved them towards one of the wooden stalls where a bleary eyed slave began doling out small loaves of black bread.

When each man had been served the chaouch shouted an order and the line of prisoners were marched over to and out of the arch to begin the gradual descent towards the city gate.

Outside, the still sleeping streets were eerily silent, with only the odd barking dog to complain at the noise of dragging chains along the stone road that led down to the harbour.

"Eat," John Thompson muttered through a mouthful of the stale black bread, "for you will have no time later." James and the other Baltimore men did as suggested.

"Tis not fit for dogs," Robert Harris complained as he forced a mouthful of the bread down his gullet.

"Aye, but it is still food . . . of sorts," John Davis muttered, "and I fear we will dine on nothing better this day." His words had no sooner left his mouth when a huge explosion detonated somewhere in front of them and a thick plume of dust climbed into the air above the rooftops.

"It is an attack!" Robert Harris cried. "We may yet be freed!" Two paces in front of him, John Thompson turned and smiled thinly. "If only it were so," he said ruefully. From their position near the head of the line James turned, looked back and saw that the explosion had not registered on the faces of any but his own companions.

"The stone quarry," John Thompson muttered calmly.

"Stone quarry?" James said.

"Aye, the stone quarry; the place of breaking backs and crushed bones," Thompson replied.

James was about to ask more, but before he could the line of prisoners began to round a bend in the road and in the middle distance over the tops of the city walls he saw the reason for the dust plume. There, a mile or so past the harbour, on the lower slopes of a towering cliff, beneath a rising dust cloud, a raw pale wound showed where tons of rock had over time been blasted away.

Once they had been ushered through the city gate the chaouch barked a command and the Janissary escorts with cracking whips forced the line of prisoners into a steady dog trot which within minutes had taken them past the harbour entrance and up towards the mutilated cliff. Five more minutes and the chaouch called a halt as the line of prisoners approached a jumbled mass of shattered rock and scree at the base of the cliff.

The chaouch issued another command and the prisoners were quickly split into four groups of about twenty men. Two of the groups which contained the older and less fit looking prisoners were marched to one end of the quarry where they were put to work dressing the smaller scree stone.

James' group, which included the rest of his fellow captives were marched over to one of four 12 foot long flat wooden sledges on which were piled a selection of heavy hammers, metal chisels and longer metal crowbars. Once one of the Janissaries had handed out the tools they and the other gangs were marched back to the jumble of rocks and put to work as the dawning sun crept over the horizon.

The work was hard and the guards were merciless in their determination to wring every last ounce of effort out of the prisoners. Within the first two hours most of the men, including the newcomers had felt the biting sting of the whip on their backs.

They dug out huge rocks from the scree with their bare hands and when that was impossible they used the long crowbars to lever them out and then with the hammers and chisels set to knocking off jagged edges before manhandling the heavy rocks onto the sledges.

As each sledge was loaded the prisoners split into two lines of ten men and each man took up one of the two ropes attached to the front of each sledge. At an order from the chaouch the Janissary guards cracked their whips and on their wooden runners the sledges at first inched forward and then gathered a little momentum on the downward slope towards the harbour a mile away.

Several times on the way the sledges ground to a halt over rough ground and the guards resorted to the whip. Twice, James felt the hornet sting and a trickle of blood run down his back. Some, like Samuel Carter, tasted it more.

After what seemed like hours of cruel torture the sledges finally reached the harbour and the stone was unloaded close to the mole's landward edge.

As soon as the sleds were empty each man then took up one of the heavy stones and struggled up onto the 400 yard long and five yard wide breakwater, where they placed them where ordered. As soon as the last stones were placed they were then given a five minute break and allowed several mouthfuls of water from goatskin carafes that the guards carried, before, break over, they turned the sledges around and made their way back to the base of the cliff.

Three more times they repeated the ordeal before, on the

last return with the sun blazing down on their sweat grimed heads they were allowed a ten minute break for another drink of water.

Sat on a large rock, James wiped his forehead and massaged his aching arms and shoulders with raw skin stripped hands. He was young and very fit but this work was totally different to what he was used to.

"How long must we suffer this?" he asked John Thompson, who had had been assigned to the older, less strong group dressing the smaller stones and who had walked over to James' side during the brief break. The other man smiled thinly.

"Until the sun deserts the heavens this day." James groaned.

"And tomorrow?"

"And tomorrow and a hundred tomorrows . . . or until your departed soul takes flight."

Two backbreaking trips more and in the gathering gloom the chaouch called a halt; the tools were loaded back onto the sledges and the leg weary return to the bagnio began.

Inside the courtyard they were given another small loaf of stale black bread that was softened with a little oil and then locked up for the night.

Although they were exhausted by the physical and mental trauma brought on by the day, the little group of new prisoners sat in a tight circle on the cell floor to discuss their situation.

Samuel Carter, who because of his creeping infirmity had suffered more physically and tasted more of the lash than the others, spoke first. "We are in a desperate position," he said gravely. "How are we now to make the best of it?" Robert Mould shook his head.

"It would seem from looking at the rest of our fellow prisoners trapped in this place of despair that we do not have the power to do anything other than to pray to our Lord for strength and possible deliverance." James, who, since their capture had always tried to be positive decided to speak out.

"The others are beaten, they have accepted their fate. They are not like us these men of a dozen tongues. We will prevail . . ." Robert shook his head again.

"Prevail how," he said quietly. "Are we not as beasts,

shackled and driven to the will of these heathens?" Even though exhausted Robert's defeatist words ignited a spark of anger in James' breast.

"We will find a way!" he said forcefully. But it will be a way of our own making – for our Lord has not done anything to help these other poor Christians who languish in this filthy dungeon!" James' words that teetered on the edge of blasphemy in the minds of most of the devout little circle caused an uneasy stir. Robert Harris rose unsteadily to his feet

"We are all of fraught mind," he said glancing at James. "It is best that we get what rest we can now." The others, realising that his words made sense followed his example.

Minutes later as he lay in his hammock James' mind slipped back to the harbour edge where they had offloaded the rocks from the sledges – back to the harbour and the seemingly empty vessels that rode gently in a soft swell tantalisingly close to the shore.

14

"You are ready?" Zahid Ali said with the edge of a sneer creeping into his voice. Alice glanced across at Erin who stood stone-faced.

"Yes," she said quietly, "we are ready." The eunuch nodded.

"Then we begin."

For the next two hours they were schooled in the mysterious arts of courtesan ship. They were told what to do what not to do; what to say and when to say it; what to wear and how to wear it. They were also given their first lessons in the language of their new Ottoman masters. This latter proved difficult for the rustic mind of Anna, who despite frequent and increasingly angry prompts from Zahid Ali, struggled desperately to master even simple short phrases. Eventually, the eunuch flew into a rage and strode over to the cabin door.

"Today there will be no food or water!" he shouted as he stormed out. As the cabin door slammed Anna burst into tears.

"It is too hard!" she wailed. "My mind is not quick enough!" Erin and Alice rushed to comfort the stricken girl.

"We will help you little sister," Alice said softly.

"Yes, you will soon grasp it," Erin added, failing to add that an empty belly was a wonderful aid to learning, and particularly so for a girl like Anna who relished her food.

The next few days saw a repeat of the eunuch's tantrums and more missed meals. Eventually Anna's stomach triumphed over her head; she began to pay closer attention to the lessons and with the evening promptings of her 'sisters' she managed to gain at least a very rough grasp of the language.

A full week into the voyage passed before they were allowed to leave the cabin and enter the company of someone other than Zahid Ali. And that someone was Ali Bichnin, the Admiral of the Pasha's fleet. The women had been expecting the usual early morning arrival of the eunuch and his sneering remarks, so were surprised when the key turned in the cabin door and a white renegado crew member entered instead.

"Come," the man said simply. The women, who were glad of anything that would at least break the monotony even temporarily, glanced briefly at each other and followed the man out of the cabin door. On the small deck they stood for a brief moment, drew the fresh bracing air into their lungs and enjoyed the stiff breeze that caressed their faces and played through their hair.

"Come!" the man ordered. They followed him down the steps onto the mid deck and passed the rows of empty wooden benches and then up another four steps to the stern platform where, beneath the red silk canopy the helmsman, another white renegado was piloting a course.

They were led past the helmsman to the side of the canopy and their guide rapped softly on a cabin door. There was an immediate muffled response from inside the cabin and the renegado opened the door and from outside ushered them in before quickly shutting the door again.

Inside, the first thing that struck them was the sheer opulence of the cabin in total contrast to the Spartan starkness of their own accommodation. The dark polished wood panelling gleamed; there was an ornate brass framed mirror hung round with crimson and deep blue silks drapes; three large multi-coloured Hamadan Persian rugs were strewn across the floor; a large polished brass oil lamp with a crystal glass bowl hanging from the ceiling and two smaller brass and crystal wall mounted lamps sat either side of a polished mahogany desk strewn with charts . . . behind which stood a tall, lightly bearded, dark haired and deeply tanned white man dressed in Moorish garb.

The man, who appeared to be entering his middle years, held out a hand, smiled and said: "Welcome," in English. Erin gasped.

"You are English!" she said. The man's smile never wavered.

"No, I am . . . was Italian," he answered. "Now I am Ali Bichnin Admiral of the Pasha's fleet." Erin's eyes widened.

"You have turned Turk!" she said with a thick edge of amazement and accusation in her voice. Ali Bichnin's smile faded and his deep blue eyes narrowed slightly.

"I have embraced the true faith," he said coolly; then in a slightly warmer voice continued: "but I accept your right to honour your own god." Erin was not about to let it go at that.

"But surely you are . . . were; born to honour His Holiness, our father in Rome!" The Admiral smiled thinly.

"Rome means nothing to me," he replied. Erin's face registered her dismay and then she lowered her eyes slightly.

"I will pray for your soul," she said softly. The Admiral's laugh was genuine and warm, but his accuser took it for one of scorn.

"You mock me and my faith sir!" Ali Bichnin, impressed by the spirit of this slip of a girl held up a placating hand.

"Forgive me," he said sincerely but with the slightest edge of indulgent humour, "I meant to give no offence." Erin's stiff backed stance relaxed a little and the Admiral took the chance to move on to a less contentious subject.

"Your cabin is comfortable?" Alice, who had been slightly alarmed by Erin's verbal attack decided to intervene.

"It is hardly so sir, there is very little of comfort." Ali Bichnin nodded. He had left the details of the cabin's furnishing to the Pasha's eunuch who he knew was a man of mean temperament.

"I will see to it that your needs are attended to," the Admiral said. Alice attempted a smile. It would seem that this man was one of breeding, she thought; so perhaps it would be of benefit if she took over the lead from her fiery 'sister'.

"Our thanks sir," she said demurely. "And would you tell us whither we are taken?"

"We are on our way to pay tribute in taxes to his Serene Highness Sultan Murad IV of Constantinople."

"And what is to be our part in this venture?"

"The tribute," Ali Bichnin said evenly, "is not one purely of gold coin . . ." Alice nodded. So it was as they had thought; they were to be the mere playthings of a heathen in a heathen land. She glanced across at Erin, who nodded in understanding, and then at Anna, who simply looked on wide eyed.

For the next few minutes their charming host asked them where they had come from and listened with seeming sympathy as they briefly related their capture and treatment. Finally he sighed.

"The ways of this world are often cruel," he said. "Your own lives will change greatly; but know this you are in many ways fortunate . . . Erin, who had been content to let Alice do most of the talking up to now, could not help herself.

"Fortunate!" she exclaimed. "How so, *fortunate* sir!" The Admiral shrugged lightly.

"You, by your own mouths tell me that you have come from hard lives. Soon you will want for nothing. You will live in splendour in a magnificent palace. You will eat the best food, be clothed in the finest garments and will know none of life's hardships that other women have to endure." Erin shook her head violently.

"And unlike other women we will be slaves without freedom, without choice!" Ali Bichnin nodded.

"It is so," he conceded. "But as I have said, the ways of the world are often cruel and freedom is not a natural condition of man, *or* woman." With these words Erin knew that their captor's interest in their plight was for now, at an end. She was forced to admit to herself that he seemed to be a man of some intelligence and of more than a little compassion; but he was also a man, she was sure, who had much more to concern him self with than the well-being of three young Christian women.

As they left the Admiral's cabin and were returned to their humbler quarters Anna, as the door was locked behind them, said breathlessly: "A real palace with beautiful clothes!"

As the days turned into weeks and dragged wearily by, the Baltimore men's collective mood slowly changed. Almost to a man their initial feelings of shock morphed into a kind of numbness. Before, they had suffered the agonies of loss of loved ones and loss of freedom; now the only emotion that ruled almost all of their waking hours was the basic will to survive.

Some exercised this will better than others. Samuel Carter's rapidly failing health became a concern. He was often seen to cough bright specks of blood and he became increasingly withdrawn and sank into a deep depression. Every evening when they wearily trudged back to the bagnio he almost immediately took to his hammock with barely a word to any of his companions.

Tall, thin and stoop shouldered Adam Thomas, also suffered. He seemed to shrink as his stoop became more pronounced and his watery blue eyes sank deeper into their bony sockets.

One man alone quietly raged. James saw the effect that imprisonment and the cruel back breaking labour was having on the others and he steeled himself to fight back; as fight back he must if he was to have any chance of finding and rescuing his stolen love. So, where the others had become less animated, more docile and because of it tasted more of the lash, he doubled his efforts at the quarry.

Within two months and in spite of a meagre diet, his already muscular body had been transformed. His forearms and biceps became knotted and bulged with iron hard muscle; his slightly soft stomach disappeared and was replaced with a flat corrugated washboard; his broad shoulders widened and his chest swelled. And with the honing of his body his mind too sharpened and the germ of a plan began to form.

On their daily journeys from the quarry to the mole he had often studied the vessels that lay at anchor inside the breakwater. There never seemed to be any sign of crew on any of the dozen or so decks. If only, he thought, they could get on board one of those craft his and his companions skills would surely be enough to sail and pilot that craft to safety.

15

The female slave knelt head bowed at the seated Queen Mother and Valide Sultan's bare feet and with a small brush added the finishing touches to the black nail dye. She raised her eyes respectfully and received a slight nod. Relieved at the sign of approval, she reached for the gem-encrusted open-toed sandals and slipped them onto Kosem's feet while taking extreme care not to smudge her work. A casual wave of a ring-bedecked hand signalled a dismissal and the girl with head still bowed got up from her knees and backed slowly out of the dressing room.

Kosem sat for a minute on the low divan listening to the tinkling of jasmine scented water that splashed into a marble fountain in accompaniment to the soft lyre music being played by one of her female musicians, before standing up and studying herself in the full length Italian mirror.

Her dark brown almost black eyes took in a pleasing sight. Lustrous deep chestnut shoulder length hair framed a line-free high cheek-boned olive heart-shaped face – a gift from Greek parentage – that belied her 40 years age. The body was of a tall and pleasantly curvy nature with full breasts, narrow waist and wide hips accentuated by a long transparent, loose sleeved deeply v-necked chemise which was overlaid by a tight white silken shalvar. Satisfied with her reflection, she nodded and clapped her hands. Immediately, another of her personal slave girls strode forward with her arms full of clothes.

Kosem selected a short sleeved yellow-beige silk dress with a flower bouquet pattern of damask on a satin background and held her arms up as the girl slipped the garment over her head and did up the eight large pear shaped silk covered buttons down to her waist.

The slave then fitted a wide gold belt around Kosem's middle and held out a dagger in a decorated sheath which the Sultan's mother slipped into the belt. Finally, the slave girl carefully placed a round gem studded platiin hat onto Kosem's head. The hat, similar to ones worn by Jewish women had a large feather high on either side and bunches of black feathers that hung down at ear level onto her chest.

Her dressing complete, Kosem clapped her hands sharply and her attendants quickly left the room. Alone, she turned her attention back to the imported mirror and nodded again. It was a good choice.

She resumed her seat on the divan and from a gilded side table reached for and took a sip from a crystal goblet of cherry sherbet. She placed the drink back on the table and her blank expression suddenly darkened as troubled thoughts crept back into her head.

The Sultan was proving to be a problem. He had ascended the throne at 11 years of age when his insane uncle, Mad Mustapha I, had been removed from power. She had been able to manipulate her son without trouble for a number of years; but lately at aged 20 - and grown into a hulking and physically powerful man - he had shown a worrying tendency to ignore her political advice. He also increasingly plunged into frightening tempers brought on by drinking huge amounts of alcohol . . . tempers that were rarely extinguished without copious amounts of bloodshed.

For a time she had managed to control his savage outbursts through making sure that his thoughts were turned temporarily from drink towards young beautiful flesh. She had her people scour the land, with much success, for suitable girls; but after a while this had proved an unwise move.

Concubines had their place, but too many of them at once bred competition for favour; which in turn led to tensions in the Sultan's harem and, as the Valide Sultan, she was responsible not only for providing guidance and teaching to the Sultan on the intricacies of state politics, but also for the maintenance of order and peace inside the harem. Kosem did not need more problems to occupy her mind.

She sought an answer in the form of exchanging beautiful girls for pretty young boys.

For a time this also was successful and she made sure that she lost no opportunity to impress on him the wisdom of exchanging a scheming sex for one that had no pretensions to power.

Unfortunately she had underestimated the power that alcohol had gained over him, as once again his moods had begun to swing alarmingly.

The situation was, if not yet critical, then it was fast approaching a point where some action needed to be considered before the matter was taken out of her hands by forces outside her control; for in addition to the worries concerning the increasingly erratic behaviour of her son, rumours of unrest among the Janissary corps, the military and some of the viziers due to what they saw as a state of near anarchy due to entrenched corruption – coupled with a recent decision to debase coinage brought about by financial constraints – had also reached her . . . rumours that had set alarm bells ringing.

She shook her head and sighed. What was to be done with him? She could perhaps put in motion a subtle plot against him which might lead to his removal; but then what? Beyazid, her favourite and most able son, had incurred the fatal wrath of Murad by beating him in a joust and had been murdered on his brother's orders. Her only other living son was unofficially known as 'Ibrahim the Mad' who, in order to remove any chance of intrigue against the Sultan, was confined with his retinue of slaves and sterile concubines to the *Kafes* – a large two storey apartment building separated from the harem by a securely locked and guarded door.

Although Ibrahim would be much easier to manipulate than his brother, Kosem knew it would be difficult because of his mental state – he was lately seen feeding gold coins to fish in one of the apartment pools – to gain support for him among the viziers, Janissaries and high Military.

She sighed again then stood up and momentarily glanced in the mirror to adjust her headdress. The problems with the Sultan and other rumours of unrest would not go away, but for the present she had to put them out of her mind; for now she had a tiresome duty to oversee.

Three sides of the large audience chamber were lined with over 300 palace servants, lower ranking odalisques (concubines) and eunuchs. There was a muted hum of conversation that was suddenly cut off as a side door opened and two eunuchs entered carrying between them a glowing iron brazier that had a long thin metal carrying rod thrust through the middle.

The eunuchs placed the brazier down some ten feet in front of an ornate raised throne. One of them removed the rod and placed in on the marble floor, while the other left the room briefly before returning carrying a pair of leather bellows, a lipped crucible and a pair of long double handled metal tongs.

The eunuch who had removed the carrying rod placed the crucible on top of the brazier, placed the tongues at his feet then took up the bellows and began to blow the charcoal in the brazier until it glowed almost white hot.

Silence reined for several minutes save for the rhythmic wheezing of the bellows before the side door was suddenly flung open and two more eunuchs entered carrying a six foot long x-shaped wooden crucifix which bore a gagged naked girl with her four limbs firmly bound to the arms with thick leather thongs.

The silence broke and a muted whisper of voices filled the chamber as the eunuchs bore the crucifix to within ten feet of the throne, planted its 'feet' on the marble floor and stood mutely holding on to it's arms.

The girl's head jerked from side to side as she scanned the room with terrified, pleading eyes.

Rumours had spread around the palace for the last two days that one of the Keeper of the Jewel's slave girls had been caught trying to steal a gem by secreting it in her vagina. This then must be that girl whose fate was now surely sealed.

Another two minutes passed before the doors were again flung open and flanked by two huge scimitar wielding black eunuchs, the Valide Sultan swept into the chamber. The muted hum of conversation was immediately choked off as over 300 pairs of eyes were obediently lowered momentarily to the floor.

Now the only sound in the room was the soft silken swish of Kosem's dress and the cold tap of sandals on marble as she strode over to and mounted the ornate throne . . . those sounds only; plus the muted sobs of terror that issued from the bound girl's gagged throat.

Kosem looked slowly round the room and where her gaze lingered eyes were swiftly lowered and hands were crossed over chests and breasts.

Satisfied that she had their total attention, she glanced down into the brazier and saw that it now contained a slowly bubbling charge of molten lead. She nodded her head and the two eunuchs holding the wooden frame swiftly inverted it to leave the captive hanging upside down facing the room's audience.

She nodded again and one of the two original eunuchs took up the metal funnel, strode over to the captive and inserted it roughly into her vagina, before moving back to the other eunuch's side where they both took up the long two handled tongs, removed the crucible from the brazier, strode over to the girl and poised the slowly bubbling vessel above the rim of the funnel.

Another nod from the Valide Sultan and the crucible was tipped. The girl's whole body arched in a paroxysm of agony that threatened to burst the leather thongs, her blood filled face contorted into a hideous mask, a fine spray of pink bloody bubbles from a bit through tongue shot from her nose into her bulging eyes and a strangled scream welled from her throat to tremble round the chamber before mercifully dying as the straining body relaxed and hung loosely against the leather thongs.

Kosem sat with one arm casually draped over an arm of the throne and made a point of resting her other hand on the hilt of the dagger in her belt as she scanned the room again.

Satisfied with the sea of ashen faces she took a scented handkerchief from the sleeve of her dress, held it briefly under her nose to counter the stench of burnt flesh and accompanied by her retinue, swept regally from the room. The message had been delivered and certainly received.

At the same time of Kosem's exit, in a curtained off ante room above the domed council chamber in the Imperial Council building, a sitting scowling giant watched and listened to the proceedings taking place below. The play of state carried out by the Grand Vizier, the viziers, judiciary officials, various Ministers and a host of scribes charged with recording the four times weekly meeting, did not fully hold his attention. Murad had other things on his mind . . . disturbing things. His spies had for weeks reported strong undercurrents of unrest among some of the military and elements of the Janissaries.

Those who entertain thought of treachery will be well rewarded, he thought as his scowl deepened and his huge hands bunched into fists. He held the power of life and death and any who dared challenge him would very soon be made fatally aware of that fact. The thought had barely flashed across his mind when he was suddenly startled by a crashing open of the doors of the Council Hall and a tide of screaming, yatagan waving Janissaries surged through the opening.

Murad leapt to his feet and stood rigidly, impotently, to attention as below him the flashing blades left a trail of panic in their wake. The Grand Vizier, three viziers, the Minister of Finance and the Head of the Treasury were left in bloody heaps on the marble floor as the rest of the council members and scribes ran for their lives towards a rear door that opened up onto a porch and a courtyard.

They were not pursued. A statement had been made. The Sultan had been sent a message. Above the blood drenched floor Murad's fiery black eyes looked down at the scene of carnage and his bearded face twisted into a mask of fury.

16

Thanks to the Admiral's orders their living accommodation was much improved. Those orders however, had not sat lightly with their 'tutor', who took every opportunity he could to prolong their lessons and impose frequent penalties when he decided that their responses were not up to the standard he demanded.

"He is truly the devil's spawn!" Erin said loudly at the eunuch's back as he edged his fat frame out through the cabin door.

The long days drifted into weeks as the vessel ploughed its way through apparently endless seas and boredom became their companion. True, they had a little more freedom to leave their cabin and promenade the main deck; but this was only on the too infrequent times when the sails were billowing with a fair wind and the deck was not thronged with slave rowers and their brutal whip happy torturers

"I can not bear to look upon those poor souls!" Alice had exclaimed on the one occasion they had witnessed the scene. Erin had shaken her head sadly and agreed, while Anna had not been too happy at their insistence that they would not venture out of their cabin again when the vessel was more or less becalmed.

Two days later when the sails were again pregnant with stiff breezes and the oar slaves had been herded back below decks, Erin had accosted the Admiral on the poop deck.

"Those poor devils!" she had said sharply. "Why must they be treated so vilely?" The Admiral had smiled thinly. He was coming to expect barbs from the fiery-headed young woman.

"Madam," he had replied calmly, "such is the way of life in this harsh world; indeed your own English navy is renowned for its brutal treatment of regular and press ganged sailors, is it not?"

Erin had admitted that she had heard tales of harsh treatment in His Majesty's service, "But", she insisted, "press ganged or not, English sailors were not chained to benches and whipped like dogs." The Admiral could have supplied details of 'cat o nine tails' punishments, regularly handed out for petty infringements in His Majesty's senior service, but instead had shrugged and said simply: "Different cultures have different ways."

On the occasions when they did step out onto the main deck the women were struck by the professional way that the Admiral's motley crew went about their duties. Every man among them be he black, brown or white, seemed to take pride in his actions.

"The Admiral must be very well liked . . . or very much feared," Alice had commented. Erin had nodded. "He is a different man indeed to the rogue who we had the pleasure of sailing with before," she said. "But sister be aware, for a rapier is as deadly as a blunt axe."

Erin and her companions were also in thrall to the professionalism of the Janissary troops who frequently practised their intricate combat moves on deck. Their brown arms and faces, their fierce moustaches, their outlandish alien dress, their wicked flashing blades and their terrifying battle screams left the women wide eyed and huddled closely together whenever they witnessed them in mock action. "Tis little wonder," Alice said, "that we were so easily stolen, for who taken by surprise could best such devils?"

Although they agreed that the Janissaries in action were a truly frightening spectacle, they also admitted that they were surprised at the way these fierce warriors went out of their way to show respect to their female captives. Even on the vessel that they were first imprisoned on all those months ago, the Janissaries had acted, unlike some of the renegade crew, if not nobly, then at least with no ill intent. They had even shown a positive liking for some of the children by on occasion providing them with warm clothing from their own backs.

A week later the Admiral gave them the double-edged news that their journey would soon be at an end. "We are entering the Sea of Marinara," he had said casually. "From there the Bosporus and Constantinople is a mere two days sailing away."

The captives were pleased to hear that the long voyage would soon be over; but that very knowledge re-awakened the suppressed fears of an unknown future. "We knew this day would come sisters, so now we must steel ourselves with the resolve of true Christians to face whatever may lie in wait," Erin said quietly.

The pre-dawn shouted order to rise from their hammocks and the crack of the whip that accompanied it, bounced off the walls of the sleeping room.

James groaned lightly and eased himself out of the hammock and down onto the bare stone floor. All around him the other heavily sagging canvas cocoons began to open and slowly reveal their contents.

Within five minutes the bleary eyed line of prisoners stood loosely to attention as the guard made his morning count. The man finished and then spat out an alien curse. He moved back to the head of the line and began a recount. Count done, he cursed again and cast his eyes around the room until they rested on a lone sagging hammock that hung some six feet above the floor.

He shouted a curse and striding over to the canvas bed, raised his arms and tipped it roughly. The loose limbed body tumbled out and landed with a meaty smack upon the floor.

The horrible sound drew all eyes towards it and James' heart skipped a beat as he looked into the white, bright blood flecked face of Samuel Carter. "Samuel. . . No!" He shouted, and followed immediately by the other Baltimore captives, he strode quickly forward.

The guard turned quickly towards them and his whip split the air in front of their faces.

"Dead!" he yelled, then: "Back!" James stopped and looked down into the once keen now sightless eyes of the man who he had known and admired for all the 20 years of his life. He bunched his fists and through compressed lips snarled "Bring a priest!"

The guard shrugged. John Thompson detached himself from the line and moving to the guard's side said something in Sabir. The guard sighed lightly turned on his heel and left the cell.

As they heard the outer grill slam shut John Thompson moved to James' side.

"He has gone to the middle building to fetch a Trinitarian man of the cloth," he said quietly as James knelt and straightened Samuel's limbs, gently closed his eyes and folded the cold hands over his chest.

Two minutes passed before they heard the outer grill open and followed by the jailer, a tall middle-aged European man in an ankle length light brown habit embossed with a large dark brown stitched cross and wearing a round wide brimmed hat strode into their midst. The priest looked down at Samuel's body and made a rapid sign of the cross. James noticed the sign.

"He is a Christian," he said softly, "though not one with allegiance to Rome." The tall man shook his head lightly.

"Then I am not able to offer him the last rites in accordance with the Church's doctrine," he answered in accented English.

"But you will pray for the delivery of this good man's soul to his Maker?" James asked. The priest nodded.

"I will attend his laying to rest in the quick lime pits and offer my prayers for his salvation." James' face hardened.

"He will not be buried in accordance with the Christian faith's teachings!" he said sharply. The priest shook his head again.

"I regret, no. All slaves of whatever faith are consigned to the quick lime." James' frown faded and he nodded slowly. *Does it really matter*, he thought. He had been brought up to believe strongly in God's goodness; but the recent traumatic and tragic events in his life had begun to cause him to question whether that faith was truly justified.

"Our thanks to you father," James said softly. "He was a man of standing in our lost community and will be sorely missed by all here that admired him." The priest was about to reply, but was stopped by a barked order from the guard and the line of prisoners began to shuffle their way forward and out into the chill early morning air.

As their turn came to move, the Baltimore men first cast a lingering look back at their fallen companion. The last in line, James briefly caught the priest's eye and nodded slowly before turning and following the others.

At the end of their gruelling day and with their thoughts still on their sudden loss, the Baltimore men sat quietly in their customary little circle out of earshot of the other captives. James took in the sombre mood and decided that the time was right to introduce his ideas on escape.

"We have all been sorely shaken today," he said softly. "Samuel's was a voice that all in Baltimore listened to; but that voice has been stilled and it now falls on us to bear witnesses to his and other tragic deaths that would else wise go unreported should we not take steps to effect our salvation." Robert Mould raised his eyes from the bare stone floor.

"What steps are we able to take?" he said quietly. James nodded and began to briefly outline his plan to the sitting circle before, at some prompting, going into detail. He was asked how they could, for a start, shed the shackles that signalled to all outside the bagnio their slave status.

"We all work closely together so it would not be difficult for one of us while shaping rock with hammer and chisel to strike through the brass pin of the ankle manacle of a companion. The manacle's design would not allow it to fall loose and it would be easy to keep it firmly in place by knotting a thin strip of torn cloth through the holes that receive the pin." As he spoke he looked keenly around the little circle of shadowed faces. He saw a mixture of slowly blossoming hope and bitter resignation.

"Tis pure folly," Robert Harris said tiredly. "Even if we could shed these irons," he muttered, rattling the heavy chain around his ankle, "how could we hope to escape from this room and make our way unchallenged to the harbour?"

"And from there take over a vessel?" Adam Thomas added shaking his head.

"The guard comes alone in the morning to unlock the bagnio gate," James said. "If we hide in the small side room where we are shaved we can remove our anklets and chains, overpower him after he has opened the gate, bind and gag him, lock the gate behind us to gain time and make our way out into the courtyard."

"Which will be filling with traders and a goodly number of Janissaries . . ." Robert Harris said shaking his head. James nodded.

"Yes and many general, *unchained* slaves!" James replied. "So, a few more such slaves would not cause remark. We would simply mingle then make our way in ones and twos over to and through the arched entrance to the courtyard where others will be entering and leaving."

"But then there is the city gate . . ." Robert Mould added. James shrugged.

"The gate is closed at sundown and opened at first light to

admit and let out all manner of people. Unchained slaves going about their master's business in bringing in fruit, vegetables and other goods from outside would, again, cause no remark."

"And if all this could be accomplished without raising alarm, what then of taking over a vessel which none of us has experience of sailing?" John Davis said quietly.

"We are all of us in one way or another, men of the sea," James countered. "Hauling sail and steering a vessel would not tax us unduly."

"And navigation. Who among us has the skills to pilot a vessel over a distance that surely exceeds well over one thousand miles?

"We do not strike westwards as expected; instead we steer north east and make for one of the nearer Spanish islands where we will find refuge," James said. After he had spoken he looked from face to face to judge the impact of his words. John Davis, Stephen Ryder and Richard Evans all displayed a bright eyed look about them, while Robert Mould, William Fletcher, Robert Harris, John Cartwright and Adam Thomas were plainly not convinced. Robert Harris put words to his feelings.

"Tis a plan with too many chances to go awry," he said firmly as the other doubters nodded in agreement. "Even if your plan worked as far as securing a vessel," he continued, "surely the start you gained would be counted in mere minutes before the alarm was raised." James nodded.

"Yes, but there would be much confusion before a search could be organised and put in action." Harris was still not convinced.

"Even so, surely once they realised that a pirate vessel had been taken they would swiftly run you down." James shook his head.

"We do not take a pirate vessel. There are always a number of small trader and fishing vessels moored at the mole. We board one of these and with any luck the vessel's owner will be about his business in the city and will not be aware of the hue and cry; and once he is made aware, he will find it hard to convince anyone in authority to give chase." Robert Mould was still far from convinced.

"There is great risk even so. You have heard of the punishments meted out to slaves who fall foul of these heathens. Some have been hung, some crucified, some beheaded, some burnt to death, and some nailed to the city gate." James was aware of the risks that his plan carried; but unlike some of them he was of a mind that to do nothing and simply sit with one's finger for ever on one's pulse was not an option.

"And if we do nothing, what then?" he said with a sharp edge to his words. Before anyone had a chance to answer he continued. "Well then we rot here in a living death with no chance of redeeming our loved ones - until we embark upon the final journey to the lime pit."

"Surely there will have been petitions for our release," Adam Thomas said quickly. James' face hardened.

"And who will petition for us?" he said bitterly. "Will King Charles act for those his Government were pleased to be rid of? There are many men in this bagnio who have been rotting here years because, like us, they are common men with no ransom value." There were a few firm nods at his words. Robert Harris spoke next.

"You are young James, young and impetuous. Yes we suffer, but suffering is the lot of man. In time and with God's help I am sure that we will be rescued." James snorted.

"Tis a lot I am not willing to bear without challenge. So who then feels as I?" he added firmly in a determined push to bring the matter to a head.

"I do," John Davis said quietly.

"And I," Stephen Ryder added. After a moment's hesitation Richard Evans also gave his support to James' plan.

Minutes later in his hammock James ran the plan over again in his mind. Yes, there was risk, great risk; but the alternative of miserable years stretching ahead into a bleak hopeless future that decreed he never saw her beloved face again made, in his mind, the risk well worth the taking.

He had also wrestled with the fact that his escape would mean him leaving her behind. Was that the right thing to do? She, like the other kidnapped villagers was somewhere in this huge city, perhaps even not far away. And although the thought of the possibility of her nearness caused him mental agony, he knew that she might as well have been a hundred miles distant for all the chance he had of single-handedly coming to her rescue.

No; if he could get back home he, as an actual escapee, stood a better chance of helping to set in motion a rescue through ransom by making sure that his voice was heard in high places.

The morning came swiftly and the march to the quarry, with a firm goal to aim for after months of physical and mental misery, saw a slight spring added to his step.

On each of their tortuous trips down to the mole he made keen note of the activity there and that of any comings and goings from the moored vessels. In particular he studied the smaller craft, of which there were three. The two much larger ones were, he knew, trading vessels typical of those that paid fairly regular visits to the city, while the smaller was a fishing vessel that landed a daily catch and so was ideal for his plan. If they took this craft they could if approached at sea dampen any suspicion by simply laying net like honest fishermen going about their business.

The long day wore on and as they were toiling to roughly dress the stone for the last sleds of the day he made a move.

With John Davis close by his side and Stephen Ryder and Richard Evans providing blocking cover, James quickly knelt and forced the narrow edge of his chisel between the two sides of the shackle. John Davis glanced around quickly to make sure that they were not attracting attention from their guards then struck swiftly.

The ringing hammer blow of metal on metal sheared the connecting pin and caused them all to wince; but once again the guards, standing a good two dozen yards away and idly chatting under a temporary canvas awning, showed no sign of interest.

James quickly undid the thin strip of cloth from around his wrist, twisted it tightly for extra strength, threaded it through the shackle's eye holes and knotted it in position.

Two minute's later they reversed roles and he used the hammer on John Davis' shackle. Fifteen minutes later still and the others had followed suit and within the hour they were on their way down to the mole dragging the final sleds of the day.

17

As the Admiral's vessel edged its way into a berth in the busy harbour, Erin, Alice and Anna stared with eyes that registered pure shock. Their first sight of Algiers had stunned them; but Algiers was a mere village compared to Constantinople. Protected by gigantic fortified walls the city rose halfway to the heavens and seemed to stretch almost to the eastern horizon!

From their position on the raised poop deck they looked out at what seemed to be dozens of towering minarets that pricked the sky, blue domed mosques, palaces and thousands of smaller buildings ranged around a multitude of green parks and open squares. And above all, they looked upon a monstrous palace surrounded by its own walls and set on higher ground, against which the palace of the Pasha of Algiers was no more substantial than one of their tiny thatched roof lost cottages back in Baltimore!

"Surely London itself can not be as big as this city!" Anna marvelled before adding breathlessly, "And that palace! It must surely be where we are bound!" Erin nodded. She, herself was stunned by the sight, but Anna's childish fascination did not strike a chord within her.

"Yes," she said quietly, "Tis a wondrous place to be sure; but it will be a prison none the less." Alice agreed but young Anna merely continued to gaze bright eyed at the amazing sight.

As soon as their vessel was securely moored the Admiral, who had been standing on the main deck with the Pasha's chief eunuch, made his way down onto the dock where he was immediately approached by what was obviously a high ranking official. There was an animated conversation before the official turned his back and beckoned to the black driver of an ornate carriage. As the carriage pulled forward the Admiral strode purposely back up the gangplank.

"He is much disturbed," Alice remarked as she saw the marked frown that clouded Ali Bichnin's features. The Admiral stopped at Zahid Ali's side and spoke to the eunuch for a minute and, even though they could not hear the words, the watchers on the poop deck saw a strong reaction to them as Zahid Ali's fat ring be-decked hands jumped up to his mouth in shock.

"There is bad news ashore," Erin said softly.

"And how will this bad news affect us I wonder . . ." Alice mused.

Down on the main deck the Admiral wrestled with the dilemma that the Harbour Master had presented him with. There had been a recent attempt at an uprising and several high officials, including the Grand Vizier had been slain and a new Grand Vizier had been forced on Murad by sections of the Janissaries and the military. He had asked the Harbour Master how the Sultan had reacted to events and the man had smiled grimly and said that when he ventured into the city he would soon see for himself, as on almost every corner bloated corpses hung rotting in the sun.

The Admiral, knowing of the Sultan's blossoming reputation would have expecting nothing less of his majesty Murad IV. The dilemma now was how to approach the enraged Sultan. Should he keep himself well out of range of Murad's black moods by sending the Pasha's chief eunuch alone with the taxes and tributes, or should he go with the eunuch and offer his moral support of the Sultan?

Self preservation said that he should follow the first course, but then Murad would very likely see it as a snub if the Admiral of the Pasha's fleet did not present himself. No, he reasoned, he must go himself. And further, he must offer more than simple moral support.

The tributes to the Sultan, with their linen clothes bags at their feet watched from the poop deck as a six man Janissary guard brought a large obviously heavy wooden chest up from below decks and loaded it onto the waiting carriage then ranged themselves three either side of the vehicle.

From the main deck Ali Bichnin made a beckoning gesture at the women and waited as they slowly made their way down.

"We must soon part company ladies," he said lightly; then under his breath added: *and may your God look kindly upon you.*

Within minutes, with the Admiral and Zahid Ali sitting opposite them, they left the dockside and approached a gate built into the side of the enormous city walls.

Their carriage was obviously well known, as at its approach the huge wood and iron banded portal was drawn back and they drove through only to stop within 40 feet outside another door set into a second, slightly less impressive city wall. Two guards standing either side of this door stepped quickly forward and drew the portal open. Inside the city proper the women were again stunned by the size of everything they saw and by the sheer torrent of alien humanity that thronged the streets.

"Surely there can not be this many souls in the whole of Ireland!" Anna said shaking her head. "They are..." her words trailed off and the look of wonderment on her face suddenly faded and was replaced by one of shock. Erin and Alice turned their heads to follow Anna's stricken stare and her shock was immediately mirrored on their faces.

The headless and handless body hung by its feet from a wooden gibbet erected at a wide crossroads. As the carriage drew closer they saw that a swarm of fat flies was crawling over clotted black gore that clung to the severed neck like a living beard.

Sickened by the sight, they averted their eyes. Seven more times they came upon similar scenes and each time although disgusted by the sights, perverse fascination forced them to look, before ingrained sensibilities allowed them to turn ashen-faced away.

Thankfully, they soon left the public streets behind and approached a gate in the walls that protected the huge palace complex. The portal was opened and the carriage rumbled onto a stone-paved road that bisected a large tree-lined courtyard.

At the end of the road, some hundred yards ahead a huge crenelated gate with large octagonal pointed towers at either side stood in their way. As they approached the high central arched gateway they could make out that its sides and roof were decorated in all manner of Moorish inscriptions.

Immediately in front of the entrance and to the right of the gate there was a small marble fountain. Zahid. Ali pointed to the fountain and looking directly at the women, who were sat holding hands in an effort to offer and gain some measure of comfort, he said: "It is the Fountain of the Executioner. It is here that he washes his hands and sword after his work." His words had the desired affect and he smiled thinly at the looks on the women's faces.

The carriage rolled through the gate and entered another courtyard. This courtyard, which was surrounded by a number of impressive looking buildings, to the women's utter amazement contained rolling green lawns and on those lawns there were a great number of fantastic strutting birds with enormous and gorgeous iridescent blue and green fan-tailed feathers that were decorated with what seemed to be eyes!

At the far end of the long courtyard they approached a long marble colonnade that had a huge central gate, above which and supported on slim marble columns was a pale blue dome topped with a golden crescent moon. The carriage pulled up in front of the gate and waited while two Janissary guards who were stationed either side of the portal approached and entered into a brief conversation with the driver.

"We are not allowed to enter until the Sultan's chief black eunuch, the Kizlar Agha, has been summoned," Zahid Ali said to the Admiral. "When permission is given we must dismount and continue on foot." Ali Bichnin nodded. He had never visited the palace before and was as curious as the young women.

"What lies beyond this gate?" he asked. The Pasha's chief eunuch puffed himself up. Here he was the fount of wisdom.

"Beyond this gate – the *Gate of Felicity* – is the Third Courtyard, the *Endurun Avlusa*, the heart of the palace. There we will find the *Has Oda*, the Hall of the Privy Chamber, the Harem, the Treasury and the magnificent library of Ahmed III." The Admiral's face showed a modicum of respect for the eunuch's knowledge.

"You have been to this place before, eunuch?" he asked. Zahid Ali smiled.

"I spent many years here before I was sent to assist his Excellency Pasha Hussain in Algiers two years ago."

The women, who had only been able to understand parts of the conversation, sat quietly holding hands. After a wait of several minutes a small gate built into one side of the marble colonnade opened and a heavy set, bald headed black man dressed in baggy sky blue silk pantaloons and a short sleeved red waistcoat strode out towards them.

As the man approached the carriage Zahid Ali stepped down and went to meet him, then, while the other occupants of the carriage looked on the two entered into a lengthy conversation, after which Zahid Ali, with a serious look on his face, waddled back to the carriage and turned to the Admiral.

"There is deep unrest at the palace. The Kizlar Agha tells me that the Sultan sees treachery everywhere he turns and that his monstrous sword is never far from his side." The Admiral nodded.

"We must then take care not to try his temper lest we feel that weapon's sharp edge ourselves," he muttered trying to sound as casual as he could.

The eunuch swallowed hard. He had himself seen the Sultan's favourite weapons in action. The five foot long two handed broadsword weighed over a hundred pounds, while his huge mace, which he wielded with one hand, weighed even more! Zahid Ali's mental musings were then cut short as the Sultan's Chief Eunuch strode up to the carriage.

"You are to dismount and follow me," he said with an edge of authority to his voice. The Admiral smiled thinly as the passengers climbed down from the carriage and followed the black eunuch over to the gate. There a Palace guard sprang to attention and the portal was swung open.

The travellers passed through into a lush garden setting, at the back of which they walked towards a square building surrounded by a colonnade of 22 columns supporting a large roof with overhanging eaves. The Chief Eunuch opened the building's door and they crossed an ornately patterned marble floor to an open arched doorway that sat behind two huge green columns decorated at the top and base with gold. There the Chief Eunuch turned and held up a hand.

"You are to carry no arms through into the Inner Council Hall," he said. Ali Bichnin signalled to his Janissary guards who reluctantly removed their yatagans from the sashes around their waists and placed them on the marble floor. Satisfied, the Chief Eunuch ushered them through into the empty audience chamber.

The women's eyes widened as they took in the splendour before them. The ceiling of the chamber was painted in ultramarine blue and studded with golden stars, while the walls were lined with blue, white and turquoise tiles spangled with gold and at their feet the marble floor was strewn with precious carpets and silk pillows in a riot of colours.

At the far end of the chamber a huge raised throne with a dark wooden overhanging canopy sat imperiously as the only furniture in the chamber. As they moved in closer they saw that the underside of the lacquered canopy was studded with jewels and covered in green foliage patterns in the middle of which there was a depiction of a dragon engaged in a death struggle with a mythical bird. The throne itself was covered with golden brocade cloth studded with emerald and ruby plaques and pearls.

At one side of the raised throne they noticed a large solid silver fireplace inlaid with gold; while at the other there was a jade green marble fountain set against the wall from which scented water gushed.

"You will wait here," the black eunuch said simply as he left the audience chamber through a small door which sat directly behind the throne. As the door closed behind the eunuch, the Admiral signalled the Janissary guards carrying the heavy chest to place it on the marble floor in front of the throne and then to move back towards the chamber entrance.

Several minutes dragged by before the door sprung open and a bearded red faced and red eyed giant standing at least six and a half feet tall, wearing a yellow cotton turban, yellow silk shirt and white baggy cotton trousers and carrying a huge sword, strode through. Scurrying at his elbow the Chief Eunuch shouted: "Kneel!" The six Janissaries immediately flung themselves to their knees, lowered their heads and clasped their hands under their chins in obedience. Ali Bichnin and Zahid Ali quickly followed suit. Momentarily bemused, the women stood alone for a second or two before Anna and Alice also knelt. They were followed a long second later by Erin.

As he lowered his huge frame onto the throne and propped his sword against a gilded arm, the Sultan glared at the kneeling newcomers.

"Why does my uncle not present him self?" he demanded. The Admiral raised his head.

"I can not say your Highness. The Pasha has entrusted me with the honour of delivering the taxes." Murad scowled.

"And who are you that carry this honour?"

"Your humble servant, Ali Bichnin. I am Admiral of the Pasha's fleet your Highness." The Sultan nodded lightly. He had heard of the Admiral and his tactical brilliance. He had also had reports that this Ali Bichnin was looked upon by many in Algiers as the real power in the city state.

His head throbbing with the after affects of alcohol, the Sultan considered the Admiral's brief statement. *I am beset with traitors,* he thought, *some of whom have escaped my just revenge and will continue to plot against me. This Admiral may be of use.* He nodded again and then seemed to notice for the first time Zahid Ali's presence.

"Ah, eunuch," he said loudly. Zahid Ali raised his head a little.

"Your servant, your Highness," he replied meekly before tucking his head back down and raising his shoulders a little. The Sultan wore yellow and had his sword at his side; a sword that his Highness had used many times to remove heads from necks – and particularly from fat necks which presented a challenge. The eunuch lowered his chin and raised his shoulders another inch.

"My uncle is well?" Murad asked smoothly. Zahid Ali swallowed nervously.

"He is in good health Highness and has charged me to deliver his felicitations." Murad's face hardened.

"Felicitations are better received when delivered in person," he said sourly as one of his huge hands reached sideways and thick fingers folded around the handle of his sword. Zahid Ali saw the movement and his head almost disappeared into his shoulders. The Sultan, who had noticed the eunuch's reaction smiled thinly as he toyed briefly with the notion of removing that bald head from its shoulders, then in a quick change of mood said: "Ah, and what is this that you have brought me eunuch?" He removed his hand from the sword and casually indicated the kneeling women. Relieved, Zahid Ali gushed:

"These are virgin tributes from your uncle, Highness!" Murad cast his bloodshot eyes briefly over the women and rated their suitability. The taller dark haired, brown eyed tribute was comely enough, although he had many such already. The smallest, the one with hair the colour of ripe corn and with bright blue eyes was much more interesting. Yes she would be a welcome addition to stimulate his jaded appetite. And the other, the one with wild flame red hair, alabaster skin and emerald eyes; yes, she too could prove a welcome distraction. As his gaze landed briefly on Erin his drink fogged mind belatedly registered a fact - the flame haired one had been slower than the others to fall to her knees when ordered. *Spirit*, he thought, then, *a rough breaking is called for with this one.*

From his place standing beside the seated Sultan, the Chief Eunuch noticed a smile blossom briefly on Murad's lips and allowed him self to breathe a small sigh of relief as his trained eye and ear told him that no volcanic eruptions were on the near horizon. The past days had been fraught with tension and the palace's inhabitants had trod very carefully about their duties as the Sultan's moods swung wildly to and fro.

Towering rages had culminated in savage torture and summary executions. His Highness had personally dispatched over fifty men with sword or mace and had seen a hundred others have their hands, then feet, then legs sawn off. For now at least there seemed to be a levelling out to his moods. His thoughts were then interrupted by a steady voiced command from Murad to the Kizlar Agha.

"Take the eunuch and the Pasha's tributes to the Queen Mother and the taxes to the treasury. The Admiral will accompany me, we have things to discuss," he said.

As the little party followed the Chief Eunuch out of the audience chamber Zahid Ali was mightily relieved. He had been charged by the Pasha to keep his eyes and ears open where the Admiral was concerned, but now his summary dismissal had thankfully removed him from the immediate danger of being parted from his head. He could now rest easy in the knowledge that anything that the Admiral got up to could not be laid at his own feet.

18

In the pre-dawn gloom James waited until the third shadowy figure had passed then climbed silently out of his hammock and with his shackle chain in hand groped his way over to and through the open arch. Out in the dimly lit corridor he quickly reached the small door less ante-room that lay five yards before the barred gate. Inside the room the prisoners quietly prised open and removed their ankle shackles and untied the torn strips of rough cotton cloth from their wrists which were to be used to bind and gag the guard.

"We will now have a long wait, for the hour is still early yet," James whispered to the others. None of them answered, for the tension was too great. Instead they each went through the plan of action in their minds; some of them several times.

The plan was for them to casually walk out one at a time into the courtyard with an interval of some 30 seconds between them. Each man was then to pass as close as possible to those with a legitimate reason to be in the courtyard without raising any suspicion and then make his way casually over to and through the arched entrance gate. Once outside the courtyard each was to walk at a leisurely pace singly down to the city gate where they were to wait out of sight of the gate men until there was human and cart traffic distraction for them to slip out virtually unnoticed and make their way to the harbour.

After what, to their strained nerves seemed hours, they heard the sound of metal on metal as the heavy key was inserted in the lock and a low creak as the grill was folded back against the wall. They heard the grill creak again as it was closed, followed by a soft click as the lock was engaged again.

Footsteps sounded down the corridor. At the ante-room entrance James held his arms up at chest height, flexed his fists once and opened his hands ready to pounce.

The guard's head appeared in the open doorway and James struck. He lunged forward and wrapped his left hand around the man's mouth while with his right he dragged the startled man into the ante-room, whirled him round and delivered a crunching blow to his temple. The guard's legs folded and James lowered him gently to the floor where John Davis stuffed a bunched piece of cloth into his mouth, Stephen Ryder quickly flipped him over onto his stomach and bound his hands behind his back while Richard Evans tied his feet together. James then removed the key from the man's pocket.

The whole attack had taken barely a minute and now there was no going back.

James took a deep breath bent over and dragged the unconscious guard deeper into the ante-room he then straightened up and looked deeply into the eyes of his companions and saw commitment reflected there. He followed the others' example and stripped off the red sleeveless jacket that marked them out as quarry slaves, nodded and with them at his back he made his way silently over to the gate. There he peered out through the bars into the early dawn gloom and saw that there was much activity in the courtyard as traders and their slaves scurried back and forth setting up and provisioning the many stalls.

He inserted the key into the lock, turned it and gently pulled the gate towards him, wincing slightly as the metal protested. He carefully leaned forward through the partially opened gate and saw that there was no-one looking in his direction. Satisfied, he ducked back inside and signalled for John Davis to go.

Within another two minutes James stood alone with the key in his hand. He took a deep breath, slid through the gate, pulled it closed behind him, locked it and pocketed the key. Sure now that no-one would be able to get into or out of the bagnio for some considerable time, he sauntered across the busy courtyard, stopping briefly to stoop to pick up a large empty wicker fruit basket from the side of an unattended stall.

With the basket in hand he made his way across the courtyard and reached the arch - and collided with the quarry Janissary guard detail on their way in. The leading guard cuffed him around the head and swore an oath. James, with his heart pounding in his ears slipped quickly to his knees in abject apology. The Janissary snarled down at him briefly and made another threatening movement with his arm, James cowered before the blow that never came, and the guard snorted his contempt before, with the others close behind him he strode on into the courtyard.

James climbed swiftly to his feet and with the empty basket swinging from a hand he entered the quiet streets - just another slave going about his master's business.

Five minutes later as he approached the city gate he stopped for a few seconds and peered intently ahead. There was a reasonable amount of activity, with carts loaded with goods and foodstuffs rolling in and empty vehicles passing out. He saw two guards stood to one side of the gate who were engaged in apparent casual conversation and displaying no interest in the comings and goings. "It can be done!" he muttered as he also saw that there was no sign of the others who must have passed through without any problems.

He raised the wicker basket to chest height and strode purposely forward. He drew almost level with the gate just as another cart loaded with fruit rolled in and there was a barked order from one of the guards. His heart almost leaped up into his mouth as the guard left his companion and strode over. *No!* He thought. *It can not end here, not now not so close!* The guard drew level with James' shoulder, then passed casually in front of him and reached into the cart and took two large apples. Heart pounding and head lowered James waited for the man to pass back in front of him then carried on through the gate.

Once outside the city walls his hammering heart quieted. He dropped the basket and stretching his legs he was soon at the harbour mouth.

"James!" The urgent whisper came from behind a large stack of rough logs of timber sitting in front of a low stone built block house that faced onto the harbour. Richard Evans stepped out from behind the logs and in the gloom his pale face radiated anxiety.

"Come," he said quickly, "we have little time." James nodded in agreement and then noticed that Richard was alone.

"Where are the..."

"They are aboard," Richard interrupted, "Come we must

make all haste!"

The rickety little vessel was not built for speed and as a gentle zephyr caught her sail and she began to slowly limp towards the break in the mole her passengers prayed for a strong wind. At the tiller, James cast frequent anxious looks back to shore over his shoulder and muttered a word of thanks when there was no sign of pursuit. He knew that their escape must - if not yet be discovered - would be made known any minute and that a hue and cry would follow.

The discovery of their discarded shackles and red tunics might lead pursuers down to the dockside, so a swift retreat was vital. These thoughts had no sooner raced through his mind when the little sail suddenly filled with a firm breath of wind and they picked up speed. Within a minute they breached the gap in the mole and the little vessel staggered slightly as she left the breakwater behind and pointed her nose out into the deeper and much rougher wide expanse of water.

With the Kizlar Agha in the lead, Zahid Ali, the women and the Janissary guard carrying the wooden chest, made their way back into the courtyard where the Chief Eunuch turned and spoke to Zahid Ali.

"You will wait here while the taxes are delivered to the treasury." The eunuch bowed as the Kizlar Agha turned and with the Janissary guard carrying the chest at his side, made his way over to one of the perimeter buildings and disappeared inside. Zahid Ali had not been part of the palace staff for more than two years but he still retained total respect for the Kizlar Agha, who was in fact the third highest ranking officer of the empire behind the Sultan and the Grand Vizier. His was a position that Zahid Ali could never have aspired to - as unlike the Chief Eunuch who was 'clean shaven', he had had only his testes removed.

Anna, who had looked on in wonder at everything they had seen since passing through the first palace gate, couldn't contain herself. "This wondrous palace," she said breathlessly, "is surely a city within a city!" Zahid Ali nodded and his voice carried an overtone of religious superiority as he answered.

"Nothing in the lands of the infidel can come close. There are more than two thousand rooms within these walls and the Harem alone has over 400 rooms." Anna's mouth dropped open. She had known only cottage life, where four rooms were considered grand and the number so blandly stated by the eunuch was to her simple mind, almost incomprehensible.

Erin, had also been stunned by the sights she had witnessed since entering the palace complex, but was not about to feed the eunuch's sense of superiority by showing it. Instead, she looked casually around the courtyard and her gaze fell on one of several two storey buildings that lined the perimeter, where a number of young boys had just emerged to march solemnly in silence across to and then enter another of the buildings.

"Who are those boys," she asked, "are they more poor unfortunates stolen from their families?" Zahid Ali smiled thinly he was going to miss chastising this infidel female.

"They are the Sultan's *Agas*, or in your language, Pages. Here they are schooled in languages and the arts, such as music and painting - something that your peasant's minds perhaps cannot understand. As they progress they could become *Has Odali Aga*, Keepers of the Holy Relics of the Prophet and personal servants of the Sultan. With dedication they may even become officers or high-ranking officials."

The eunuch's dismissive tone stung Erin but she had to admit to herself that even though she could never overestimate the degree of barbarity that she had so far witnessed in this heathen land, perhaps she had wrongly dismissed the possibility that barbarians could display any appetite for the nobler arts, or indeed, to her mind, for the Christian ethic of advancement through hard work and merit rather than inherited status. She decided not to bandy words further with the eunuch.

Alice, who had kept her own council since they entered the palace, was also impressed by the scale and grandeur but her mind operated on a more practical level than those of her companions. Whereas Erin was intent on maintaining a stoic Christian ethic and Anna seemed to care less for her moral well being than for beautiful clothes, she saw things a little differently. Their old life was gone and she was under no illusions as to what lay ahead. They were to be like songbirds in gilded cages. They would live in physical splendour but would be shackled by golden chains. *My life before capture was hard and with little chance of improvement,* she thought, *but it was the only life I knew. Now I must somehow adapt to a new one.*

"The harem you speak of," she said quietly turning to Zahid Ali. "It has many women?"

"There are over 100 women in the Pasha's harem. In the Sultan's harem there will be many more," the eunuch answered. Alice nodded. *Perhaps,* she thought, *the Sultan might never even set eyes, let alone other parts on us among such a great number of women?*

Zahid Ali seemed to read her thoughts.

"Many hundreds of women," he said smoothly. "But the Sultan has a great appetite for white flesh," he added with a smirk. Any further discussion was cut short as the portly body of the Chief Eunuch emerged from one of the buildings and made his way back over to them.

"The taxes are in order," the Kizlar Agha said lightly. "Now you will follow me to the apartments of the Valide Sultan."

Behind the Chief Eunuch the little party entered one of the perimeter buildings and found themselves in another world of wondrous splendour.

They passed down passages richly lined with silk hangings in a riot of colours; through huge rooms with silver chandeliers; red, blue and green velvet covered divans and low Ottomans; ornately decorated carpets and softly murmuring marble fountains.

They entered a vast hall with a green marbled floor and covered by a huge blue dome richly edged with gold, from which three enormous cut crystal chandeliers hung. To the left there was a slightly raised annexe fronted by three ornately painted arches supported on slender porphyry columns. The annexe was furnished with a mixture of striped silk divans and low Ottomans at the feet of which there were a multitude of plump purple, blue and green velvet cushions strewn over the sky blue marble floor.

The walls of the hall were decorated with blue-and-white and coral-red Iznik tiles with rich floral designs framed in thick orange borders. At the far end of the hall sat a huge canopy covered ebony throne that was inlaid with nacre and ivory and at the sides of the throne there was a large fireplace with gilded hood and a two-tiered fountain skilfully decorated in marble.

Noticing the looks of wonder on his charges faces, Zahid Ali said: "This is the Imperial Hall. It is the official reception hall of the Sultan as well as for the entertainment of the Harem. Here the Sultan welcomes family and guests. It is also used for religious festivals and wedding ceremonies which take place in the presence of the members of his Highnesses' dynasty. The Chief Eunuch nodded.

"Your memory serves you well Zahid Ali; perhaps we should approach the Pasha for your return as you seem to hold deep affection for your former residence?" The eunuch smiled weakly. The thought of leaving behind his comfortable life in Algiers – and returning to a life where his every footstep would be on tiptoes for fear of falling foul of a yellow garbed madman who took great delight in severing heads from fat necks – was one that certainly held no charms.

He lowered his head slightly, and steepled his hands under his chin. "It would of course be a great honour," he said meekly, "but my Pasha relies heavily on my guiding hand and would be bereft were I to leave his service." The Chief Eunuch nodded and a thin smile creased his lips. *Yes*, he thought, *but not as bereft as Zahid Ali, who has no desire to re-enter the lion's den.*

They passed through the great hall and the Kizlar Agha led them to and up a grand marble staircase that led to another level. "On this level," Zahid Ali said smugly, "are the apartments of the Sultan himself and those of his favourite concubines." At his final words Erin and her companions exchanged quick looks. As the eunuch saw what passed between them he sniffed disdainfully. "You infidels, of course, can only hope to attain this level after much hard work and after undergoing many harsh lessons in servitude and respect."

They were taken up to the next level and the Chief Eunuch led the way down a short corridor and then turned sharply right onto a smaller but equally grand staircase. At the top of this they stepped off onto another corridor which led to an imposing ebony door that had an ivory latticework panel set at eye level. To the side of the door there was a hanging purple velvet tasselled cord. The Kizlar Agha tugged sharply on the cord and the women heard the faint tinkle of a bell from somewhere inside.

Two minutes passed and then a dark face appeared at the lattice and briefly scrutinised the Chief Eunuch, before a bolt was withdrawn and the door yawned open.

Inside the ornately decorated room, the black eunuch who had opened the door bowed deeply to the Kizlar Agha and without a word led the party to a pair of large low Ottomans and signalled for them to sit, before bowing again and leaving through a beaded curtain.

"You will soon be in the presence of her Highness the Valide Sultan," Zahid Ali said sternly. "When she enters you will rise to your feet, bow deeply and will not raise your eyes. You will not speak unless she asks a question of you. If you speak you will do so with eyes lowered and will address her as 'Your Royal Highness'. When he had finished his instructions the eunuch made a point of glaring at Erin, who coolly returned his gaze causing him to bite his lip in agitation. The girl had been a constant aggravation during their long voyage and here in the waiting room of the Valide Sultan's apartments he was worried that she would ignore his orders and by so doing it would reflect badly on his patient tuition.

For a long minute his mind raced with distressing visions of ignominy, with Royal rebuke and with gigantic swords and gargantuan maces. He swallowed nervously and then leapt to his feet as the beaded curtain was drawn aside by two hand maidens and Kosem swept into the room.

19

Ali Bichnin bowed respectfully as Murad, from his own slightly elevated seat made a languid hand motion towards the lower seat. As the Admiral sat, the Sultan smiled lightly and his voice was almost conversationally normal.

"Your voyage was a pleasant one?" Murad asked. The

Admiral hesitated for a second as he glanced at the huge sword that rested against the arm of the Sultan's chair. He had been told that Murad's moods could swing violently from the benign to the murderous within a heartbeat. He must weigh his own words very carefully.

"Pleasant yes, your Highness, but overly long as the honour of being charged with the bringing of taxes and tributes was much anticipated." The Sultan nodded again, but his next words carried a rough edge.

"And my uncle? Speak plainly; why does he not honour me personally?" Ali Bichnin swallowed nervously and thought: *He sees treachery everywhere; it is well that I put distance between the Pasha and myself.*

"Your Highness I am simply a man of the sea who obeys the orders of his Pasha and so am not privy to the motives of those above me." Murad smiled thinly.

"A simple man of the sea indeed? My spies inform me Admiral, that you are much more. I am told that my uncle is the Pasha in name only and that Ali Bichnin, the Head of the Corsair Council and with his fleet of pirate vessels is the true ruler of Algiers." The Admiral risked a slight shrug.

"It is true your Highness that I have risen to a certain level of high standing through my efforts to contribute to the Empire's coffers."

"Your efforts in these troubled times are much appreciated Admiral," the Sultan said lightly. The Admiral lowered his head humbly. "My ships are yours to command Highness, as am I and my corsair captains."

"And should my wishes run counter to your Pasha's commands, what then would be your response Admiral?" Bichnin hesitated for a long second in order that his next words would have the Sultan's full attention.

"Your Highness has but to speak and your words will carry more import than had the Prophet himself spoken contrary," he said with a deliberate note of strong conviction to his voice. The Sultan nodded.

"Well spoken Admiral," he said softly, before his face hardened, his fleshy lips narrowed into two tight lines, his voice took on a flinty edge and a huge hand tightened its grip on the handle of the great sword by his side. "You have heard have you not Admiral of the black treachery that has been laid at your Sultan's door?" The Admiral nodded.

"I have your Highness and if this loyal subject can do anything to help bring to justice those who have transgressed he will do so with all the power that he commands." Murad lifted his right hand from the pommel of his sword, lightly stroked his bearded chin and for a good half minute seemed deep in thought, before he nodded firmly.

"Good," he said. "I have received word that those who escaped my wrath have fled to a fortification on the border overlooking Macedonian Alexandroupolis where they have either overrun the small garrison or," and his face hardened and his eyes blazed, "they have found allies to aid their plans for further havoc. I would have you lead a fleet of your prime vessels to their lair and in my name exact revenge and bring back their dogs of leaders that I might personally see to their despatch." Ali Bichnin's eyes widened. He had offered what he thought were words of mere moral support; but now the Sultan was laying on him a heavy burden that would surely carry dire personal consequences should he fail to bring his task to a successful conclusion.

"And how great or small are the numbers of these traitors Highness?" the Admiral asked casually.

"They number no more than two hundred and their leaders no more than five, prime among which is Jafar Ben Ali a General of my Army." Ali Bichnin nodded. Two hundred was not an insignificant number and especially not if many of that number were Janissaries; but the die was cast and he was committed . . . unless he could introduce a practical reason for not undertaking such a risky venture.

"I am honoured that your Highness places such trust in this humble servant," the Admiral said. "But to strip Algiers of much of its corsair fleet for what might prove a protracted engagement would lead to a great reduction in revenues to the Empire's treasury." Murad's eyes narrowed and his right hand dropped back onto the pommel of the sword at his side.

"Your heart and head do not belong to your Sultan Admiral?" he said slowly. The Admiral, noting the hand movement and the reference to heads, was quick to respond.

"Highness I am your servant unto death! My words were meant only to highlight practical matters." The Sultan's bloodshot eyes blazed with sudden anger.

"Practical matters are of no concern. There has been foul treachery and the dogs must be brought to heel!" The Admiral nodded quickly.

"As you say Highness; and your will shall be done." The fierce light dimmed in Murad's eyes and his voice softened.

"Good. You will return immediately at full speed to Algiers to marshal your forces and drag the curs back to me; but," he added, "you will not sail with Janissaries in your company. Such can not be trusted to take up arms against their fellow Janissaries and Moslems. You will only sail with your European dogs of war and you are free to make promise to these of rich rewards for their service. You will order the Pasha to advance 20,000 Spanish dollars and with a successful outcome I will pay an additional 30,000 Spanish dollars." Ali Bichnin nodded, but then steepled his fingers together beneath his lips as though in sudden thought. Murad frowned.

"You wish to speak Admiral?" Ali Bichnin's hands moved apart and his head tilted slightly to one side.

"Highness, I do not know if I have the authority to speak."

"Speak." The Sultan ordered.

"The reward you offer is very generous Highness, but. . ." he hesitated for a few seconds before continuing. "The Pasha does not, for some reason, hold your servant in very high regard. Were I to demand 20,000 Spanish dollars from his treasury he might baulk." Murad's eyes narrowed and his right hand moved again to rest on the pommel of his huge sword.

"The treasury is not his Admiral," he said slowly. Ali Bichnin was quick to nod in agreement.

"Of course not highness, but to remove any chance of obstruction would your Highness prepare an order in the form of a personal letter that I might present?" Murad removed his hand from the sword's pommel and nodded lightly.

"It will be done Admiral and then you will move quickly fulfil your Sultan's wishes."

"As you say Highness; so shall it be." Murad's fleshy lips twitched into a thin fleeting smile.

"Yes Admiral, so shall it be. And when it is done your Sultan will be deeply in your debt; perhaps even to such an extent that his absent uncle might regret the day he failed to show his nephew the due respect shown by yourself." Ali Bichnin lowered his head in a show of humility . . . but mainly to hide the slow smile that blossomed on his own lips.

James, with his hand on the tiller, glanced back over his shoulder at the sight of the breakwater that was fading into the background of hills. There was no sign of pursuit and he was sure that none would now come. He turned to face the wide expanse of sea and then glanced up at the little sail that billowed bravely with a wind that held the promise of freedom.

Each mile would take him further away from his love and the bitter thought caused him pain; but he told himself that it was the price to be paid if he was ever to have a real chance of seeing her beautiful face again. "I will not rest," he muttered, as once more he turned briefly toward the retreating shore, "until I hold you in my arms again."

"What say you?" James turned quickly to see Richard Evans emerge from the little cabin.

"I pondered on one left behind," he said simply. Richard nodded.

"And I also, my dear wife and two darling sons are ever in my tortured thoughts." James felt a little stab of guilt at his own selfish words. Yes his precious one had been stolen from his side, but all of them had suffered as deeply if not even more deeply than he. All aboard this little vessel and those who languished on the fading shore had had family ripped from their lives and now the only hope of reuniting the Baltimore stolen with their loved ones lay in their making a dire thousand mile journey - and at the end of it, praying that the strength of their voices in suing for release would fall on powerful and receptive ears.

The shoreline had become a dark grey blue smudge beneath a cloudless sky when James stood and handed the tiller over to John Davis. Back down in the tiny cabin he took a sip from a carafe of water that was hanging by a leather thong from a hook on the cabin wall then shook the goatskin container. It felt almost empty. "There is no more water aboard?" he asked, hoping not to hear the response that came from Richard Evans.

"No James, nary a drop; nor is there any food." James bit his lip. The lack of food was not a problem; after several weeks of suffering the brooding ferocity of hunger – against which feelings and principles such as honour, disgust and fear had been relegated to no more than a handful of chaff blowing in the wind – they were now resigned to its bite. Water though was another matter altogether.

"We must then pray to God for rain," Stephen Ryder said softly from the rough wooden bunk on which he reclined. James nodded, but for him prayers to a deaf God were little more than wasted words. There was too much raw remembered loss in his short life. His father, his brother, young Jonathan, Samuel Carter – all dead; and his love snatched away.

He recognised that every man's life accumulated memories of bitter loss; but where most were accumulated over time and over time those swift and final passages became vague shadows, his were too newly clad in flesh and blood, in smiling eyes, remembered words and gestures. God would have to get by without his prayers.

Each of them had taken a turn at the tiller by the time the land astern had disappeared, the westering sun had sunk below the horizon, and a full moon had risen to spread a thin film of silver over the gently rolling waves, before Richard Evans furled the little sail and James dropped the vessel's anchor over the side to slow any drift. Back down in the cramped cabin they made themselves as comfortable as possible and settled down to wait for dawn.

The nerve shredding tensions of the day had slowly subsided and now in the deep shadows of the little cabin, lit only by a sprinkling of starlight through the open hatch, they listened to the soft lapping of waves against the vessel's hull and thought thoughts of loved ones now miles astern yet never more than a heartbeat away.

Dawn brought them out on deck where they raised the anchor, unfurled the sail and, taking bearings from the newly risen sun, set off again.

At the tiller James looked up at a cloudless sky that held not even a distant promise of rain and ran his tongue over his lips. None of them had any real idea of the distance they had to travel to reach any of the Spanish islands that lay to the north and a little to the east. All they knew from snatches of conversation they had picked up on in the bagnio was that they were perhaps eight to ten days sailing from Algiers. Eight to ten days with barely a few mouthfuls of water each.

James ran his tongue over his lips again as a fiery red ball rose higher in the sky and the decking beneath his bare feet began to radiate heat.

Three hours later, his shift at the tiller over, he lay below on one of the two little bunks. Stephen Ryder lay in the other and John Davis sat on the decking with his knees drawn up and his back to the hull. Because of the stifling heat their conversation had tailed off as the cabin had got uncomfortably sticky and now each of them was lost in their own thoughts.

Suddenly they were brought back to the present by a shout from Richard Evans up on deck. Together they scrambled to their feet and made their way to Richard's side. "The wind," the helmsman said simply, pointing to the little sail. James and the others looked up and saw a patched and sun bleached canvas that lay as limp as a crucified body against the mast's cross spar. "We are becalmed," Richard said as the others looked from the sail down to a sea that was as flat and still as a mill pond.

Erin rose to her feet and lowered her eyes as ordered; but not before she had time to take in the tall, exquisitely dressed figure that had entered the room.

The statuesque woman wore a long dark green dress embossed with a silver gilded cloud pattern. It had a deep v neck that exposed three thick gold necklaces and loose sleeves that reached almost to her wrists. On top of the dress she wore a snugly fitted brown velvet hip length jacket with short sleeves, which was fastened with pearl buttons and pulled in at the waist by a wide gold belt that carried a jewel encrusted dagger. Her long dark brown hair was piled up on her head framing an olive skinned heart shaped high cheek boned face, and was kept in place by a large gold and emerald studded pin that held a tall black plume. Her feet were shod in yellow gem encrusted open toed sandals and on the little finger of each hand she wore a ring with a huge blue sapphire stone.

"Your Highness," the Chief Eunuch said in greeting, "we bring you tributes from your brother in law, the Pasha of Algiers. The Queen Mother's black eyes took in the fair skinned women and she nodded.

"They are on first sight acceptable," she said, before adding, "Have they been schooled in what is required of them?" Zahid Ali stepped forward.

"Highness," he said bowing deeply, "your humble servant has taken it upon himself to give instruction during the too short journey from Algiers. They are still unfortunately lacking in adequate language, but have gained rudimentary skills in what their duties will entail." Kosem nodded.

"We have instructors who will complete their education," she said coolly before adding: "And you Zahid Ali, you come in place of the Pasha?"

"Yes your Highness, the Pasha has entrusted me with delivering taxes and these tributes."

"The Sultan was not displeased at his uncle's absence?" The eunuch hesitated for a second before deciding that his Pasha's future well being was no concern of his.

"Highness, this humble servant has not the authority to comment on the Sultan's mood; but if pressed, I must say that his Highness did indeed seem displeased." The Queen Mother nodded to herself then changed the subject.

"And my son, has he seen these tributes?"

"Yes he has your Highness, and his Supreme Highness seemed satisfied." Kosem thought: *Perhaps his mind might be briefly turned away from black thoughts of bloody revenge by new fair flesh.*

But then she added mentally: *But no female flesh can hold back his moods for long.* Erin and her companions, understanding little of the conversation, looked on mutely.

The Kizlar Agha, who had stood back while Kosem and Zahid Ali were talking, coughed lightly to attract the Queen Mother's attention.

"With your permission Highness," he said softly, "if you have no further need of our presence we will withdraw and deliver the tributes to the Keeper of the Harem." Kosem's shoulders lifted slightly and she gave a little wave of her right hand as sign of dismissal.

The Kizlar Agha's face showed no sign of emotion as the little party left the reception room but the summary dismissal was not well received. He was after all the Kizlar Agha, the third highest ranking officer of the empire behind the Sultan and the Grand Vizier.

Zahid Ali, who held the Chief Eunuch in high regard, was astute enough to notice that the Kizla Agha's's stony countenance was a practised mask concealing annoyance. It was another sign of the deteriorating state of affairs that had gained pace since he himself had left the palace.

The Sultan's addiction to alcohol and his alarming mood swings that so often led to butchery, coupled with Kosem's apparent increasing meddling in the Empire's affairs had no doubt played a major part in the recent mutiny of elements of the military and the Janissary Corps. It was a developing situation that he himself was now anxious to be far away from as soon as possible and to that end he wasted no time in asking to be excused.

"With my duties now discharged concerning delivery of the taxes and tributes," he said bowing deeply to the Kizla Agha, "I would ask leave to return to the Admiral's vessel." The Head Eunuch briefly toyed with the idea of denying the request, just to see the look on the other's face. He pursed his lips and tilted his head sideways in apparent deep thought and was rewarded with the sight of Zahid Ali unconsciously wringing folded hands in front of a corpulent belly.

"Permission is given," he said after a lengthy pause, before adding: "Unless I petition the Sultan for your return to palace duties here..." A look of panic skittered across Zahid Ali's face and he swallowed hard before answering.

"To serve his Highness again would be a great honour of course; but I fear that even short absence from my duties in the Pasha's household will have led to many problems that need urgent attention." The Chief Eunuch smiled.

"Yes," he said softly, "I am sure you are much missed. The Sultan's loss then will be your Pasha's gain. You may go." The words had barely left the Kizla Agha's lips before Zahid Ali bowed, turned quickly and without a backward glance waddled off towards, and fairly skipped down, the staircase.

With oddly conflicting emotions Erin watched the eunuch disappear. She in particular had no reason to regret his leaving; but somehow his had been a constant, if irritating presence in the last few turbulent weeks and months of her life. Now, with his departure she and her sisters were once again facing the unknown.

She had scant seconds to consider her feelings before the Chief Eunuch marched them along the corridor and passed several closed doors, to another staircase that led down and opened up onto a large open space. The airy room was furnished with a number of Ottoman divans, low tables and chairs and scattered rugs. To their right three tall windows with clear and coloured panels cast white, red and cobalt blue splashes of light onto a pale green marble floor. On the far side of the room and directly across from where they were standing there was another imposing portal with an ivory latticework grill set at head height. The Kizla Agha led them over to the door and again reached for and tugged on a thick hanging tasselled cord. A minute later a brown face appeared behind the lattice and the door swung open.

They entered into another reception room furnished much the same as that of the Queen Mother and after being signalled to sit on one of the long divans, the eunuch doorman spoke briefly to the still standing Chief Eunuch before leaving through an inner door.

From her seat Erin reached out to her left and right to hold her sister's hands. At the touch Anna glanced briefly sideways and smiled a wide genuine smile. *She is enraptured,* Erin thought. *Her pretty little head is full of great palaces and gaudy clothes, with no thought to her moral welfare.* She glanced to her left and Alice also smiled back; but this time there was no wonder in her smile, it was only a brave attempt to offer comfort, which was followed by a little reassuring - to both of them - squeeze of a hand.

Once more the door opened and the captives rose to their feet as another exotically dressed woman entered the room. She looked to be a few years older and she was less imposing than the Valide Sultan, but her confident bearing said that she was another personage of some authority. She wore a long pale rose silk dress with a tight bodice that was open at the front with no collar and short sleeves. Her dark brown hair carried faint streaks of grey and was partially covered by a conical hat that had pink and green pale gauzy fabric wound around it that dropped onto her shoulders and was held in place by a jasper and pearl studded pin.

On sight of the Kizlar Agha the woman bowed respectfully and the Chief Eunuch nodded slowly in response.

"You are to discover if these odalisques are suitable candidates to be presented to the Sultan," he said. "If they are you will tutor them in language, religion and the arts. If they are not suitable you will assign them as you see fit." The woman bowed again and the Kizlar Agha turned to the women who had been struggling to follow his words, and spoke in English.

"The Haznedar Usta, Head Treasurer, of the Sultan's Harem, will be your examiner and guide. You will address her as Mistress and always speak with total respect. You will obey always. You will risk severe punishment if you do not." With that, he turned on his heel and left.

As the door closed behind him their new Mistress, with a blank expression on her face, ushered them through the interior door to begin their examination.

20

James ran the back of a hand across his sweating forehead. For the last three days they had managed to lessen the effects of the relentless heat in the little cabin and up on deck by stripping off their clothes and going over the side into the cooling water – but this was only a very temporary relief.

The heat though was the least of their worries. The empty carafe on the cabin's wall – a constant taunting reminder of their thirst – was what continually occupied their thoughts. They had spread the sail out on the deck each night that they had been becalmed in an attempt to trap any moisture from the cooling air, but had been rewarded with nothing in the morning but small patches of dampness that they had licked dry.

Now the night lay heavy upon them again and John Davis, lying on the cabin deck alongside Stephen Ryder, said through cracked lips: "Surely this torment must soon end. God must hear our prayers and send us rain and a breeze to set us back on our way." From his bunk James smiled mirthlessly to himself. *Yes*, he thought, *God will hear your prayers, he is after all our Father and fathers always watch over their children.* He shook his head in a weak effort to evict his blasphemous thoughts, but his mood held.

From the other bunk, Richard Evans echoed John Davis' words. "We must keep faith John. Our Lord will soon send an end to our suffering . . . of this we can be certain."

James drifted off into a fitful sleep that was plagued by shadowy faces of the lost, by spurting blood from gaping wounds, green eyes that shed crystal tears and the rhythmic beating of a pulsing heart. The pulsing chased away the other visions and in the darkness, where time lays more heavily than in the light, he woke like a sick man whose wicked torment makes him weary. He shook his head but the rhythmic pulse persisted and grew stronger. It was coming from somewhere outside the vessel.

Gently, he eased himself out of the bunk and carefully strode over the sleeping forms of John Davis and Stephen Ryder and made his way up onto the deck.

The shadowy outline of a huge many oared vessel that bore down on them was no more than twenty feet away. He shouted a strangled warning just as the vessel's iron shod prow rammed into the midsection of their little craft, flipped it onto its side and catapulted him into the sea.

He hit the water, sank and then struggled upwards to surface between a bank of dipping oars. He reached out and wrapped an arm around one of the oars as a loud warning shout from the deck of the vessel rang out and the lowered blades froze.

Holding on tightly he turned his head to look for their stricken vessel. All he saw was a series of large bubbles rising slowly to the surface.

From above a rope was swiftly lowered to him and he was lifted out of the water and rough hands dragged him aboard. As he lay on the deck getting his breath back Richard Evans' last words tripped through his mind *"Our Lord will soon send an end to our suffering . . .of this we can be certain,"* and to the amazement of those who looked down on him they heard a laugh that was rimmed with ice.

In his cabin Ali Bichnin felt the impact, heard the shouts and noted that his vessel had suddenly stopped. He climbed out of his bunk, threw on a topcoat over his night attire and went to investigate. Down on the main deck he saw a little group of shadowy figures clustered round another figure that was struggling to its feet.

"What have we hit," he demanded of the black slave master.

"A small vessel Admiral," the man replied.

"And this man?" the Admiral asked taking in the figure that had stumbled to its feet.

"From the vessel Admiral."

"And the vessel?"

"Gone to the bottom Admiral; with any crew on board." Ali Bichnin nodded.

"Then there is nothing more to do here, strike up the beat to 30 to the minute." The slave master nodded, cracked his whip and the galley began to inch forward again.

In the dim dawn light the Admiral turned his attention briefly to the survivor who was leaning over the side and peering intently into the dark water. "Your vessel has gone," he said in Sabir. The man turned slowly and Ali Bichnin's eyes narrowed in an effort to focus more clearly in the gloom. Surely his eyes were deceiving him! No, the man's face and arms were burnt deep brown, but his head and jaw was covered in fine, almost blond, stubble. He moved closer and peered directly into the man's eyes – they were blue.

"You are European!" the Admiral said in surprise. James did not need to speak fluent Sabir to understand what this other man, who from his looks was also a European, was saying. He had intended to remain dumb when pulled aboard the vessel, but the corsair captain, as a fellow European would surely be inclined to show some sympathy.

"Yes," James said quietly in English, "I am, like you a European." Ali Bichnin nodded and replied in the same language.

"You are English?" James shrugged.

"I am by heritage, but I was born in Baltimore, Ireland" The Admiral's eyes widened slightly as the familiar place name registered.

"Come," he ordered, we will speak more."

In the cabin the Admiral came straight to the point. "You are an escaped slave," he said indicating James' right ankle where the manacle had rubbed the skin to leave a raw red mark. James glanced down quickly then nodded.

The Admiral returned the nod. "You know the penalty meted out to escaped slaves." It was a statement rather than a question. Again James nodded mutely, but his eyes grew hard and bright. Ali Bichnin noted the look and his lips twitched upwards in a sardonic smile. *This slave had backbone to go with his physical strength* he thought, taking in the man's broad chest and heavily muscled arms. He was intrigued and wanted to know more.

"How came you to be in the unfortunate vessel," he asked. James decided that there was nothing to be gained by staying mute.

"We escaped from an Algiers bagnio four days ago and were left becalmed." The Admiral nodded.

"A feat of some cunning and daring," he said. "And one very rarely successful - as can be seen," he added pointedly. James shrugged.

"We chose the chance of freedom against a lifetime of misery."

"You say we, who were the others who now lie in their watery graves?" James' eyes lost their flinty look and misted over.

"They were three good fellow Baltimore men stolen with their families," he answered sadly. The Admiral nodded.

"Yes," he said simply, before adding: "And there were also a number of comely young women taken, was there not." Again it was a statement rather than a question. James lifted his head and stared directly into the other's eyes.

"You know of these women?" he said sharply. Ali Bichnin nodded.

"I had the pleasure of the company of three such recently."

"Who! When! James demanded. The Admiral's face hardened.

"You do not make demands of the Admiral of the Pasha's fleet slave!" James lowered his head.

"Apologies Admiral, I meant no disrespect," he said softly, deciding that a show of humility was called for. Ali Bichnin nodded but he was not taken in by the change of tone. *He is a man's man this one*, he thought, *and one with fire in his belly but with the brains to temper it in his speech*.

"Your apology is accepted," he said casually before adding, "Perhaps your tone was prompted by a very personal interest?"

"It was sir; I have lost my betrothed."

"And how looks this maiden?" James swallowed hard and ran his tongue over his lips.

"She is of great beauty sir, with flaming red hair and eyes the colour of purest jade."

"And with a fiery temper perhaps?" the Admiral said casually. James' heart leapt.

"You have seen her sir!" Ali Bichnin nodded.

"Indeed. She was with two other comely young women from Baltimore who I have just delivered to the harem of his Highness the Sultan of Constantinople." James' mind whirled in a welter of confused thoughts and emotions. She was safe and well. But she had been taken even further away. Unlike the men of Baltimore she would not suffer physical privation; but she was in moral danger at the hands of a Moorish devil.

He made an effort to check the rush of emotion. She was

well, that was the main consideration. Yes there was moral danger, but there was nothing that he could do to remove or even lessen that danger. He took two deep breaths and his voice was calm when he spoke again.

"I thank you sir for giving me that information." The Admiral shrugged.

"It can be of little comfort I am sure, for your betrothed might as well be removed to the moon for all you can do to return her to your side." James shook his head.

"Where there is life there is hope," he said firmly. Ali Bichnin took in the words and the steely determination behind them and his slowly growing admiration for this young slave grew, before a wry smile clouded his features.

"And therein lies a dilemma, for the life of a re-captured slave in Algiers where we are bound is not worth a candle."

The Head Treasurer, Fekriye, proved to be a harsh and impatient language and religious studies tutor and as the weeks went by Anna, in particular, was a frequent victim of punishment in the form of strokes from a light bamboo cane meted out by one of the Mistress's black eunuchs. Erin and Alice were much quicker to expand the basic vocabulary gained under Zahid Ali's instructions. They were also quick – under duress – to learn the basics of Islam and were soon passed on to one of the junior tutors, the Mistress of Dance.

Erin found this parting – though it was only during the long daily hours of tuition before they were returned to their small apartment – difficult. She had grown to look upon pretty empty headed Anna as a little sister who was in constant need of support and guidance; even though her little sister often seemed more interested in the more material side of life. "She needs our guidance," Erin said to Alice during a short break in lessons. Alice was not so sure.

"Sister, the cane aside she is as happy with her lot as can be possible in our situation. Her wants extend no further than for fine clothes and foods and a style of life a world away from her earlier life in Baltimore."

Erin sighed. She knew that Alice's words made sense. Anna's life in Baltimore had been a mundane one. Their own lives had also been mundane, but the difference between them had been that while she and Alice had at least had the benefit of a family upbringing to lean on, young Alice had been removed from such an environment much earlier in her short life.

"Yes sister," she replied. "You are right; but nevertheless I feel we must still do all in our power to offer guidance."

Fekriye studied the report from the Mistress of Dance. The two new odalisques were performing well. They had mastered the less intricate movements and were now being taught the more complex moves. They would soon, the report said, be ready to move on to the Mistress of Music and ultimately, from there to training in the erotic arts.

The tiny golden-haired one was another matter. Fekriye sighed. She had tutored Georgians, Armenians and Caucasians from many areas in language and religious studies, but this one was proving difficult. She was half inclined to give up and pass the girl on to the Mistress of Robes or the Keeper of Baths, who would surely have more success in training her in menial tasks; but she persevered because the girl's striking yellow hair, blue eyes, delicate fair skin and elfin figure were a rarity. The Sultan's seraglio had many dark haired, brown eyed, olive and dark skinned beauties and there were also a number of fair haired and skinned captives from the Land of Ice in far northern Europe; but none of these displayed both the physical attributes and the simple and strangely beguiling childlike innocence that this girl offered.

Fekriye knew that the girl was never going to become truly fluent in language but she decided to persevere for a while, before passing her on to the Mistresses of Dance and Music. Once she had sufficiently mastered those skills she would then undergo the ultimate training; a training that would finally decide if she was capable of mastering the critical skill of bringing pleasure to her master.

"I felt the cane only three times today," Anna said brightly. "And the Mistress says that I will soon move on to join you in dance!" Erin smiled indulgently.

"You see; did we not say that you would succeed? Did we not say that if you put your mind to it you would win?" Alice nodded in accompaniment to Erin's words and Anna, pleased with her self grinned.

"I will find dance more to my liking," she said gaily, "It will come much more naturally, than having to concentrate my mind so hard my head aches!"

"You will excel sister," Erin said confidently for Anna's benefit, "But sadly you will have to do it alone, for we are soon to be moved on to the Mistress of Music who is to instruct us in the playing of instruments." The smile on Anna's face faded and Alice stepped forward to take up the young girl's hand.

"You will be alone for only a short time Anna," she said brightly. "For did you not just say that dancing will come much more naturally to you? Indeed, you will pass through Dance to join us, I feel, before Erin and I have learned to master even a penny whistle!" At Alice's words the smile blossomed once more.

"You are indeed my sisters," Anna gushed. "For you are always ready to lay my silly mind to rest!"

Away from the long daily lessons their evenings were spent in their second floor apartment with its little veranda that opened out onto a small grassed courtyard below and where they breathed in the heady fragrance of planted frangipani shrubs, jasmine and purple blue flowered hyacinths wafted up by the rising warm evening air currents. Their food and hygiene needs were met by serving women, none of whom could be drawn into any meaningful conversation and, although the door to their apartment was never locked, they were told that any evening or night excursions would be dealt with severely. It seemed that even though they lived in relative luxury, they were still prisoners.

21

The hatch cover drew back and James squinted as the sudden burst of light stabbed his eyes. He had been confined to the small forward hold for two days while the vessel completed the last leg of its journey and now, obviously, the end was in sight.

His imprisonment had not been harsh and water and food had been lowered down to him at regular intervals. Even so, in the dark he suffered. He was tormented by the cruel misfortunes that had overwhelmed him and those he loved and admired.

A few short months ago he had been a carefree young man with his whole life spread before him. There had been no trace of struggle in that life, nothing in particular to strive after, to aim for or to desire – other than perhaps a wife and family sometime in the future; but now even that simple undefined wish had been rendered improbable by the nightmare that his life had become.

In the dark, he briefly wondered how his brother, Thomas, would be thinking, if their roles had been reversed and he was here now. Thomas had always been the bright one with an agile mind and sharp irreverent wit. Would he have thought something like: *'God's only excuse for abandoning him was that He, God, did not exist.* That would have been Thomas, James thought; whereas he had always considered himself to be a God-fearing Christian who held a simple faith and a belief that a life well lived would ultimately, in the final reckoning, be rewarded by eternal happiness.

"Fool!" He had bounced the bitter word off the walls of the little hold a dozen times in the last two days. "God-fearing fool!" had followed accompanied by a sneering laugh. Well if there was a God, He was one who cared nothing for those who blindly worshipped Him. So, he decided that whatever short life that remained to him would not be spent in prayer but in the knowledge that he would stand defiantly alone.

Up in his cabin the Admiral gathered up his personal effects and made ready to disembark. His vessel was minutes away from docking and he was already rehearsing what he was going to say to the Pasha. He smiled as he imagined the look on Hussain's face as he related the Sultan's deep annoyance and the slight felt at his uncle's absence. He also looked forward to telling the Sultan that his coffers would be severely depleted due to the possible long term loss of much of his fleet.

He nodded and smiled again as he reached for the cabin

door, only to stop as another loosely related thought came into his head. *The escaped prisoner, what should I do with him?* The man had told him that he had been forced to work at the quarry cutting and hauling rock to maintain the mole. As such he was a civil slave owned by the Pasha himself. The Admiral smiled again. *He is too good to be returned to the Pasha's care. It is better that he be added to my own slaves where his strength and character may be put to better use.*

James took a deep breath and placed his foot on the bottom rung of the ladder that had been lowered to him. "If I am to die I will do so with all the dignity I can summon forth," he said quietly as he reached his hands up and began to climb.

Up on deck he was a little surprised to find that there was no armed guard waiting to escort him off the vessel. In fact, while there was a bustle of activity with people milling around, there appeared to be no-one - apart from the crewman who had lowered the ladder - taking any particular interest in him. The man, a tall thin dark skinned half-caste reached for his arm and spoke in Sabir.

"Come," he ordered. James allowed the man to lead him down the gangplank and onto the dockside from where he and his dear friends had so recently set sail on their tragic voyage. The man led him to a waiting horse drawn wagon and signalled for him to climb into the back while he himself took a seat beside the driver, who flicked the reins.

This is strange, James thought as the wagon began to roll forward. The half-caste and the driver were not paying him the slightest attention; instead they were chatting together in Sabir. The wagon rolled on towards the main gate, but then rattled by with out stopping and turned onto a road that followed the curve of the city wall to the east. *We do not make our way to the bagnio?*, James thought, *so where do we go?*

The wagon trundled on alongside the city wall at a steady pace for a good fifteen minutes before it drew abreast of another, slightly smaller gate. The driver pulled sharply on the left rein and the wagon rolled through the open portal where it was waved forward by a solitary Janissary guard.

James was now in a part of the city that he was not familiar with. There were no narrow streets with crowded overhanging buildings and no mad press of people going about their daily business; instead they passed a number of green spaces surrounded by large detached two and three storey what looked to be domestic dwellings, before the driver turned onto a wide palm tree lined approach road at the end of which on a softly rising grassy plateau and behind blindingly white lime washed eight foot high walls, sat a huge palace.

The driver brought the wagon to a halt in front of an impressive double-door portal built into the wall and dismounted. James, in a confused state of mind looked on. He had steeled himself to face the fate that prisoners' tales had told him lay in store for all those re-captured once they had been returned through the city walls. But this palace was no bagnio. Behind these walls there was surely another fate to be revealed.

The driver removed a short stout cudgel from his belt and rapped loudly on the door. Within seconds the portal swung open, the driver strode back to the wagon and they drove through into a landscaped courtyard fringed with cherry, orange and lemon trees. As the gate man slammed the door shut behind them the half-caste turned in his seat and signalled for James to climb down. *Whatever lies ahead*, James thought as he did as ordered, *must surely be better than to be returned to the bagnio.*

With James at his back the half caste crossed the courtyard and made his way through a high open archway that led into a smaller paved courtyard, in the centre of which there was a circular flower bed, a perfumed oasis containing two dozen carefully cultivated white, pink and yellow dwarf rose bushes surrounded by beds of exotic herbs.

The man strode purposely across this courtyard and with an outstretched arm swept aside a heavily beaded curtain, then turned, and with his other arm, beckoned James through. The pleasantly cool reception room was furnished with four large rosewood chairs and two low Ottomans upholstered in red and cream striped satin. The floor was clad in slabs of polished pink marble and the white interior walls glittered with encrusted powdered gold. His guide motioned for him to sit in one of the chairs before leaving the reception room through another beaded curtain.

James shook his head in confusion. *Why am I here and not back in the bagnio?* The thought kept repeating in his head as the minutes slowly crawled by; before the curtain drew back and the half caste crewman beckoned him through into a large circular room with three doors leading off it that featured only a number of large potted fern-like plants and a softly murmuring marble fountain. They crossed the floor towards one of the doors which the crewman opened and then motioned him through. They had entered another smaller open space at the rear of which an ornate staircase rose to a landing.

"Come," the crewman ordered as he strode towards and onto the stairs. James who had made a conscious effort to empty his mind of fruitless thoughts, meekly followed. What would be would be and his future would soon be revealed.

They reached the landing and passed a number of doors, before the crewman stopped outside one and rapped sharply before opening it and entering.

"This is a slave that the Admiral bids you employ," he said firmly in Sabir. The seated Negro rose to his feet and came round from behind the desk.

"Does he speak the language?" he asked looking into James' blue eyes. The crewman shrugged

"You, you know Sabir?" The Negro asked.

"A little," James admitted. The Negro nodded.

"Take him to the kitchens and put him to work, the Admiral will decide his fate when he returns."

With a languid hand movement the Pasha signalled Ali Bichnin to sit. The Admiral smiled. He was going to enjoy imparting his news.

"Your journey was without incident Admiral?" the Pasha asked casually as Ali Bichnin took the proffered seat. *You know it was*, the Admiral thought. *Your lapdog Zahid Ali has given you chapter and verse.*

"It was without incident, but certainly not without import." The Pasha frowned lightly at the Admiral's cryptic response. Zahid Ali had told him that Constantinople had been in a state of near anarchy with mutilated corpses hanging on every street corner and that the Sultan's sword and mace had seen heavy use. He had also reported that he had not been privy to any conversations between the Sultan and the Admiral due to being ordered from their company early in their meeting.

"And what was this thing of import Admiral?" Ali Bichnin smiled again.

"The Sultan has charged me to put together a naval force consisting of the best of our fleet and to lead that fleet to Macedonian Alexandropoulos where I am to capture the leaders of a revolt against the Empire ... and to return those leaders to the Sultan to face his wrath." The Pasha's mouth dropped open.

"Impossible!" he shouted. "Such a venture could take many months!" Ali Bichnin shrugged.

"True, many months . . ."

"And our own treasury . . . months without substantial income from slaves . . . it would be drained!

"True it very well might be . . ." The Admiral shook his head sadly. "And of course we might lose much of our fleet in the action," he added with another little shake of his head. The Pasha's face blanched.

"Oh, and the Sultan has told me to inform you that you are to advance 20,000 Spanish dollars towards the venture for provisioning the fleet and payment for the men." The Pasha's eyes almost started out from his head.

"Impossible!" he ranted. "We do not have such a sum freely available . . . I would have to use coin from my own resources . . . It can not be done!" The Admiral shrugged lightly and then removed a rolled parchment from a coat pocket.

"His Highness said that his demands might meet with resistance; so he told me to give this to you so there would be no misunderstanding." He handed the parchment over to the seething Pasha.

Hussain's defiant look slowly faded as he read the document and was replaced by one of bitter resignation. The

Admiral knew why. He had taken the liberty of reading it too and the dire threat at the end relating to impaling on a thick sharpened stake had been responsible for an about turn in attitude.

From his seat at the head of the table in the offices of the Captains Guild, Ali Bichnin related his conversation with the Sultan and now awaited the response of the pirate captains who he had summoned. As usual, Morat Rais was the first to speak.

"Why should we embark on such a risky venture that carries no guarantee of success, when we are secure and sure of continued success here in Algiers? Some of the other captains nodded in agreement. The Admiral pushed his chair back, rose to his feet and leaning forward, placed his palms on the table.

"Yes we grow slowly richer here by harvesting an easy crop, but our continued success is only guaranteed through the Empire's good will and that good will is dependent on the Sultan's favour.

"He has charged me to bring to justice those who have sorely wronged him and for my part I commit my own vessels, their captains and crews to that end." Morat Rais rose to his feet.

"And the rest of us, did you commit our vessels also to this venture Admiral?" The Admiral shrugged.

"Your vessels are your own concern captain. I was elected by my fellow corsairs as leader of the Captains' Guild and am thus obliged to outline any venture that would lead to great profit for its members." Morat's eyebrows lifted at mention of the words 'great profit'.

"Great profit you say? And what might this great profit amount to Admiral?" Ali Bichnin smiled inwardly.

"The Sultan has charged the Pasha to pay an initial 20,000 Spanish dollars." There was a murmur of interest from around the table before Morat spoke again.

"A generous offer Admiral, but such a venture is fraught with danger. We do not know of the strength of these so called traitors, nor do we know how firmly they are entrenched." The Admiral nodded.

"You speak truly captain . . . and that is why the Sultan, in addition to the initial sum provided by our esteemed Pasha, has promised to pay, for a successful venture, the sum of 30,000 Spanish dollars to be shared among those who answer his summons for assistance." Ali Bichnin glanced around the table to gauge the impact of his words and saw the glint of gold reflected in their eyes.

"My two vessels are yours to command Admiral," Morat Rais said quickly and his words were echoed immediately by the other independent captains. The Admiral nodded. He knew that the chance to earn at least treble what each man stood to gain in a whole year, would strike the right chord in their mercenary souls.

Morat Rais' smile suddenly faded and a second later his face registered a slightly concerned look.

"The offer is a most generous one Admiral, but what guarantee do we have that the Sultan will honour the bargain? He is known for his contrary temperament, is he not?" The Admiral nodded.

"His contrary temperament and his murderous moods, captain. But he is in a dangerous position. The Empire itself could descend into chaos if he does not act swiftly and decisively to quell the seeds of rebellion. He cannot risk sending his own military for fear of leaving himself open to further attack on his own doorstep. Our Sultan is many things captain but he is not a fool. He will willingly honour the bargain . . . and then increase taxes to recover his outlay."

As he looked once more into the faces around the table Ali Bichnin saw that his words and the firm manner of their delivery had been well received, with even the notoriously independent Morat Rais apparently convinced.

"We are of one mind then gentlemen?" The Admiral's question received nods.

"Good, then I will make ready for a return to the Pasha to secure the 20,000 Spanish dollars. Once the money has been secured we must then make haste, for the adventure awaits and good fortune for us all surely lies ahead!

22

Ever since their capture Erin's nature had marked her out as being the stubborn one. Her determination to remain steadfast in her religion and not to appear subservient had cost her many verbal and physical rebukes; now though her attitude had mellowed slightly. She still held to her faith but she had realised that battling against the fates was, at least for the time being, a fruitless undertaking. She, like Alice, would make the best of their situation.

They had completed their tuition under the Mistress of Dance and had been moved on to lessons under the Mistress of Music, who now stood before them and was proving to be a hard taskmistress.

Erin slipped on the finger cymbals and began to dance while Alice from behind shook her tambourine. They had not gone more than ten seconds before the Mistress clapped her hands in annoyance.

"Stop!" she ordered. "I have heard better music from the mouths of copulating cats! You," she turned to Alice, "treat the tambourine like you are shaking your fist at a fishwife. You must caress not shake the life out of the instrument. And you," she turned to Erin, "These instruments are as toys for children. How are you going to learn the lute and the saz if you find these so hard to master?" The two young women's newly acquired grasp of language had some gaps in it, but the Mistress' meaning was fully understood. Erin's finger cymbals tinkled as she raised her hands in a gesture that said 'I don't know'.

"We have never tried to play any musical instrument before Mistress, but we will learn." The Mistress nodded. She had taught many odalisques over the years. These two were not, by far, the worst pupils, but it was her duty to make sure that they mastered the art of music; otherwise their failure would reflect badly on her and in the present Palace climate that could prove most costly.

"Yes, you will learn," she said firmly. "Now begin again!"

The days stretched into weeks and true to her words, the Mistress managed to turn them into passable musicians.

Anna had joined them on the third week and much to Erin and Alice's surprise the young girl had taken to dance to such a degree that their own laboured attempts suffered by comparison. The Mistress had made her perform first without the finger cymbals and as she watched the petite young girl's lithe body gyrate she had nodded.

"Now put on the finger cymbals and begin again," she had ordered. Anna did as told and Erin and Alice had looked on in wonder as Anna performed. Where Erin and in particular Alice, had found it hard to marry the dance and the music together, Anna's sensual performance did just that.

The Mistress had been impressed, but she was not about to let it show. "The dance is very adequate," she admitted, "but the thumb cymbals are heavy and slow."

Anna's blossoming talent meant that she soon caught up to Erin and Alice and although she found the lute difficult to master, she eventually reached the Mistress' minimum standards. "You have all somehow managed to gain a modest grasp of music," she told them. "And tomorrow you will move on to the final phase of your education - you will be taught how to fulfil a woman's role in life . . . that of pleasing a man."

Back in their apartment Erin and Alice fretted, while Anna seemed totally at ease. She had enjoyed the dance and to a lesser degree the music. Yes, the language had been difficult and had caused her much early distress, but she could now understand much of what was said and could respond if not fluently, then well enough to get by. *I have a new life*, she thought. *And it is much more pleasant than the one I left behind.*

Out on the little balcony Erin breathed in the heady scent that drifted up from the courtyard below. She sighed deeply and turned to Alice. "We have come to the point sister that I have long dreaded," she said quietly. "I have pledged my body in marriage to my one true love; how am I to honour that pledge now?" Alice shook her head.

"I do not know sister. All you can do is keep true to your love in heart and mind, if not in body." Erin's shoulders sagged.

"Yes, but my maidenhead is a precious gift and one that I so dearly wanted to offer to my beloved James." Alice nodded.

"Yes sister that is how it should be between lovers. But your James would understand should that gift be stolen away." It was Erin's turn to nod.

"He would sister, for he is a good man; but in his heart it would surely cause pain." Alice tried her best to put on a brave face.

"It may not come to pass," she said as brightly as she could muster. "Do you not recall the reply given by that fat rascal, Zahid Ali, when I asked about the numbers in the Sultan's harem?" Erin frowned lightly.

"What words sister?"

"I asked how many women were in the harem and he said there were hundreds! Perhaps then we may never have to face the ordeal." Erin's frown faded and was replaced by a weak smile.

"Sister, you are as usual, a comfort in trying times. I apologise for my selfish feelings, for you also must be deeply worried by what the future holds." Alice returned the smile.

"I have no man to save the gift for sister; so for me although it would still be a loss, that loss would not weigh as heavy as yours."

They sat on the balcony for another half hour before they were joined by Anna whose light mood was in sharp contrast to their own.

"Tomorrow," Anna said," we enter the last step of our training sisters; it has been a remarkable journey, has it not!" Erin pinched her lips together in an effort to hold back a sharp response, but failed.

"Do you not realise what may now await us little sister!" she said sharply. Anna looked startled as Erin continued.

"We are to be taught practices that only a married woman should entertain; and perhaps, practices as undertaken by such as these heretics, that no modest married Christian woman should *ever* entertain!" Anna shrugged

"We are women Erin and women must adapt in a man's world." Erin shook her head.

"Sister, we may be women, but we have minds of our own

and the power to use them!" Anna shrugged.

"Yes, we are women Erin and we do have power, but it is the power to bend men to our will, through womanly wiles." Erin could hardly believe her own ears. Was this the empty headed slip of a girl that she had taken under her wing? And another thing, Anna had called her 'Erin' twice in the last minute instead of using the term 'sister' that they had settled on ever since they had suffered the nightmare of abduction.

"You have changed sister and it pains me greatly," Erin said sadly. Anna shrugged again.

"I will do what I must do to make life as a captive as comfortable as possible," the young woman said flatly.

The rest of the evening was spent in near silence. Erin was stung by what she thought of as Anna's betrayal; Anna kept her own council and preferred to think thoughts of pretty clothes and of ways to exert her new found womanhood, while Alice often glanced across at her two sisters with a heavy heart that the bond that had tied them so closely together seemed to be loosening.

The slave girl appeared early with their breakfast next morning and was soon followed by a huge, heavily muscled and silent, black eunuch who signalled for them to follow him. They were taken through parts of the palace that they had not seen before and bright eyed Anna marvelled at the amazing riches on show in the form of the exotic architecture, fantastic furniture and beautiful fabrics. For their part the sights that so intrigued and thrilled Anna passed Erin and Alice by. They were more concerned with what lay ahead.

The black eunuch led them to a large circular room that was furnished with several chairs, two low divans an ornately carved mahogany desk and in the very centre, a large canopied bed. The eunuch signalled for them to sit and left through a heavily beaded curtain.

They had sat in silence for perhaps two minutes when Erin and Alice together, glanced at the bed, then at each other and twin blushes blossomed on their cheeks. Anna giggled, rose to her feet, ran over to the bed, leapt onto it and bounced up and down. Erin started to voice a rebuke but her words were cut off by a sudden parting of the beaded curtain and the reappearance of the eunuch, closely followed by a woman.

She was tall and slim and her hair which was parted in the middle fell in glossy cascades onto her shoulders and was as black as a raven's wing. Her dark long lashed eyes were highlighted in pale green kohl which matched a long green, short sleeved velvet dress that was pulled in at the waist by a wide tasselled brown leather belt studded with emeralds. Her high cheek-boned face and bare arms were the colour of wild honey and she glided into the room like a stalking cheetah.

The woman's cold feline gaze fell immediately on Anna. She snapped her fingers and made a languid 'get down' motion with a tawny arm; Anna leaped off the bed and moved quickly to Erin and Alice's side. The woman then turned her attention to the three young women.

"I am Nubana, the Sultan's favourite Ikbal. You will attend my every word and address me as Mistress." Anna nodded obediently, while Alice and Erin looked blankly on.

"You three odalisques are said to be possible candidates for concubinage . . . That is for me alone to decide." Erin and Alice exchanged quick glances and Anna nodded again, this time more vigorously.

"I will educate you in the many ways to give pleasure," Nubana continued. "Ways that have been practised for a hundred years and which peasants and slaves such as you can have no knowledge of.

You will learn the art of sensual massage using fragrant oils such as jasmine and sandalwood.

I will teach you how to re-awaken passion by use of the bark and berries of certain trees and shrubs.

You will learn which foods are love foods and ways to make a man's shaft hard as ebony." Her last words caused Erin and Alice's cheeks to burn with embarrassment, while Anna's merely glowed with a much cooler flow of blood.

23

Ali Bichnin secured the 20,000 Spanish dollars from a sour faced Pasha Hussain and left his second in command, Jan van Reebek to the task of provisioning and recruiting the extra men needed from the renegado dregs that frequented the city's bars and brothels. He knew that the standard of recruits would not come close to matching the fighting skills of the Janissaries or military that they had to overcome, but they were expendable cannon fodder and as such their numbers would be much depleted when it came to the final sharing of the Sultan's bounty.

As he and his fellow passenger, Morat Rais, climbed out of the carriage in the courtyard, the Admiral breathed in the bouquet of scents that greeted him and smiled. He had made a fine life for himself in this once foreign land. He was rich beyond the dreams of common men. He owned thousands of slaves; he had built a magnificent palace and an equally magnificent mosque as testament to his conversion to Islam and now he was about to embark on a venture that could result in him perhaps becoming the new Pasha of Algiers.

With Morat at his side he made his way through the palace complex to his apartments on the second floor. There, he poured two large brandies from a crystal decanter and offered one to his companion who gratefully accepted.

"So, captain," he said as they took seats and sipped the drinks, "what say you to this turn of events?" Morat shrugged.

"It could go well for all of us, or it could end in disaster." Ali Bichnin smiled thinly.

"Such is life captain. We are in an occupation that is ruled by the gods, are we not?"

"Gods?" Morat said raising an eyebrow. "Surely Admiral you mean the one true God?"

"Ah, yes of course captain; a careless slip of the tongue . . ." The Admiral smiled and Morat followed suit. He, like the Admiral, had accepted the circumcision knife a number of years ago and his foreskin was, he often thought, a small price to pay for the wealth that he had amassed. The Admiral's profile and standing in Algiers had of course demanded he openly proclaimed his new faith, as in the building of a new mosque, but Morat Rais suspected that like himself, Ali Bichnin's faith was little more than a flag of convenience; a flag that Morat had increasingly had thoughts of abandoning. The brandy and the

Admiral's response to his question of faith loosened his tongue.

"You have been here for many years Admiral," he said quietly.

"Yes, it was 14 years ago when I arrived in Algiers with one vessel and no idea of what my future held."

"And have you ever regretted that arrival Admiral?" Ali Bichnin considered the question carefully.

"There are always regrets in men's lives captain; but had I not pitched up on these shores I would as like have ended up swinging from a gibbet somewhere."

"And you have amassed great fortune and respect." The Admiral nodded.

"Yes, I have everything a man could desire." Morat lowered his eyes slightly and swirled the dark liquid in his glass, before taking a sip and raising his eyes again.

"I too have great wealth, gained over the eight years that I have been in the Pasha's service; but as my fiftieth year approaches, I oft times think of a quieter life back home in Scotland, where I could reclaim the birth name of Robert Fleck." Ali Bichnin smiled.

"I do not know of your Scotland," he said, "but I have heard that it is a land of biting winds and acid tongued women who find it hard to obey their masters." Morat's huge head shook as a belly laugh issued from his mouth.

"Just so Admiral, but I would get much satisfaction from teaching them to obey!"

During the course of emptying the brandy decanter they moved on to discuss logistics and battle plans for the upcoming campaign, before the Admiral rose from his seat and tugged on a bell cord that hung nearby.

"The hour grows late captain," Ali Bichnin said, "You will stay and share a meal and then a bed with a companion of choice?"

"A generous offer Admiral and one gratefully received."

The Admiral's black head of palace staff answered the summons almost immediately and after taking note of their choice of food he scurried down to the kitchens to rouse one of the cooks.

In the little ante room behind the kitchens James was awakened by a hefty kick in the ribs. He rolled out of the rough blanket and staggered to his feet in front of the cook.

"Move dog and follow me. The master has demanded food." James rubbed the sleep from his eyes and followed the cook back into the huge kitchens where two large silver trays bearing hot cuts of meat, bread and a selection of fruits sat on a table. The delicious aromas given off by the meat caused the juices in his belly to flow. He had been in the palace for two days now and had been fed only on meagre scraps left over from the meals of others.

He lifted one of the trays and, as ordered, fell into step behind the cook. *I could take a piece of this lamb*, he thought and his stomach gurgled in response.

He shifted his hold on the tray and carefully balanced it on one open palm, while with the other hand he liberated a piece of meat and quickly put it into his mouth. The sensation was intense and he had to fight back a groan of pleasure as the tender meat almost melted before it was quickly chewed and swallowed. *Another!* His stomach demanded; but his brain overruled the demand. *The food I get is not much, but it is better than the foul fare of the bagnio*, he thought as he placed his hand back under the tray and out of the range of temptation.

A minute later the cook stopped in front of a door and balancing his tray on one hand softly rapped on it. There was a muffled response and the door was opened by a familiar figure.

James' startled look was not picked up by the huge black bearded man who ushered them into the room and directed them to place the trays on a table. Ali Bichnin was about to dismiss the newcomers when he noticed that the man accompanying the cook was James and there was a sudden connection in his mind. The slave was one of those who were taken recently by Morat at Baltimore.

"Ah, step forward," he ordered James before dismissing the cook. James, with his face set hard and his eyes firmly on Morat Rais did as ordered.

"This slave," the Admiral said to Morat in English, "is one who you should know." The captain looked at James and shook his shaggy head.

"He is not familiar," he mused, before there was a dawning light in his eyes. "Wait; yes Admiral you are right. You," he said to James, "You are the one from Baltimore who had the gall to accost me at the palace of the Pasha to speak on behalf of a captured boy." James nodded.

"Yes, and you are the one who stole a whole village and was responsible for the death of my brother and an innocent boy." Morat's mouth dropped open at the slave's temerity, but a belly laugh then filled the room.

"You are still an insolent dog, slave," he roared. "But a dog is better than a mouse!" The Admiral nodded. He too had been taken by the flinty look and the almost arrogant bearing of the man; or why else had he brought him here rather than sending him back to the bagnio?

James kept his eyes firmly on the captain and said:

"And the boy; did you keep your word?" Morat's dawning admiration for James' spirit grew and he nodded.

"Yes," he said. "The boy is settled and his duties are as stated." James returned the captain's nod.

"I thank you," he said simply.

"Your thanks are accepted slave," Morat said coolly, but then with a smile he said: "As for your accusation that I was responsible for your misfortunes . . . I am a corsair and my business is one that offers risk to me and to those I engage with. But if you want to aim your spite at anyone perhaps you should direct it towards your fellow countryman who organised the raid on your village . . ." James frowned.

"My fellow countryman?" he said shaking his head.

"A man of means and standing," the captain replied.

"Which man?"

"Walter Coppinger," Morat said simply. James' eyes widened and his mouth hardened.

"Walter Coppinger was behind the raid!"

"The very same; a man with a burning desire, apparently, to be rid of the village." James stood speechless for several seconds as he tried to digest Morat's words. The captain assuming that the slave had nothing more to add, turned to the Admiral and changed the subject.

"How comes this slave to your palace Admiral, surely he was marked for the bagnio?"

"Marked for the bagnio and from there escaped captain," Ali Bichnin answered.

"Escaped! How so escaped?" While James stood mutely to attention the Admiral related the story and Morat was impressed.

"A tale of derring do Admiral and one that by rights should end with a body nailed to the city wall." Ali Bichnin smiled.

"By rights, yes, but the man has spirit and such men are too valuable to waste. Also," he added with a light laugh, "he was property of the Pasha so I do not regret stealing him to my own purpose." Morat's laughter filled the room again. He was well aware of the mutual disdain shared between his Admiral and the Pasha and he came down firmly on Ali Bichnin's side in that regard.

James who had soon gotten over the shock of Morat's revelation, had listened intently to the conversation and now questions were answered. He would not be going back to the bagnio. He was now the property of the Admiral, who for some reason took delight in acting against the Pasha. *So be it*, he thought. *At least freedom from the bagnio allows for the possibility, even though a remote one, of reunion somehow with Erin.*

They were taught which foods aided a man's abilities and which held those abilities back. Nubana also showed them a range of roots, berries and barks and demonstrated how to prepare them as powerful potions. They were given lessons in coyness and showed when a fluttering eyelid and slightly bowed head could, just as well as a lustful look, be used to ignite flame in the male heart.

Now, as Erin and her sisters looked on Nubana unlocked and opened a drawer in the desk and took out a long narrow, blue velvet covered box. She placed the box on the desk top and then opened it and removed a nine inch long carved ivory object. Anna giggled and Erin and Alice's blushes suddenly blossomed again as they recognised what it was.

"This," Nubana said matter-of-factly, "is the only one of its kind allowed in the harem and it is kept locked in this desk. It will be the instrument that you will use to gain mastery of the erotic arts."

She took the phallus, moved over to the bed in the centre of the room and signalled to the black eunuch who was stood to attention against a wall to lie on the bed. Once he was positioned, she slipped the object between the top of his legs so that it stood proud then moved back to the desk and opened up another drawer and removed a small glass stoppered bottle. "This", she said as she moved back to the bed, "is sandalwood oil. Attend me and I will show you how it is to be used."

With Anna firmly in the lead they moved over to the bed and watched while Nubana uncorked the bottle, tipped a little of the aromatic oil onto the palm of her right hand and then rubbed it into both hands before placing the bottle carefully on the floor and moving over to the phallus between the eunuch's thighs.

"Now," she said, "watch closely as I show you ways to delight a man."

She arched her thumb and forefinger into a ring and slipped it over the head of the phallus.

"Now you will tighten your grip around the shaft a little and slide up and down like this; at first gently and then with more and more pressure." Anna watched very closely as Nubana demonstrated, while Erin and Alice tried not to look too closely.

"Now," Nubana said, stooping to pour a little more oil onto her hands, "this next method is also very good. Gently pull the skin down towards the base, like so; then hold the phallus with one hand with the head exposed above the fingers. With the other hand massage the head with just the palm, like so, going round and round and change pressure and the speed of your movement."

Next, rub the phallus between the palms of both hands as if you are trying to warm them, like so . . ." Anna giggled and earned a quick look of rebuke from Nubana, which caused her to offer a hasty "Sorry Mistress."

"Next, place hands either side of the phallus. Keep them straight and squeeze them together as you continue to move them up and down the shaft, squeezing and releasing as you go."

When she had finished Nubana straightened and turned to the women. "These are just some of the ways in which you can use your hands to give much pleasure - and to maintain that pleasure you must make sure your palms are well oiled and that they remain so." Anna nodded and took half a pace forward.

"Mistress? She said coyly, "You say they are 'just 'some ways' . . . are there many more?" Nubana nodded. "Yes," she replied, "there are more with hand and mouth; but before I show you, you must all now demonstrate that you have paid attention." She stooped quickly, took up the bottle and handed it to Anna, who grinned.

Erin and Alice, with their faces showing a mixture of shock and embarrassment, stood back and watched as the young girl enthusiastically followed Nubana's instructions. When she had gone through the four lessons she turned quickly to the Mistress to seek her approval. Nubana nodded lightly and thought: *This little one needs watching. She has the innocent face of a child, behind which there lies a mind of one who will use it to advantage if allowed.*

Later back in their apartment Erin and Alice both looked at Anna who it was obvious, had taken delight in performing those acts that, when it became their turn, had so mortified her older sisters. "How could you," Erin said shaking her head, "do such things with a smile on your face?" Anna shrugged.

"It was just a game played with a toy," she replied.

"A game? A toy? Surely you know that it was a lesson preparing you for the day that *toy* is replaced by a man." Anna shrugged again.

"Then it is best that lesson is well learned if I am to secure a safe future."

"Your thoughts, little sister, should be directed towards hope of rescue and a return to a Christian life and . . ." She was interrupted by a mirthless little laugh.

"There will be no rescue. And my Christian life gave me nothing but hard toil and poverty in return for my pious prayers!" Erin shook her head again but saw that it was useless to argue further.

She is a child and children are always stubborn of mind, she thought. *But I will not abandon my role as a big sister.*

While Anna sat moodily alone inside Erin and Alice moved out to sit on the little balcony and take in the cooler evening air. The sun had disappeared and the darkening cloudless sky carried a pale crescent moon and a heavy sprinkling of bright stars. Below, in the trees, bushes and shrubs of the cultivated courtyard the night creatures had awakened and the chirruping of crickets, cicadas and the plaintive call of a nesting wood pigeon drifted up to them. Alice was the first to speak.

"What do you make of the new Mistress, sister?" she said quietly.

"She is a person of high standing and with a powerful presence." Alice nodded.

"And is she not the most beautiful and graceful of women!"

"She has great beauty;" Erin conceded, "but there is coldness behind the form and grace."

"Yes, perhaps so," Alice said. Erin moved to change the subject.

"And our little sister, what must we do to place her feet back firmly onto the path of Christian modesty?"

"She is younger than her years Erin, we should make allowance." Erin shook her head slowly.

"She is younger in some ways Alice, but I have seen a sudden side to her that is cold and bleakly calculating far beyond her tender years."

"Life has been hard for her with the loss of her family . . ."

"And our lives sister; what of those, are we both not orphans? Have we not suffered loss?"

"Yes, you are right; but we both have someone at least. You have your James. I have a family of sorts. She has no-one." In the gloom a soft smile formed on Erin's lips.

"Sister, if you were of the Catholic faith you would surely dwell in a convent with other holy women!" Alice laughed and climbed to her feet

"Come then, let us go back in and mend some fences with our young headstrong sister!"

The days that followed brought more embarrassment for Erin and Alice. It also brought them several rebukes from the

Mistress who was constantly irked at their heavy handed attempts at mastering the exotic arts. "You are not wringing the head of a chicken!" she shouted at Erin and Alice was told that "It has only one small eye and no mouth, it will not bite you!" Anna, though, was given only praise. "Follow her example," Nubana told them, "and you will move quickly on." And it was the thought of what could result from them 'moving on' that made them hold back.

The Mistress had to accept the fact that Erin and Alice would never come close to matching the erotic skills of Anna. She had taught them as best she could the hand and mouth skills and she had taught them, with the assistance of the black eunuch, the varied positions they could be expected to take up during sexual congress. It would have to do.

Kosem rose from her chair and nodded a greeting as Nubana was ushered into her presence by one of her handmaidens. She had a special relationship with the Sultan's favoured Ikbal who acted as her eyes and ears in the harem and in the Sultan's bedchamber. Nubana had carried a son to term for the Sultan but the child had been stillborn and so the Ikbal had not been elevated to the position of Kadin or Wife; a position that would have diluted Kosem's power over the Sultan.

The Queen Mother had gone out of her way to offer her deep condolences for the still birth, but had been privately delighted. She had also decided – with the help of a trusted Jewish maker of special potions – that neither Kosem nor the Sultan's other Ikbal, Besma, would provide her son with a male heir.

"So tell me Mistress," Kosem said conversationally, "how fares my son's temper, is it as changeable as always?" Nubana nodded.

"It would seem so Highness. But at least his lust for blood has abated somewhat since he talked with the Pasha's Admiral." The Valide Sultan frowned lightly.

"And what was discussed?"

"I was not party to it, but the Sultan told me in his bedchamber that the discussion was directed towards revenge against the traitors who have plotted against him."

"How so, revenge?"

"He has charged the Admiral to mount an attack on the traitor's stronghold and to carry back their leaders to Constantinople so that he can personally mete out justice." Kosem nodded and then changed the subject.

"And the harem; is there anything afoot there that should concern me?"

"No Highness everything is as it should be and the three latest odalisques have almost completed their training."

"And what is the level of their success?"

"The tiny one with the golden hair shows great promise in dance and the erotic arts and is adequate in language, religion and music; the other two are more than adequate in language, religion, dance and music but are no match for the golden haired one in the erotic arts."

Kosem was ultimately responsible for the smooth running of the harem so she digested Nubana's words for half a minute.

"Can the other two be advanced in the erotic arts?" Nubana shook her head slowly.

"I think not Highness, their nature is not suited and I think the will is not present." Kosem nodded.

"Then the golden haired one will be advanced to the position of gedikli and will be placed in the Sultan's court. The other two must be sent back to the Mistresses of Dance and Music; we must turn their adequacy into proficiency to make up for the lack of skill in the erotic arts."

"And what will we do with them once they have advanced further Highness?"

"You may assign them to your oda to join your ladies in waiting, or pass them on to the oda of Besma."

As she made her way back to her own apartments Nubana considered the Valide Sultan's orders. As Mistress of the Erotic Arts dozens of odalisques had passed through her hands on their way to the Sultan's court. She had trained them well but did not consider that any of her previous pupils were capable of posing a threat to her own position. The golden haired one however needed careful watching. She was different enough in beauty, size and personality to intrigue the Sultan, who very well might be captivated by that difference. She cast her mind back to the first meeting with the new odalisques and to her first impression of the tiny one. *Yes*, she thought, *I saw it in you right away, hidden beneath the golden hair and. innocent blue eyes . . . that inner diamond bright hardness.*

The other two did not give her cause for concern. The fiery haired one with the green eyes had the complexion and the beauty to almost match the tiny one, but her manner was too brittle and unbending. The taller dark haired one though was of interest. *She possesses a captivating serenity and a thoughtful nature that hints at wisdom* she thought. *A combination of attributes that is rare in one so young. Yes, that one I will personally tutor further.*

24

James was awakened not by a kick in the ribs, but by an almost gentle shake of the shoulder. He looked up into the face of the Admiral's black head of palace staff.

"Come," the man said. "The Admiral commands your presence."

As the door closed behind the head of staff, Ali Bichnin motioned James forward.

"You owe me your life slave," he said simply and waited for James' slow nod of agreement. "So," the Admiral continued, "how do you propose to repay my generosity?" James considered the question for a few seconds.

"I am it seems yours to command Admiral. So I will serve you in any way that I can . . . . until the day I regain my freedom." Ali Bichnin smiled. It was the kind of response that he had come to expect.

"You are proficient in arms?" James frowned at the odd question.

"Weapons? No Admiral, I am but a simple fisherman." The Admiral looked James up and down.

"You carry the build of a fighting man," he said slowly,

"and there is steel in your eye and a touch of devil may care in your bearing; where does that come from slave?"

"I was a boy; now through the actions of others I have grown to become a man." Ali Bichnin nodded and smiled again.

"Yes," he said. "Cruel fate will either make or break a man." James said nothing and the Admiral continued.

"Know you slave that I am a man of great wealth and standing in this city?" James nodded.

"So much is evident," he said simply.

"And because of that wealth and standing I am known to sometimes engage in whimsy; to indulge myself in actions that would seem contrary for one who holds such power; and in your case slave," he said lightly, "I am about to indulge myself again." A light frown creased James' brow and he raised his shoulders slightly in a sign of mild confusion. Ali Bichnin smiled. "You wonder slave why I prattle so?" James nodded as the Admiral reached for and tugged on the bell cord.

The black head of house appeared within a minute and the Admiral pointed a finger in James' direction. "Take this man," he ordered, "Have the filth washed from his body, burn the rags he wears and fit him into decent clothing, then feed him well and return him to me within the hour."

An hour later James stood once again in front of the Admiral who casually looked him up and down.

"A change for the better," Ali Bichnin said. "Now look sharp and follow me."

Down in the courtyard they climbed onto a waiting carriage and were driven out through the palace gate and then through the palm fringed suburbs towards the central city. In his seat opposite the Admiral James' mind struggled to take in the strange state of affairs that saw him, a wretched slave, washed, fed and clothed in sweet smelling cotton and sitting across from perhaps the most important man in this huge city.

The carriage was eventually brought to a stop in the heart of the Medina close to a huge domed mosque. "My gift to the true believers of Algiers," the Admiral said with a smile in his voice and on his face as he nodded towards the building. "And here," he added as he climbed down from the carriage in front of a narrow alleyway, "is one of my other interests in the city." Puzzled, James got out of the carriage and followed Ali Bichnin into the alley, which opened out into a courtyard, at the rear of which a large two-storied flat-roofed building loomed.

"My bagnio," the Admiral said. The word sent a shock through James and halted him in his tracks. Was he then to escape one bagnio to end up in another after all? Ali Bichnin noticed James' reaction and smiled lightly. "Do not concern yourself," he said, "You will find this bagnio much less arduous than the other you have endured."

They entered the building through a normal looking and sized front door and James found himself in a large arcade. On the busy ground floor, which was thronged with at least a hundred men in various styles of clothing, there were a number of stalls set up on the open floor. There were also taverns built into alcoves similar to the ones he had seen in the other bagnio and in the first courtyard the Baltimore men had passed through on the day of their arrival. He glanced up to the second floor balustraded gallery that ran fully round the building and saw that it too was busy.

"Some of my city enterprises," the Admiral said as they passed through to the rear of the building and through a door that led to a downward flight of stone steps. At the bottom of the steps they entered a large open dimly torch lit area which contained a similar number of hammocks suspended on poles as were in the other bagnio.

"You will wait here until someone comes for you," Ali Bichnin said. James nodded dumbly as the Admiral turned and made his way back up the stairs. Alone, he tried once more to make sense of the situation. He was in another slave compound, but this one held no locked doors; so he could, if the mood took him, simply walk out! The thought to do that briefly crossed his mind; but then, what could he walk out to? No, he had been brought to this place by a man of power who for some reason had taken a liking to him, but to what end he could not even conjecture. What he was sure of was the fact that he was in an infinitely better position than he had been in the other bagnio. He decided he would wait here, *my future will unfold when it is ready* he thought as he eased himself into one of the hammocks.

He had lain in the hammock for perhaps an hour when he heard the door open and the sound of descending footsteps.

"Make yourself seen slave!" James was startled, not by the loud order, but by the voice it was delivered in: it was in rich Cornish English! He climbed quickly out of the hammock as the man approached in the dim light.

"You are English!" James exclaimed. The man shrugged.

"I was," he said. "Now I owe allegiance to no flag other than that of the crescent moon." As the newcomer halted at James' side James took in his features. He was a good half head taller than James himself, though not as well built. His dark hair was cropped short, as was his beard and he had a large gold earring in his right ear and a zigzag scar down his left cheek that stood out boldly white against his tanned skin.

"What are you called slave?"

"My name is James Pallow and who asks?" The tall man smiled thinly.

"I am Ezra Johnstone, Boson to his Excellency, Admiral Ali Bichnin and I am here to teach you how a man fights." James took a half step backwards, tucked his chin down and slowly raised his fists. The man smiled.

"Ah, the Admiral said that you had spirit mister Pallow. That is good; but I am not here to trade fist blows. Come," he ordered, as he turned to make his way back up the stairs.

Back on the ground floor of the building Ezra Johnstone led the way to a rear door that let out into a small walled-in paved courtyard. Blinking in the strong sunlight James followed the tall man over to a small wooden table that had two cutlasses resting on its top.

"Take up one," Johnstone ordered. James reluctantly took up the weapon.

"I have no skill in swordplay," he said softly. Johnstone nodded.

"And that is why I am here; for you have need to learn quickly if you wish to hold on to your life." James frowned.

"What need?" The tall man smiled again.

"Because mister Pallow a fortnight hence you will be sailing with me and the Admiral in a battle fleet of several hundred men; now take guard." Bemused, James took up the sword and stood loosely to attention.

"Attack me!" James made a hesitant lunge towards Johnstone's chest that was dismissively turned aside.

"Again! And this time attack with true intent!" James took in a deep breath and lunged forward. Once more his attack was turned effortlessly aside; but this time he found the other man's cutlass pricking his throat.

"You are now dead," Johnstone said casually.

For the next nine mornings Ezra Johnstone arrived early to tutor his pupil and they spent an increasingly energetic two hours at cut, thrust and parry, until on the last morning Ezra finally nodded.

"You advance well mister Pallow, you may even survive our coming adventure," he said. James grinned. The hard physical exertion had given him something to look forward to each day and his already honed body had become even firmer. He had also gotten to like the tall man with the bluff manner who had opened up to him a little.

James learned that Ezra had been taken, along with the rest of the crew of a Penzance merchantman carrying a cargo of tea en route to the Americas, eight years earlier. He had spent the first year of capture chained to the oar before being sold to the Admiral.

He told James how, soon after being bought, Ali Bichnin had been approached by a fat merchant who wanted the Admiral to let him kill a Christian slave as an offering before a big commercial venture he was due to embark on. The merchant commented that killing a Christian was surely the most acceptable sacrifice that could be made to the Prophet.

The Admiral had cheerfully agreed and had brought forth Ezra, who he armed with a cutlass and a dagger and ordered to chase the merchant away. When the man had gathered up the courage to return to complain, the Admiral had laughed at him and said there was no honour in killing an unarmed man who was not able to defend himself; and that the merchant should go away and learn the true message delivered by the Alcoran. It was a story that James could well believe and one that led to a growing, if slightly grudging respect for the enigmatic Admiral.

James soon drifted into a routine. On each morning when Ezra arrived he brought with him a freshly baked loaf, cheese and black olives, which they shared. When the daily lesson was over Ezra took James through to the busy bagnio where he left him in the hands of one of Ali Bichnin's merchant slaves, a Spaniard named Juan Mendoza, who ran a rope making business for the Admiral.

James was shown the process by Mendoza then put to work alongside two other slaves, an Italian and a Sardinian, plaiting sisal into ropes of various length and thickness. The work was not complicated and within a day or so he became reasonably adept and his grasp of their common language, Sabir, slowly grew.

Mendoza kept them busy for five hours then allowed them to slip out into the city to steal what food they could, before returning for five more hours of work, after which they were allowed to spend the rest of the evening and night as they chose.

On the first free evening James had made his way up onto the second floor level, where he found more taverns and stalls and two more of Ali Bichnin's businesses, a tinsmiths and a gunsmiths. He also, much to his surprise, discovered a Christian church that could hold at least 300 slaves and which was run by a fat Dominican friar, Brother Antonio, who celebrated mass on Sundays and got uproariously drunk on each weekday.

In addition to large numbers of Catholics Brother Antonio also ministered to Lutherans, Puritans and even some of James' fellow Calvinists, who he included in his Sunday masses. On the two Sundays that he spent in the bagnio James did not attend.

A dozen days after his introduction to the bagnio Ezra appeared at his regular hour, but this time he arrived with a canvas bag slung over his shoulder and a jaunty spring in his step.

"The time is come and we will soon find if your lessons have been well learned" he said with a hearty laugh.

Erin and Alice had mixed feelings when they were told that

they would be sent back to the Mistresses of Dance and Music. They were quietly pleased that they would not be joining the Sultan's Court, but were both dismayed that their little 'sister' would be leaving them to act as an gedikli or maid in waiting at that Court. Erin in particular felt heartsick. Throughout their ordeals she had tried her best to be a caring big sister to Anna and even the young girl's apparent gradual change in character from frightened child to bright eyed, hard headed young woman did not alter those protective feelings.

"We will miss you so much little sister," Erin said quietly as the young girl gathered up her clothes, made her way over to the apartment door and reached for the handle, before turning and smiling brightly.

"Of course," she said lightly, "and I will miss you both also, but we must all move on." And with that, she was gone.

As the door closed behind her a light sob was forced from Erin's throat and Alice moved quickly to her side and threw a comforting arm across her shoulder.

"She is young and without care sister," she said, before adding, "And perhaps that is a blessing." Erin forced a weak smile.

"Yes, she is without care, and we must pray that whatever fate has in store for her she will cope well." Alice nodded in agreement.

The weeks drifted by and Erin and Alice's worries for Anna's well being slowly faded. She was far from forgotten; but they both realised that there was nothing that they, two insignificant slaves among a palace containing hundreds or perhaps thousands of others, could do to affect the situation.

Their skills in dance and music improved and after a month they were summoned to Nubana's apartments where the raven haired Ikbal coolly addressed them.

"You have gained more skills in music and dance and now you must be assigned to your new stations." Erin and Alice exchanged quick glances as Nubana continued. "Your skills in the erotic arts however - for whatever reason," she said pointedly, "fall short of what is required. You will therefore be assigned to act as ladies in waiting." A quick look of relief passed between the two young women.

"You," Nubana said to Alice, "will join my oda. You," she added, looking at Erin, "will join the ladies in waiting of Ikbal Besma." Relief fled from Erin's face as Nubana's words registered.

"Mistress!" she pleaded, "we have endured much together may we not stay together?" Nubana's lips twitched into the faintest semblance of a smile. It was the first time that she had seen any sign of servility in the fiery headed one. The smile then faded to be replaced by a stony look.

"You," she said coldly, pointing a red nailed finger at Erin "will join the ladies in waiting of Ikbal Besma. I have spoken. You will now be escorted back to your apartment to gather up your belongings," she snapped, signalling forward a black eunuch who was standing to attention against a wall.

Back in the apartment and in stunned silence they packed their clothes and toiletry items into linen bags, before Erin spoke.

"So sister, we are now to be parted," she said quietly. Alice swallowed the rising lump in her throat.

"Yes sister, but they can not break our bond by moving our bodies apart. We will prevail." Erin nodded and reached for Alice's hand as the eunuch opened the apartment door and ushered them through.

25

With Ezra in the lead they made their way on foot down to the harbour which was teeming with activity. There was a long line of horse drawn wagons with their impatient drivers queuing up to offload powder, cannonballs, foodstuff, spare sails, rigging and water in iron ringed wooden barrels; all of which was organised by a sweating cursing overseer who directed a team to place everything in equal measure into eight piles spaced out along the harbour road, where men were starting to load longboats ready to ferry the supplies out to the vessels that lay at anchor alongside the mole. While this activity was progressing a ragged file of what seemed to be hundreds of men carrying canvas sacks over their shoulders were making their way along the rough road that ended at the landward edge of the breakwater and from there on to the waiting vessels.

Ezra pointed to the largest vessel which was first in the anchored line where Ali Bichnin could be seen standing on the mole directing the line of men with extravagant arm gestures.

"The Admiral is anxious for the off," Ezra said smiling. James nodded.

"Yes he is obviously a man of action."

"Aye, he is that, so we too better get a move on!"

They joined the moving file and within minutes they were level with the Admiral who had boarded his vessel.

"Good day Admiral," Ezra said lightly as he looked up towards Ali Bichnin. The Admiral nodded.

"And a very good day to you mister Johnstone and are you and your pupil set fair for the adventure?" Ezra grinned.

"Aye Admiral those traitorous dogs will soon be whining with their tails tucked between their legs when they catch sight of Ezra Johnstone and the fearsome James Pallow!" Ali Bichnin laughed.

"Well then gentlemen come aboard. We will be ready to sail," he said, as he looked back along the shortening line of approaching men, "in less than an hour."

When the hour had passed and all the vessels were fully loaded and complemented Ali Bichnin had a tethered goat brought on deck where a local *marabout* slit its throat. The holy man then held the carcass over the vessel's side and as the hot blood spurted out and down into the water intoned: *There is no other God than God and Mohammed is His messenger; may this sacrifice ensure His believers find success*. He then slit the goats belly and removed the entrails, one half of which he threw over the port side and the other over the starboard.

If, months ago, James had witnessed such an alien ceremony he would have been appalled. Now though as he watched impassively by the vessel's rail he felt nothing. His connections to the Christian faith had ultimately been severed with the neck of his brother and the tragedies that had followed.

Now he stood isolated and aloof, with no allegiance to Christianity or to Islam. *I am my own man,* he thought, *I will stand or fall through my own strength and will and shall not plead protection from any deity.*

The rite concluded, the *marabout* left the vessel, the mooring ropes were cast off and the Admiral gave the order for the slave master to count the beat. The banked oars dipped and the vessel moved slowly towards the opening in the mole.

For the first few days in her new environment Alice had felt totally lost and sorely missed the comforting presence of her 'sisters' and their shared history of upheaval and loss. But with her immediate future seemingly mapped out, and as the days drifted by, her practical nature took over and she began to accept things. *I will make the best of it*, she thought, *because I can do nothing more.*

The Mistress had almost fifty handmaidens and a dozen eunuchs whose sole role in life was to pander to her every whim. The lower ranked were charged with menial duties such as keepers of wardrobe, baths, or kitchens. Many of the higher ranked women treated Alice with cold indifference, while more were openly hostile to the newcomer who they suspected might try to climb above them in status. And this latter group's suspicions were hardened when the Mistress was seen to favour the newcomer with her attention.

Alice it was who was almost immediately stationed at Nubana's side during the day, where with a small selected group she attended to the Mistress' needs. She might be ordered to dance or to play the lyre, or simply to sit attentively at Nubana's feet to await her commands.

When dismissed from the Mistress' personal apartments in the evening most of the handmaidens returned to their own small rooms for the night or congregated in small groups in a large lavishly furnished common room where they could engage in gossip. Alice was given a small two-roomed apartment annexed to Nubana's opulent suite and it was there that she was surprised by a late evening visit from one of the eunuchs who told her that the Mistress commanded her presence.

Nubana, from her reclined position on an Ottoman dismissed the eunuch with a wave of her hand. "Come sit," she ordered, motioning Alice to a gold painted and brocaded chair that sat alongside a low table by her side. "We will speak." Alice was confused.

"Mistress?" she said quietly. Nubana smiled and the tip of her tongue flicked over her painted lips.

"Come," she said reaching out and patting the arm of the chair, "I do not bite." Alice sat.

"Slave, tell me what were you called," Nubana asked casually.

"Mistress?"

"Your name before capture."

"Alice, Mistress." Nubana nodded lightly.

"And tell me...Alice...why did you not excel in the erotic arts?" At the sudden personal question a slight roseate flush tinged Alice's cheeks.

"It was not in my nature Mistress," she replied softly.

"And is it not in your nature because you fear being taken by the Sultan?" Alice raised her shoulders slightly but didn't reply.

"Or perhaps," Nubana continued, arching a sculpted eyebrow, "is it because you fear being taken by any man?"

"I do not know mistress, I have never thought deeply on the matter of men and women." Nubana smiled thinly and reached out a hand to the table by her side where two crystal goblets filled with rose pink liquid sat on a silver tray. She took up one of the goblets and motioned Alice to take up the other. Nubana took a sip of her drink and then languidly raised a finger towards the other goblet in Alice's hand.

"Drink," she said. "It is most refreshing." Alice took a sip as Nubana watched her closely.

"It is pleasant?" Nubana asked. Alice nodded.

"Yes Mistress, it is unusual, but most refreshing."

"Good, drink up," she said, draining her own glass. "We will send for some more presently." Alice, as ordered drained her glass.

She had never tasted strong drink before but the strange

liquid quickly began to act on her in a way that she had been told that strong drink did. She experienced a curious but not unpleasant light-headed feeling that spread throughout her body. Her tenseness melted away and a soft enigmatic smile formed on her lips. Nubana leaned towards her and Alice was suddenly entranced by the other's eyes. They were tawny brown and flecked, it seemed, with gold. *You are the most beautiful woman I have ever seen!* The unformed words tripped across her mind and caused her to giggle. Nubana smiled, rose to her feet and held out a hand.

"Come Hafise," she said softly, "You are in need of a rest." Alice frowned lightly as the strange name registered.

"Hafise?" she slurred as she shook her head in an effort to clear away the clinging fog.

"It is your new name. It means the Wise One." Alice shook her head again but the fog persisted as she staggered to her feet and accepted the Mistress' supporting hand.

Nubana led her to her bedchamber and helped her onto the bed. "Rest, I will be back in a minute," she said as she turned and left the room. Alice tried shaking her head again but the effort was too much; instead, she lay back loose limbed and stared up at a crimson silk canopy and thought *this is not right. I should not be here.* Any more thoughts were then cut off as Nubana re-appeared. Alice managed to turn her head sideways and noticed that the naked and smiling Mistress was holding a long slim blue velvet covered box in her hand.

Alice opened her eyes and for a few moments tried to focus on the red silk canopy above her. She shook her head slowly and raised a bare arm to gently massage her throbbing temples. Seconds later she lowered her eyes to her bare shoulders and then her breasts. With a shock she realised she was naked! As this registered she felt a sudden movement at her side. She turned her head to the right and gasped as she saw a tumble of raven hair and the back of a smooth brown shoulder. Her heart lurched and she quickly slid out of the bed and stood dazedly looking down.

A rush of emotions - total bewilderment followed by shame

and guilt coursed through her as her mind suddenly replayed fragments of memory . . . rouge-nippled breasts . . . pink darting and probing tongue . . . tawny gold flecked cat eyes. She gasped reached forward and turned down the silk sheet - and there it was, bright spots of dried blood. Her 'gift' had been taken! And then another soft rush of emotion that began as confusion and ended with calm acceptance.

Alice, who was now Hafise, reached out, lifted the sheet and slid back into bed. She nudged herself up to the sleeping figure and gently, very gently, placed her left hand on the fiery curve of a dreaming thigh and was rewarded with a soft sigh and with two firm buttocks that pressed back into her lower abdomen.

Anna's eyes opened wide as the black eunuch flung open the double doors and ushered her through into a huge common room that was awash with colour, the sound of lyre music and many chattering female voices.

The room's midnight blue, gold star spangled domed ceiling looked down on rose pink stuccoed walls and a cool pale green marble floor strewn with at least fifty large Persian rugs in a riot of greens, blues, purples and browns. There were a similar number of richly upholstered low Ottoman couches – and reclined on these couches in languid poses or sitting casually on plump silken cushions were a host of gorgeously dressed women.

As she stood rooted to the spot in indecision one of the reclining women caught her eye and made a casual beckoning gesture. Anna crossed the dozen or so paces that separated her from the woman and stood obediently at her side.

The near middle-aged woman, who wore turquoise-blue pantaloons with a matching bodice trimmed in silver thread and lilac brocaded slippers, said: "What do you do here?" Anna swallowed nervously.

"I am sent by Mistress Nubana . . . Mistress." The woman nodded lightly.

"You have been fully trained by Nubana and are now to be gedikli?"

"Yes Mistress,"

"And how are you named?"

"Anna . . . Mistress." The woman repeated the strange name and then shook her head.

"You will be given another more fitting," she said simply before motioning Anna to sit on a purple silk cushion at her feet.

Sarina, the Kahya or Housekeeper of the Harem, was, like Nubana, another pair of eyes and ears for the Valide Sultan. Although Kosem's duties as mother to the Sultan had always included the overseeing of the smooth running of the seraglio she had - because she was now spending a great portion of her time involved in matters of State - delegated much of this duty to her trusted personal slave.

"You are gifted how?" Anna looked up at the question and saw that Sarina was not looking down at her, but with a bored look on her face was casually examining her painted fingernails.

"I am gifted in dance Mistress and, so Mistress Nubana says, also in the erotic arts..." Sarina glanced down and nodded lightly.

"Any skill in the erotic arts will only be judged by the Sultan, should you ever be blessed by his attentions" Anna bowed her head slightly in deference at Sarina's words but her response and the conviction contained within it caught the Mistress' attention.

"Yes Mistress," the girl said, "but when I am chosen I will not be found wanting." Sarina, for the first time since Anna's arrival looked closely at the newcomer. She saw an innocent face, golden hair, bright blue eyes and an elfin but alluring body. She also saw something else, and thought ... *A little bird that is eager to spread its wings and take flight*.

A minute later the Mistress clapped her hands and the chatter and music stopped suddenly and those sat on cushions or reclined on couches got to their feet and followed the Mistress to a door set at the back of the room where a black eunuch was standing to attention.

At the Mistress' approach the eunuch moved smartly to open the door, before with head bowed, stepping back into position. Anna, who was following closely behind Sarina, saw that they were entering a large common bathing area. Inside she was dazzled by the sheer opulence that confronted her.

The room was at least 150 feet in length and some 100 feet in width. The floor was laid with pale pink marble and twenty feet above her head a domed roof containing rose and pale blue glass panels shed bright shards of sun fed colour onto the marble floor below.

The walls were clad in sky blue and cream tiles and at roughly 12 feet intervals around three sides of the room there were dark blue panels of tiles from which large deep shell-like cream baths, each capable of holding half a dozen bodies in comfort were mounted at floor level on four curved gilded legs; each of these baths was fed through gold hot and cold waterspouts.

The central area of the room was taken up by about twenty rectangular islands of pale green marble that rose to a height of about 18 inches above the floor.

When all of the women had made their way into the room the black eunuch closed the door behind them and took up his station on the outside. Inside, Anna was slightly taken aback when the women, who numbered at least fifty, quickly stripped off their gaudy clothing and in little groups stepped into the shell baths. Sarina, who alone with Anna remained clothed, addressed the newcomer.

"You must remove your clothing and bathe now," she said. Anna looked around the room. Nobody seemed to be paying her any attention so she quickly stepped out of her clothes and made her way over to one of the baths that only had three other women in it. The Head Housekeeper watched her closely as she went and nodded lightly. Anna's golden hair, heart shaped face and violet eyes had captured her attention earlier; now as the girl began to make her way over to the bath her full, milk-white breasts, tiny waist, firm round buttocks and creamy skin added to the first impressions. *She has a special childlike physical beauty*, she thought, *but there is something not of the child inside.*

Anna stepped into the bath, took up a tablet of scented soap from a small lip that encircled the tub and lowered her self into the pleasantly hot water. As she began to wash one of the other young women, a coffee-coloured girl with large almost black almond shaped eyes and shoulder length black hair spoke.

"How are you named?" she asked. Anna smiled.

"I am named Anna," she said. "But the Mistress tells me that I will be given another soon." The girl inclined her head slightly.

"Yes, I too had another before I was given the name Zala."

"Zala . . . It is a pretty name . . . and how long have you been in the Sultan's Court Zala?"

"I have been in His Highness' Court for 11 moons."

"And has the Sultan blessed you with his attentions?" Zala shook her head.

"He has not." Anna nodded. *The girl is most comely,* she thought, *yet she has been here almost a year and has not been called. I must do what I can to ensure my wait is not so long.*

For the next few minutes as the young women bathed Anna got to know her bathing companions a little better. Zala was fifteen and had been sold by her parents in Egypt when she was almost ten. She had entered Palace service as a lowly odalisque and had eventually, due to her budding beauty been selected for concubinage.

Chestnut-haired, hazel-eyed Amara had been captured in a coastal raid in southern Crete when she was almost fourteen. Her training had followed the same route as Zala's and at the age of 16 she had entered the Sultan's court some six months earlier. She had not been summoned either.

Her third bath mate was very different to the other two. Shanez was tall, willowy, blonde haired and blue eyed and she exuded an air of cool aloofness. She had been captured in the north of the Baltic Sea when pirates had raided her village on the island of Saaremaa and had been in the Sultan's Court for over one year. She did not volunteer any other details about her life either before or since capture and Anna, who had taken an immediate dislike to the girl on the grounds that they were too much alike in hair and eye colour and skin tone, did not ask for any.

As the water began to cool the door to the bath chamber opened and a number of plain cotton shifted slave women entered carrying piles of fluffy white towels. Some also carried bone combs, brushes and little lidded pots. When the towels had been placed on the green marble plinths the Mistress clapped her hands and immediately the young women began to climb out of their baths and started to dry themselves. Anna followed Zala and Amara over to one of the plinths while Shanez moved to another. Anna's eyes narrowed as she watched the tall girl go.

"She is not very friendly is she?" she said to Zala as she picked up a towel and began to dry herself. The girl shrugged.

"She is Shanez," Zala replied casually.

"Has she been summoned by the Sultan?"

"Yes, two times." Anna frowned.

"And does she say what the Sultan asked of her?" Zala shook her head.

"She keeps her own council, but the Sultan must have found her pleasing for he presented her with the gift of a large pearl after their second meeting." Anna's mouth tightened and she was on the verge of passing a comment when two of the slave girls approached the marble plinth and motioned for the three girls to sit down.

"They are to do our hair and nails," Amara said as Anna looked blankly on.

Twenty minutes later with her hair washed in lemon juice, pomaded and brushed until it shone like burnished gold and her finger and toe nails clipped and painted a deep red, Anna stepped back into her beautiful clothes and a slow smile blossomed on her face.

26

Erin sat at the feet of her seated Mistress, Besma, and a little nervously took up the lyre. She had been in the Mistress' oda for over a week now and this was the first time that she had been singled out for personal attention. She ran her fingers lightly over the strings of the lyre and then after a slight hesitation, began to play a tune that was one of the first that she had mastered under the tuition of the Mistress of Music.

Besma closed her dark eyes lightly and nodded in appreciation as Erin, who had been given the new name 'Cyra' because of her 'fiery' red hair played. And as she played, Erin took the chance to study the Sultan's second Ikbal. The woman was, she guessed perhaps in her very early twenties. She was smaller in height than Nubana and fuller of figure and her flawless skin was a shade darker. Her long hair, though thick and lustrous was of a dark chestnut colour against Nubana's ebony black and her broader nose and fuller lips hinted at a mixed Moorish and Negroid parentage.

"Your music is adequate," Besma said casually as the music stopped and she opened her eyes. "Is your dance also adequate?" She added. Erin bowed her head slightly.

"The Mistress of Dance was, I think, pleased with my efforts Mistress." Besma was about to say something else when the door to her apartments was suddenly thrown open and one of her eunuchs burst through. Startled, the Mistress demanded the reason for his intrusion.

"The Sultan Mistress, he comes!" The eunuch blurted out as he stationed himself with arms folded and eyes lowered at the side of the door. Besma climbed swiftly to her feet and smoothed her dark blue silk dress over her thighs. Murad was becoming increasingly unpredictable and this sudden unannounced visit - very much against palace protocol - was another example of that.

"My Lord . . ." she managed to say as the Sultan strode into the room. Murad nodded and waved away her greeting. Besma quickly gathered her wits about her. "Your visit is, as always, a precious gift, but with a little warning I could have made myself more presentable," she said demurely. Murad shrugged.

"Your Sultan is Lord of all and comes and departs as his mood takes him," he said, his words slurring slightly as he spoke. Besma recognised the warning. He was drunk and when he was drunk it could take very little to send him teetering over the edge and into a terrifying black rage.

"Of course my Lord," she said softly. Before adding humbly, "Your servant is yours to command as are all within these walls . . . and without," she added quickly before he could say anything. As she finished speaking she turned quickly to Erin and clapped her hands in dismissal. Erin climbed to her feet and with her head bowed so as not to meet his eyes she made to leave.

"Hold!" the command stopped her in her tracks. "Hair of fire," he slurred. "I have looked upon that fire recently, have I not?" Erin with head still bowed nodded.

"Speak!" he demanded.

"Yes Lord," she said quietly. "I came with the taxes from the Pasha of Algiers."

"Ah yes, my dear uncle," he said sourly. Then after rubbing his bearded chin for a second or two: "Yes, yes, I remember now ; the fiery one who was slow to bend knee." And as the memory returned he also recalled his thought at the time that he would take pleasure in instructing her in the ways of obedience. He nodded and smiled. And then when he spoke his voice was cordially firm. "Apologies for the intrusion," he said to Besma shaking his head slowly. "I came on an errand that has quite escaped my mind." Besma smiled lightly.

"My Lord has much to concern himself with and it is without wonder that things of non-importance can sometime slip from mind." He nodded.

"Indeed," he said pleasantly as he dipped a huge hand into a pocket, withdrew an embroidered silk handkerchief, handed it to Erin and said: "Attend me as soon as you are made ready," before turning on his heel and leaving the oda as quickly as he had entered. Puzzled, Erin looked at the handkerchief then turned to Besma for explanation. The Ikbal gave her a stony look. "You have been summoned to the Sultan's bed," she said coldly.

Scant minutes later, Besma stood before the seated Valide Sultan and relayed the news. Kosem was appalled. She was the Keeper of the Harem and there was protocol at stake. Tradition decreed that the chosen were to be admitted to the Sultan's bedchamber at ten o'clock in the evening after the Valide Sultan had chance to prepare them for the honour (and also so that she could provide a friendly glass of special sherbet). Now she was informed that her son had cast aside tradition and was demanding that his choice be prepared and delivered immediately!

"Tell me again," she said tersely. Besma shrugged.

"It is as I said Highness. The Sultan arrived unannounced ."

"And what condition was he in?" Besma hesitated for a

second or two.

"He was perhaps under the influence of strong drink your Highness." Kosem's mouth hardened.

"But he was aware that this odalisque is not gedikli?"

"I think so Highness." The Valide Sultan drummed her fingers lightly on the arm of her chair. She had gone to great lengths to place trusted spies in the Sultan's Court and in the odas of Murad's Ikbals. She had also, through the aid of her Jewish mistress of potions, made sure that the chances of any of the Ikbals or concubines falling pregnant were minimised. Now here was the Sultan shunning protocol - and there was no time to take precautions. *Very well*, she thought, *this time I must take the risk; but afterwards I will remind my drunken son most forcefully of the way things must be done.*

As the long hot days slipped by the old James - the James of Baltimore - slowly faded into the past. Where once his life had been centred on community, Christian morals and work ethic; now his blood sang with the unholy joy of looming battle.

He spent hours each day sharpening his skills with wooden practice blades, until his tutor, Ezra, was forced to admit that even he could teach him nothing more.

Annoyed, James moved on to practice sword fights with any of his crew mates that accepted the challenge of measuring themselves against him. During these rough and tumbles, which often descended into brawls, he at first suffered and then learned and adopted any number of tricks using stabbing fingers, fists, heels of hands, knees, feet and occasionally, teeth. These ploys allied to a natural flair for Cornish wrestling that he had displayed during his earlier life among the fishermen of Baltimore, soon saw him hugely respected by even the most battle hardened of his shipmates.

"You are a man possessed," Ezra observed casually after one particularly bloody brawl with a hulking, bald, cannonball headed Armenian. James had grinned, wiped blood from his mouth with the back of a hand and spit out a broken tooth.

"Possessed?" he had replied. "Perhaps; but it is a possession that will keep me alive until I have attained my goal." Ezra had nodded lightly before replying:

"She must be very special indeed my friend."

Twenty days into the voyage the little armada of vessels passed east of the island of Samothraki and came in sight of the mainland. On-board as the little armada struck west and then swung east to hug the coastline James, who was stood at the rail alongside Ezra, could almost feel the sudden electric charge in the air.

"Yes," Ezra said softly," as he noted the way James' eyes were lit with the fire of nervous excitement, "You will soon be able to test your arm." James grinned.

"And it is to be hoped that my tutor has been worthy of the name!" he answered.

In his cabin the Admiral, with his captains in close attendance, studied his charts. They were now perhaps a dozen nautical miles from a narrow estuary that lay to the west on the Turkish side of the border between Macedonia and Turkey. On the east bank of this estuary their unsuspecting target sat.

The Sultan had provided him with details on the fortification which he had personally visited to administer bloody retribution during a minor outbreak of rebellion a year previously. The squat forty foot high building sat perched on the edge of a plateau looking directly out onto the estuary. It was fortified with a dozen heavy cannon all of which could be depressed in order to repel attack from the water or raised to hurl their projectiles across the inlet to the Macedonian bank. The only entrance to the fortification was through a large iron shod heavily barred door that was built into the seaward side of the building.

The Admiral had originally planned to blast open this door in a pre-dawn attack in order for his force to take the defenders by total surprise, but the Sultan's insistence that the door's sturdiness would likely lead to it resisting such an attempt caused him to abandon that plan. The breach would have to come from the water.

The estuary was too narrow for his vessels to enter *en masse* and manoeuvre safely out of range of the cannon that were trained west across the inlet towards Macedonia. He would have to rely on a quick in line thrust and cannonade from each of his vessels in the hope that they might make sufficient breaches in the walls of the fortifications for his land force to pour through. His vessels would attract heavy return fire and would more than likely sustain losses in the process but there was no other way.

"We will make landfall out of sight behind this promontory," he said, indicating a point on the map. "There is a long shingle strand there which will place us within a nautical mile of the estuary on which our target sits. You" he said indicating Morat Rais, "will lead the men with Ezra Johnstone as your second in command." Morat nodded and smiled. "You will move your men," the Admiral continued, "under cover of darkness and position them out of sight to the rear of the fortifications and within easy striking distance ready for our sea attack at dawn." Morat nodded again.

"And how are we to know from the rear that the fortifications have been breached Admiral?"

"You will station a lone lookout within your sight with a white flag on high ground close to the mouth of the estuary. He will have view of the action and I will run up a red ensign when the walls have been breached sufficient for your men to enter. Your man will signal you immediately and you will lead your men in."

"Our gunners are well trained Admiral," Morat said confidently, "and with the guiding hand of Allah, *praise be to his name*, they will soon bring the traitors' walls tumbling round their ears." The other captains around the map table nodded their agreement.

As darkness fell each of the vessels launched their laden boats towards the accessible shore where they landed their human cargo on the long shale strand and then returned to reload again. Soon over seven hundred of Algiers battle hardened renegadoes were grouped together awaiting their orders. Among them James, his heart thumping with tension, flashed a nervous smile at Ezra who was stood by his side.

"Stick close to me," Ezra said quietly "and there is a chance that you will live to be re-united with your woman one day."

James compressed his lips and nodded. He had trained hard and physically he was in the best condition of his life; but he was about to enter the unknown. When faced with it did he have the fortitude and stomach to look into a fellow human's eyes and kill that person without compunction? He would certainly have done it all those months ago outside the cottage in Baltimore when faced with his brother's killer; but then his blood had boiled and a kind of berserker madness had taken hold of him.

Now, as he stood quietly, one among hundreds in the shadows beneath a canopy of stars, with nothing but the slow rise and fall of his chest and the sound of his own breathing in his ears . . . he felt unsure. He took a few deep breaths and forced his shoulders back. *I will do whatever I must*, he thought, *for I am not the boy of a year past. I have seen and endured too much.* In the darkness he nodded to himself and the fingers of his right hand folded around the hilt of the sword at his side.

When the last ferry craft set off on its return to its mother ship Morat Rais moved to the head of the waiting men and quickly relayed the plan of action which was completed with an order that the leaders of the revolt should be taken prisoner if possible and that the man or men who captured Jafar Ben Ali would be paid a handsome reward. Satisfied that his words had been fully understood, he then gave the command for the attackers to follow closely behind as under a moonless sky he made his way up from the strand onto a low lying grassy shelf.

Within two minutes his full force were by his side and within two more they had mounted the shelf and found themselves on level stony ground. There he instructed Ezra to move quickly among the men to check that swords were sheathed against reflected light, that guns were not cocked against accidental discharge and that all knew that from henceforth silence was essential. When Ezra reported back that everything was taken care of Morat turned his face to the east and signalled for the force to follow.

The captain's attitude was on the surface one of total confident command, but in his mind there was nagging doubt. His own men he trusted totally. Most of them had been through many raids and battles with him before, but now, because of the rushed nature of the campaign he was forced to rely on many who were little more than dregs culled from the bars and brothels of Algiers.

There will be many mothers who will be ignorant of the passing of their bonny child soon, he thought before adding mentally with a little wry smile: *Though even the mothers of some of these scum would be hard put to shed a tear at that passing.*

The raiding party flowed across the rock strewn ground with nothing more than the faint sound of the odd upturned stone to mark its almost silent passing. Within minutes a large shadowy mass loomed ahead blocking out a patch of star spangled sky. Morat raised an arm to signal a halt and followed by Ezra he advanced directly to the shelter of the thick stone walls.

"There is no sign of gun emplacements on this side," he whispered, "for no defender would expect trouble to arise from within Turkey." Ezra nodded.

"Just so captain," he agreed. "The estuary and Macedonia across it would be the ground to guard against." Morat turned and raising his left arm, indicated a dense stand of trees.

"We can bring our force to within one hundred yards of the fort," he said, "and place it there safe from discovery behind that stand of trees where the ground is largely depressed. There we will await the signal."

Satisfied they backtracked and Morat picked out one of his trusted men to position himself at the tip of the promontory in line with the front of the fortification and with a good view of the estuary itself.

"Now we wait," the captain said as his force hunkered down in the depression immediately behind the thick stand of trees.

James stretched his legs out in front of him and lay back with his head against a large rock and looked up at the stars. *Where is she beneath those stars*, he thought. *Is she by chance looking up at them now and thinking of me as I think of her?*

There was another thought that tried to creep into his mind but he blocked it before it could be fully formed, before it could stab him to the heart. "No!" He whispered fiercely to the stars,

"She is safe and has come to no harm!"

The hours dragged slowly by until finally the stars began to fade, to be extinguished by a soft rosy glow from the east. And as he watched the sky lighten by degrees a sudden, all but forgotten, bible quotation from a long ago Sunday school lesson came into his mind *'He maketh the sun to rise on the evil and on the good, and sendeth rain on the just and the unjust.'* The quotation was still echoing in his head when he was startled by a quick series of loud booms, followed scant seconds later by the heavy dull sound of iron thumping stone.

"It has begun," Ezra, who was lying close by his side, muttered. Together with hundreds of others around them, they climbed stiffly to their feet and turned in the direction that the sound had come from.

Down in the mouth of the estuary Ali Bichnin trained his eye glass on the walls of the fort and nodded as he saw jagged pale grey wounds spread where the dark almost black weathered stone was being ripped away by fire from his two in line leading xebecs that had sailed down the centre of the inlet, each discharging their twelve elevated cannon as they drew level, before tacking and coming back to discharge their remaining weapons. Both vessels had raced out through the mouth of the estuary to be replaced by two more before the stunned defenders could begin to return fire.

Through his glass the Admiral watched spurts of white water erupt around the two vessels as they fired and then sailed on by the fort before turning sharply and returning to discharge another heavy salvo.

The first vessel sped safely by but the second took a direct hit at deck level where the heavy ball swept away the main mast after ploughing through flesh and bone. The Admiral cursed under his breath. The untouched vessel cleared the guns, but the damaged xebec with its mainsail gone was now almost a sitting target to the fort's gunners who had found their range.

Two more balls slammed into the vessel causing it to stagger drunkenly. The first hit amidships tearing a huge chunk out of the decking and sending a blizzard of deadly flying wooden splinters that found soft targets in heads, faces, eyes, stomachs and groins. The second hit close to the bow and just on the waterline. Ali Bichnin cursed again as water rushed into the gaping hole, the mortally wounded vessel's bow dipped sharply and tiny figures leapt over the sides in a bid to swim to safety.

Two more of his little fleet sailed into the estuary. "Use your speed and set a different course!" he mouthed and was rewarded as the steersmen took a wider channel before discharging their salvos.

In the depression behind the stand of trees the waiting men listened as balls thudded into the fort's wall and the defender's heavy cannon boomed out in reply.

"How much can the building take?" James muttered. Ezra's reply never came, as the words had barely left James' mouth before there was a heavy rumble that seemed to come from the front of the fort.

On his flagship Ali Bichnin clenched a fist and snarled "Yesss," as he saw a section of the weakened wall collapse under the weight of one of the defender's heavy cannon. He immediately turned to one of his crewmen and ordered a red ensign to be run up.

Morat smiled as he saw the white flag a hundred yards ahead and two hundred away to his left being waved urgently. "The red ensign flies," he said jubilantly to Ezra by his side, "And it is time for our swords to drink traitor's blood!" Ezra grinned and turned to James.

"Now you can put your training to the test pupil!" he said as he slid his sword from its scabbard. James took a deep breath, balled both hands into fists and swallowed hard.

Am I really here about to engage in a murderous undertaking, he thought. *Yes*, he answered himself firmly. *I am about to commit to something that the James of Baltimore would have considered totally barbaric.*

27

"But Mistress," Erin said with a note of alarm in her voice, "I am not deemed sufficiently trained to be presented to the Sultan!"

"The Sultan is lord of all he surveys," Besma replied coldly, "and his command must be obeyed." Erin swallowed nervously. She had almost resigned herself to make the best of her situation in the faint hope that sometime in the near future she might be reunited with her love and be safely returned to the land of her birth and the simple life she had become accustomed to before their abduction.

Now even that faint hope was in danger of being dashed; for she had heard that those who were summoned to the Sultan's bed were afterwards kept in a permanent confinement that was much stricter than that which she herself now endured. She was a prisoner yes, but her captivity was in some ways a gentle one. True she could not roam the palace at will, let alone leave its confines; nor could she even leave her new Mistress' apartments unless in Besma's retinue; but her life here in the oda was one without the pressing fear of physical harm.

"Mistress," Erin who was now Cyra, said plaintively, "is there no way that I might be excused?"

Besma had been brought up from the age of twelve knowing only harem life where she had progressed from a lowly servant girl to an odalisque and finally to a favoured gedikli. She had been taught that it was her duty to obey all those above her in station and that her ultimate aim must be to please the Sultan in any way that he should desire.

Her call to Murad's bed had arrived days before her twentieth birthday and she had welcomed it with open arms and with a passion that her Lord had found most pleasing. Now, before her was a girl who shrank at the thought of the honour that was about to be bestowed on her! She herself was annoyed that this slip of a girl, one not even judged ready for the honour, should be summoned in her presence, but summoned she had been; so she, Besma, was duty bound to prepare her properly.

"You will fulfil the Sultan's command," she said firmly as she beckoned the eunuch who still stood to attention by the door. "Summon the Mistress of Clothes and the Mistress of Jewels to me at once and make ready a perfumed bath," she ordered.

Word of the Sultan's unannounced visit and his selection of the new odalisque spread like wildfire throughout Besma's oda and soon some two dozen of her slaves had congregated in the large common room where the Mistresses of Clothes and Jewels had arrived to set out their wares.

Besma, with Erin at her side and much of her chattering retinue looking eagerly on, moved over to the low table that was piled high with colourful gauzy clothing. She selected a pair of long silk pantaloons that were striped in bands of gold and wide bands of green and then put them to one side before selecting a pair of green silk slippers studded with red garnets, a sheer white long sleeved blouse and a shaped short sleeved bodice of green silk that was fastened by three pearl buttons.

"Green must dominate," she said before moving to another table where the Mistress of Jewels' offerings were laid out in sparkling splendour. She lightly ran her hands over a selection of necklaces in rich ruby, golden amber, orange carnelian, pale blue aquamarine, smoky topaz and scintillating white diamond before selecting a square cut emerald offering with six stones mounted three either side of a much larger stone. Earrings were next. For these she selected a pair with a round cut ruby and three in line tear drop pearls.

Satisfied with her choices she signed her name in the Mistress of Jewels' leather bound ledger and ordered one of her servants to gather up the clothes and jewels. "Bring them through to my apartments," she threw over her shoulder as, with Erin at her back, she marched out of the common room.

"You must be shaved," the Mistress said. Erin looked a little confused.

"Shaved Mistress?" Besma shook her head and tutted.

"Of course, you cannot expect the Sultan to bed someone who looks hairier than a she goat." Erin glanced at the fine golden fuzz of hair that was barely noticeable on her forearms and nodded. If it was the practice then so be it. She took a seat while one of Besma's hand maidens left the room and then returned a few minutes later with a silver bowl of gently steaming water, a fluffy white towel and an ivory handled razor. She held out one of her arms. Besma shook her head again.

"Your arms are not in need of shaving," she said, "Stand

and remove your pantaloons." Erin blushed.

"Mistress?"

"Your legs will be shaved first and then that part of you that must sate the Sultan's ardour."

Minutes later and still with an embarrassed blush on her cheeks, Erin, who was now Cyra, slipped into the perfumed water of the Mistresses' marble bath.

Alone and in the silence of the sumptuous bath chamber her situation weighed heavily on her mind. There was no way to escape what lay ahead. She could refuse; but she knew that that was not really an option, as refusal would certainly be looked upon as a dire personal insult to the beast that held the power of life and death over all . . . and she had heard many tales of his berserker fatal response to any who had even lightly tried his temper.

"I must be strong," she murmured to herself. "The ordeal will not last over long and I will keep firmly an image of my James in mind during it." She nodded. *Yes*, she thought, *my gift will be stolen but my heart will remain pure.* She took a deep re-affirming breath as she climbed out of the bath and dried herself off before returning to Besma's living room where the seated Mistress had two of the lower odalisques dress her, attend to her hair, paint her finger and toe nails and dust subtle shades of pale green powder onto her eyelids.

Besma studied the final result and jealousy stirred within her. The girl was beautiful it was true; but she should not have been chosen. She was not gedikli! This final thought though, helped to quell the pang. The girl was a virgin and was not schooled in the ways of giving pleasure; so the Sultan – who enjoyed the expert attentions of skilled performers like herself – would surely find her lacking.

She nodded to herself but then experienced another little prick of annoyance as the girl, thinking it a nod of approval smiled wanly back at her. Any further thoughts were then cut off by a knock on the apartment door. She strode over and opened it to find that the conveyance for the chosen one was outside.

Erin, looked at the ornate gold painted and purple silk canopied and curtained palanquin – and at the four muscular black eunuchs who were carrying it – with surprise and turned to the Mistress.

"You are to be carried to the Sultan's bedchamber," Besma said as she signalled the eunuchs to lower the palanquin to the floor, swept back the purple curtaining, and motioned Erin to climb in.

Cocooned in her little purple curtained bubble Erin took a number of deep breaths as the palanquin was hoisted onto brawny shoulders and steeled herself for whatever lay in store.

Carried along by the silent crush of bodies James, with Morat in the lead and Ezra by his side, unsheathed his sword and gave himself up to the rising thrill of exhilaration tempered with trepidation that surged through his body marking his headlong rush into the unknown.

The raiding party raced round the side of the fort and then to the front, where they poured into the narrow rubble strewn breach and over the upturned fallen cannon before fanning out into a large courtyard that was filled with shocked defenders.

With Ezra to his left and Morat to his right James charged ahead and then suddenly the confused scene before his eyes wavered for a second and in his mind's eye he was standing in the doorway of their cottage staring into the alien eyes of that other Janissary, the yatagan-wielding killer of his brother.

A strangled roar leapt from his mouth as he lunged at the man who was barely four feet away and in the process of drawing his wicked blade. Their bodies collided and their eyes met. The Janissary saw icy, implacable intent. James saw instant shock followed by the slow dying of light as he leaned back from his victim and withdrew his sword.

As his mind snapped back to the present James stepped around the fallen body and became engulfed in a surging tide of shouting screaming men and became one of them himself.

The outnumbered defenders who had been concentrating on the attack from sea, had been taken by surprise, and within barely a minute the stone floor of the courtyard was awash with blood and overhead, unseen, Azerael, the Black Angel of Death swooped time and time again to lay an icy hand upon a victim's head. The defenders regrouped and with their military training, managed to check the onslaught. Now dozens of the attackers also felt Azerael's bleak heart stopping touch.

James, with Ezra and Morat by his side pressed on into the heart of the courtyard where their forward rush suddenly came up against stiffer defence.

With blades whirring around his head James ran one of the General's men through and for a few seconds found him self unopposed. He drew a breath in time to see another of the General's men who was barely two feet away raise and aim a pistol at Morat's head. The captain who was roaring his defiance and in the act of withdrawing his sword from another victim's gizzard turned his head and saw the man's trigger finger tightening on his weapon. He was dead.

But then he wasn't, as by his side a sword flashed; the man's hand was lopped off at the wrist and the discharging weapon sent a heavy ball thudding into a left thigh instead of his temple. Morat turned his head and nodded at James and then for a full minute they were being hard pressed again, before the human tide at their backs broke the resistance.

Now, in the midst of the melee a wedge of attackers formed with Morat Rais at its head, flanked by James and Ezra and backed by some fifty renegadoes. The attackers sliced their way through the middle of the main body of defenders who were almost instantly split into two smaller groups and within a very short time were overwhelmed. Many threw down their weapons in surrender, but the attackers' blood lust had to be fully sated. "Give no quarter!" Morat roared . . . and none was given.

Eyes blazing, heart thumping, James dropped his bloody sword to his side and looked about him. It was done.

He took two deep breaths and a hot pain made him wince. He looked down to see that at chest level his white shirt had been sliced open from side to side and had turned crimson.

The sight of blood welling from the wound suddenly brought home to him what he had just done. He had killed at least three or four men and had also come very close to being killed himself.

His stomach churned and a stream of hot vomit surged up and exploded from his mouth. He leaned forward, placed trembling hands on his knees and spat out the last of the sour bile.

"It is not uncommon for a battle virgin to react so and it will almost surely not occur again," Ezra said lightly with a smile on his lips as he wiped his blade on a trouser leg. James raised his head slowly. For a time he had become one of them; one of the berserker mad men with blood lust coursing through his veins . . . and the realisation shocked him.

"I have no wish to find out if it occurs again," he said quietly but firmly. Ezra's smile widened.

"Perhaps not; but did you ever before feel as alive as you did in the last few minutes?" James wiped the back of a hand across his mouth and nodded slowly.

"And that my friend," he said, "is just why I have no wish to find out . . ."

He had no sooner finished speaking when the captain limped up and stood facing him with a quizzical look on his face.

"Why?" Morat said simply as he tilted his huge head slightly sideways to reinforce the question.

"Why?" James said.

"Yes. Why did you act as you did when you had no reason to save the life of the man you blame for much of your misfortune?" James shook his head.

"I saw a man fighting by my side in peril and acted, no more, no less." Morat nodded, turned and limped away towards a grinning group of four of his men who were half dragging, half carrying an unconscious man. "The General!" one of his men shouted across the courtyard.

"The bounty is ours!" another crowed.

"And where are the other leaders of this pack of curs?" the captain shouted back.

"They decided that a quick clean death was much to be desired over the Sultan's slower and certainly more painful revenge!" the first man responded with a huge grin on his face.

Morat ordered the men to keep the unconscious man under close guard then pulled Ezra and James to one side. "Our

General must have the means to pay the wages of his men here. We will take a stroll through the fort's rooms in search of it once we have seen the remainder of our hardy troops to the strand ready for returning to their vessels." Ezra nodded and then glanced down at the captain's blood stained thigh. "Your wound captain, should it not be attended to first." Morat shrugged his huge shoulders.

"Another scratch to add to a fine collection," he said. Ezra smiled. He would not have expected anything else of Morat Rais.

"The captain's reputation for hardiness is well known and well earned," he said lightly. "As of course is his loyalty to my Admiral, who will no doubt be most pleased with a share of any gold found . . ." Morat smiled thinly through slightly clenched teeth.

The action had been costly, they had lost 124 men with at least eight more not expected to last out the day. Of the rest, a great many would be taking a souvenir of the bloody action - in the form of stab, slash or bullet wounds - back to the flesh pots of Algiers, where their heroics would doubtless be magnified many times.

"The losses are most sad," Morat said shaking his head, as with James and Ezra at his side he limped up the stone stairs that led to the fort's upper level. "But," he continued brightly, "their loss is a gain for the rest of us."

Together they had entered several rooms that revealed nothing of interest before James opened yet another door and reeled back in shock.

The sparsely furnished room was one of a small apartment and contained a rough wooden table, six wooden chairs and a large bed on which lay the naked bodies of three women frozen in grotesque attitudes of death.

Each of them had savage bite marks on their breasts. The older one's face was purple black from strangulation and her dead protruding eyes displayed a milky grey white film. The other two, who could not have been more than fifteen or sixteen years of age wore necklaces of bright blood around their throats and looks of anguish on their ashen faces. And for the second time that day James' gut lurched and he retched, before a hand fell on his shoulder and Ezra said: "Come, there is nothing we can do here."

"But why...? James managed before the captain, looking over James' shoulder said without any trace of emotion: "Blood lust and the spoils of war..."

They tried four more rooms before they came to a stout locked door. "Kick it in," Morat ordered. After half a dozen attempts the door jamb splintered and the door burst inwards to reveal a small windowless room that contained nothing but a table – and on it a dark wood iron bound box some two feet long, eighteen inches wide and a foot deep and sealed with a lock through a small hasp and staple. Morat took a dagger from his belt, prised off the hasp, lifted the lid and a wide grin split his shaggy face. "The Admiral will be pleased," Ezra said; while Murad cursed himself for including the Admiral's boson in the search.

Later, after his wound had been stitched with a sail maker's needle and fine thread, a still white faced James looked back over the battle and his part in it. He had become for a time one of them; one of those lawless dregs from the brothels and bars . . . and his blood had sung with pure raw elation! "Yes", he said quietly to himself, "I was one of them; but I know that I became one *only* to try to ensure survival . . . and with that the chance to see my Erin again."

After a journey that seemed to take many minutes the palanquin was gently lowered to the floor beside an impressive door, outside of which two armed black eunuchs stood guard. Erin drew back the purple curtain in time to see a bearer engage in a lively conversation with the guards, one of whom broke off and rapped lightly on the door. Half a minute later a small panel high up on the portal opened and a dark face appeared. Another short conversation and then the door opened and the two armed eunuchs strode over to the palanquin.

"Out," one of the guards said firmly as he swept the curtain fully back. Erin did as ordered and the other guard strode forward and swept his hands through her hair before running them down her body from chest to ankles. Satisfied that she carried no concealed weapon, he signalled for the flushed girl to enter the apartments.

Inside, the opener of the door, another black eunuch, led her through room after room of the sumptuously furnished apartment before finally bringing her to a stop outside another closed door that he rapped lightly on. His knock was answered by a muffled voice from inside and the eunuch swung the door open and standing to one side, ushered Erin through before closing the door gently behind her.

The richly furnished room was softly lit by silver glass topped wall mounted oil lamps and in one corner a huge ornately engraved silver floor standing sensor filled the air with the heady smell of fragrant burning herbs.

In the centre of the room the Sultan, dressed in a long black silk nightgown embroidered with silver crescent moons, was slumped in a large chair. His left hand was resting on one arm of the chair and in his other he gripped a dark brown bottle. He waved her forward with his right hand and she heard the bottle contents swish to his movement. She swallowed hard and approached. Murad squinted at her and for a moment seemed confused as to why she was there.

"Ah," he said, "Yes, the fiery one who needs to be taught obedience . . ." Erin swallowed again and ran her tongue over dry lips.

"My Lord," she replied "That was at my first meeting with his Lordship and I was not instructed as to the proper form of greeting." The Sultan's bloodshot eyes narrowed in an attempt to focus on the girl and he grunted, lifted the bottle and took a deep three swallow draft before wiping his left hand across his mouth.

"And now you are here and better informed as how to behave in the presence of your Lord and Master?

"Yes Lord," Erin said meekly with eyes downcast.

"Good," Murad slurred, "Now play," he ordered waving the hand with the now almost empty bottle in it towards a table on which a lyre sat.

Relieved at the chance to move onto less shaky ground Erin

took up the instrument and squatting on one of the many plump cushions that littered the floor, began to play. As she did she noticed his left hand which was tapping roughly in tempo on the arm of his chair begin to slow and his eyelids begin to droop. Suddenly he shook his huge head, raised the bottle to his lips and draining it dry grunted his annoyance before flinging it to crash and shatter against a wall.

Erin's fingers froze on the lyre's strings and she slowly climbed to her feet. As she did so a thought tiptoed into her head. *He was drunk, very drunk; perhaps if he became drunker still - and incapable - there was a slim chance that she would not have to fall prey to his beastly advances.* She replaced the lyre on the table.

"My Lord," she said softly. "May I get some more refreshment for you?" The Sultan grunted and waved an arm in the direction of a door at the far side of the room. Erin moved quickly over to the door, opened it and entered a small ante room that obviously served as a storeroom for foodstuffs. It was also the storeroom, thankfully, for liquor, as on a table there was a dozen bottles of French brandy. She lifted one of the bottles and twisted off the cork before moving quickly back into the reception room.

He was still slumped in the chair, his eyes were half hooded, his mouth was slightly open and there was a thin trickle of saliva running from his thick lips and down between the twin forks of his beard.

"My Lord!" she said loudly. He opened his eyes and shook his head. She held out the bottle of brandy and his blood shot eyes fastened onto it. *Yes*, she thought as he reached out for the bottle and lifted it up to his mouth; *there is a chance that I can see this night through intact.*

Murad's flushed face was several shades redder by the time he clumsily placed the empty bottle on a table by his side and then, much to Erin's surprise and trepidation, climbed unsteadily to his feet and said: "To bed." Her heart raced as he made his way over to a door, flung it open and staggered into his bedchamber. Erin followed slowly, as each step took a conscious effort of will.

The huge canopied bed with its gold and silver silk draped curtains was raised a foot off the floor on a pink marble plinth.

The bolster pillows were sheathed in red silk and the light covering silk sheet was of palest blue with darker blue hanging tassels.

The Sultan threw back the cover to reveal a snow white linen under-sheet, belched loudly and unfastened his black robe. As the discarded robe fell to the floor Erin's eyes, in spite of her predicament were drawn to his body and her heart lurched. He was a giant. His shoulders were almost as wide as the door they had entered by and his hairy chest was swollen with muscle. His arms too were thickly corded and laced with prominent blue veins. Her eyes were drawn down to a waist that, where once it had surely been flat and athletic, was now quickly spreading under the quantity of alcohol that had over time passed through his system.

Again, her eyes lowered and for the first time in her life she looked upon that which frightened her most. His thick, almost purple headed circumcised member hung down between his legs and was rooted in dense short black curly hair. Her appalled, but fascinated eyes lingered on it and she saw the shaft rise slightly and twitch, before almost instantly falling back into limpness. As he climbed into the bed, pulled the blue sheet loosely over him and signalled her to follow she swallowed hard.

"My Lord," she said, her voice filled with tension, "may I first entertain you with dance?" He mumbled something and before he found further voice to deny her she began her slow gyrating movements.

A bare minute into the dance she chanced a look into his face and saw that his eyelids were drooping. A minute more and they were closed and within another the chamber resonated to his snores. She was safe . . . but for how long? And what must she now do?

She stood beside the bed and was gently biting down on a lip in consternation, when her eyes lit on the mighty sword that was never far from his side and was now lay propped against the marble plinth.

Perhaps it might work? she thought as she gently lifted the corner of the bed sheet before tiptoeing over to the weapon and, running an index finger firmly over its edge, was rewarded with a sting and a slow welling of blood. She raised her finger to stop any drip, moved back to the bed and smeared the blood half way down the white under-sheet on the side opposite the loudly snoring Sultan.

Her maidenhead had now been taken. But now came the most difficult part; she would have to climb into bed beside him; and more than that she would have to disrobe first. *I must do it quickly*, she thought, *or I will not find the courage*. Half a minute later she slid in beside him and whispered a fervent prayer of protection.

For what seemed like hours she lay, without moving, quietly listening to his breathing and hoping to hear no change to the slow heavy rhythm. Once, she panicked as he turned to face her and an arm with the weight of a falling tree branch landed across her breasts. She had forced herself to breathe as shallowly as possible in case her rising and falling chest bring him back to consciousness; fortunately, within a minute he had turned back again to lie on his stomach.

Now she looked out across his hairy back and shoulders and through a high window, focused on a patch of starry sky and thin slice of moon. *Where is he now? Where is my James? Does he still live? Oh God please let him still live!* The thoughts that tripped through her mind and a final forced response of, *Of course he still lives!* released a slow rising tide of confusion that threatened to overwhelm her . . . and the stars began to shimmer and waver as hot tears welled up in her eyes and began to roll down her cheeks.

The moon and stars were eventually evicted from the sky by a blossoming dawn's light; a light that chased away black thoughts and concentrated her mind on the here and now. He would soon awake and with his awakening . . . what? Well, then she must carry through the deception. He would find a chastened slave almost overcome with awe at the memory of his magnificent masculinity.

Murad groaned and raised one hand to his throbbing temples and with the other shielded his eyes from the spears of sunlight that threatened to strike him blind.

"I will bring you water my Lord!" The loudly spoken words jarred his head and he turned quickly in the direction they had come from – and then immediately regretted his rash movement as the room spun giddily in front of his eyes.

He groaned again as the slave threw back the sheet, slid out of the bed and gathered up her discarded clothes as she made her way over to the storeroom. He squinted after her and shook his huge head in an effort to gather his scattered senses. *The virgin slave with the fiery hair and lack of manners?* Yes, he had summoned her and she had spent the night in his bed. But why was there no memory of it? Had she actually performed her duties? He glanced across to the other side of his bed, and there it was, the tell-tale rosette of dried blood. He shook his head again. He had bedded concubines, gediklis and ikbals before when he had taken drink, but always there had been at least some memory. Why no memory this time?

He pondered on the question for several seconds then nodded slowly. Of course! The slave was totally untrained and did not have the skills that were demanded of those who aspired to share his bed. She had been inadequate.

Erin now dressed emerged from the store room carrying a large onyx tumbler. She crossed over to the bed and with her eyes humbly lowered offered him the drink. Murad reached out a shaking hand took it and drained the contents in one long swallow as Erin sank to her knees and with head lowered, placed both hands palm down on her thighs. *I have no memory of it*, he thought, *but she has now learned how to act in front of her Sultan.* Erin took a deep breath before she took the risk.

"Does my mighty Lord require anything else of this servant?" she asked meekly with her heart pounding in her ears in case he might. In answer he reached an arm up and tugged on a bell cord that hung beside the bed and seconds later the black eunuch who had earlier admitted her to the apartment entered with his head bowed.

"I have no further use of this slave," he said coldly. "Have her returned to the oda of her Mistress."

Erin had only been back in Besma's oda for two hours before a eunuch arrived to escort her to the Valide Sultan's apartments. Inside, she stood with hands loosely clasped in front of her and eyes respectfully lowered knowing that she was about to be questioned and not quite certain as how to answer.

"You have been honoured," Kosem said stiffly. "But know you that the honour should not have been given?"

"Yes Highness, but when the Sultan wills it who could deny that will?" Kosem nodded, but thought: *I would have, had I been present.* Instead she said: "It is now done. And you performed your duty?" Erin hesitated for a second or two before answering.

"I had the honour of spending the night in the Sultan's bed Highness." Kosem nodded again.

"Then the honour bestowed on you means that you are elevated to my retinue as is fitting for one who has shared the Sultan's bed." What she didn't add was that it would give her the chance to watch the odalisque closely to see if the unplanned union led to unwanted consequences; consequences that would call for a stronger draft of cherry sherbet.

28

As the weeks passed Anna grew increasingly annoyed that she had not been selected by Sarina to dance for the Sultan.

He had visited his Court seven times and on each occasion she had been overlooked in favour of others, who, to her mind, were less beautiful and talented than her self.

She has taken a dislike to me she thought as on the eighth occasion, the six selected dancers performed together for Murad in front of at least 150 of his gediklis. And what irked her most was the fact that the haughty and aloof Shanez (One of Sarina's favourites?) had been honoured again with the Sultan's silk handkerchief and had been smugly parading his gifts of two more large pearls to the Court.

The female musicians finished playing and the six dancers waited with heads bowed for the Sultan's decision; a decision that did not come. Instead Murad pursed his lips and slowly shook his head. Sarina, flustered, clapped her hands and the rejected six stepped back into the waiting entourage. She would have to select six more and if none of these were pleasing to him she knew that she herself might be called upon to face his wrath. She quickly indicated five women and was about to select a sixth when the tiny golden haired one, who she had named Firousi for her turquoise eyes, pushed herself through to the front rank.

The blatant break with protocol would not normally have been tolerated by Sarina but the girl had annoyed her over the weeks since she had entered the Sultan's Court with an attitude that shouted out that she was a special one. *Very well then*, Sarina thought, *we will see if you are special. And when you are rejected I will take pleasure in that rejection and in seeing your dismay.* She pointed to Anna and nodded.

Anna, who was now Firousi, stepped out with the other five and made sure that she placed herself directly in the eye line of the Sultan. The musicians began to play and the six dancers began to dance. Five of them moved about the dance area so that they were at one time within five feet of the Sultan and at other times as much as fifteen feet away. The tiny golden haired sixth dancer however somehow kept herself always within a few paces of Murad. Five of the dancers lowered their eyes demurely to avoid personal eye contact while the sixth seemed to glory in it and in pouting her lips and smiling flirtatiously.

The music finished and the dancers stood with heads bowed as the Sultan briefly ran his eyes over them, lingering for long seconds on the tiny one. *She is interesting*, he thought, *a temptress in a child's body.* He nodded. It was a combination that intrigued him - so he stepped forward and held out his silk handkerchief.

Kosem handed the girl a welcoming glass of cherry sherbet and invited her to take a seat. "You have been honoured," she said in her imperious voice. Anna – who was now Firousi – was slightly in awe of the reputation of the Sultan's mother, so she avoided eye contact as she nodded.

"Yes, Highness, it is a great honour indeed and I will ensure that I am not found wanting." The Valide Sultan's eyes narrowed slightly. It was not the kind of response that was almost always forthcoming from a chosen virgin. "You have not known a man before?"

"No Highness."

"And yet you speak with confidence of your abilities to

please."

"Yes Highness, the Mistress Nubana has taught me well." Kosem nodded lightly.

"Yes, I would expect as much of the Sultan's favoured Ikbal . . . and yet . . ." she left the rest hanging in the air, before she continued. "You have attracted the Sultan with your dance, but you must know that there is more required to satisfy a man than ability to dance and knowledge of the erotic arts."

"Yes Highness, I am also well versed in music . . ." Kosem shook her head.

"More than music child; there is much more that is required. You must be skilled in conversation. You must be able to discuss literature and art should he desire it. You must know how to make a man feel that his will is the only will in the world and that you exist only to fulfil his every demand. Should you ever have the good fortune to attain the position of Ikbal or Kadin you must be wise enough to agree with his opinions, but clever enough to try and direct those opinions elsewhere should you feel that he is perhaps mistaken; for men, even Sultan's are, after all, only men . . ."

Kosem's words were designed to take some of the wind out of the confident one's sails, but they apparently fell well short of the desired effect.

"I am young Highness," the girl said firmly, "and the things you speak of will come with age."

The Valide Sultan looked intently into the girl's turquoise eyes and saw confidence beyond tender years reflected; confidence and a steely will to prevail - and was minded of another young girl from the past; a young Greek slave girl; a girl who rose from humble beginnings to be mother of a Sultan.

Anna took a deep breath as the palanquin was gently lowered outside the doors to the Sultan's private apartments. She had now arrived at a critical point that could decide her future and she was determined to do everything she could to ensure that future would be a golden one.

Where her 'sisters' had been embarrassed and then quietly

appalled by Nubana's lessons in the erotic arts, she had at first found them outrageously naughty; but then as she learned more she quickly began to realise that they were much more than this – they could provide a velvet road to power.

Had she not been abducted her life in Baltimore would have travelled a set and depressingly familiar path. She would have courted and married some clod and would then over a number of hard years have given birth to a brood of his children . . . and would have accepted it as a lot laid out for an empty headed girl. Well, some might say that she remained an empty headed girl, but she had glimpsed a future that any girl from her village – empty headed or not – could only dream about.

As she was ushered into the Sultan's private chamber her iron resolve began to waver. He was a giant who towered over her by at least a foot and a half. One of his hands could have totally enveloped two of hers. His huge bearded head and black beetling brows above his dark cruel eyes caused her heart to shrink within her chest. *He is just a man*, she thought desperately, *a man who can be tamed by a woman who has the knowledge and the will.*

She pushed back her shoulders, forcing her pert breasts to press forward against the sheer red silk halter top. He noticed her action and was intrigued as the sight of his interest caused her nipples to swell out against the silk. "My Lord," she said huskily, "I am your servant to do with as you will." He smiled, and thought *it is well that I moderated my drink for this little one.* And he was right because she pleased him so much that he presented her with a large emerald and sent for her three more times over the next ten days.

Alice's standing in the oda of Nubana was soon recognised by the Ikbal's retinue. Most accepted it as just another whim of their Mistress that in all probability would soon pass, others voiced their annoyance that such a recent arrival had gained favour – and one resented it bitterly.

Aiyshe had been Nubana's favoured odalisque for over a year before the arrival of Hafise, but now she had been relegated by a newcomer who was not even a true Moslem, to the position of being just another of Nubana's large retinue of odalisques, eunuchs and slaves. *I will not meekly accept it*, she frequently thought as she went about her increased load of menial daily duties. An opportunity would arise for her to strike back and when it did she would gain her revenge.

Razi Abu was one of Nubana's lesser eunuchs. He had frequently suffered lashings from his Mistress' sharp tongue and because of this held her in no great regard, so early one morning when he happened to see the new odalisque Hafise slipping quietly out of the door leading to Nubana's private bed chamber he nodded and smiled slyly to himself. The secret that his Mistress and her lover shared was now his too . . . to use as he saw fit.

The month end approached and in the common room shared by Nubana's retinue the Haznedar Usta, Fekriye, sat at the table that had been set up for her monthly visit. On the table in front of her there was a large leather bound brown ledger, a quill pen and bottle of ink and a blue velvet bag that bulged with hidden content.

Ready, she nodded to Nubana's head eunuch who then waved forward the first in line of her retinue. The girl approached the desk, curtsied and gave her name to the Head Treasurer who ran her eyes down the list of names in the ledger, noted the amount due, opened the velvet bag and tipped out a stream of silver coins. The girl signed her name in the ledger as Fekriye counted out some of the coins and handed them over to the girl who curtsied again and backed away to be replaced by the next in line.

The coins given varied from few in number and value for the menial slaves and lesser eunuchs, to reasonable amounts sufficient to purchase little luxuries for those odalisques and eunuchs of higher status.

Hafise collected her coins and followed the rest of Nubana's retinue out of a large pair of double doors that led into a cloistered courtyard where female merchants from the city had been allowed in to display their various wares on permanently sited trestle tables.

She joined the chattering women to look at bolts of coloured silks and gauzy veils, slippers decorated with sequins or coloured stones or pearls or silver or golden threads. She also saw turtle shell combs and hairbrushes, onyx, jasper, amber necklaces and earrings and little pots of nail paint, kohl and pastel face powders.

As she strolled from trestle table to table, stopping now and then to examine items another from the oda watched her movements with open hostility. Aiyshe's mouth contorted into a sneer. A sneer that was noticed by Razi Abu, who was casually leaning against a wall breathing in the scented air that filled the courtyard with the heady odours of almond blossoms, blue hyacinths and white narcissus. He smiled and pushed himself forward off the wall. "You have no love for that one?" he said, indicating Alice. Aiyshe nodded.

"She is not worthy of the Mistresses' attention," she said bitterly. Razi Abu shrugged.

"Perhaps she is," he replied enigmatically. Aiyshe looked sharply at him.

"How so!" she said. The eunuch smiled thinly.

"The Mistress must think so . . . as they share a bed." Aiyshe's eyes widened.

"How do you know this to be!" she demanded. He grinned.

"Because I have seen the odalisque creeping out of the Mistresses' bed chamber at dawn," he said casually.

Aiyshe's mind whirled with the news! *So!* She thought. *Kosem was engaged in forbidden lusts.* Lusts that the Sultan had railed against to the extent that he had banned any phallic shaped fruit or other objects from within the walls of the Harem! This news was very interesting. Now all she had to do was to make sure it reached the ever open ears and mouths of his Court . . . and she knew just what to do to make sure it did! She made her way over to a particular stall where she cheerily greeted the woman who stood behind it.

"So Fatima, business is good today?" The middle aged woman nodded and smiled.

"Fair, Aiyshe, but tomorrow will be better when I can place

my wares before richer customers!"

"Ah, yes, tomorrow you visit the ladies of the Sultan's Court do you not?" Fatima nodded again.

"Yes and perhaps your sister Ruhisar will honour me with her custom again!" Aiyshe smiled.

"I will see to it that she does Fatima! I will also suggest that she tells others of your quality goods and the bargain prices that you offer!" Fatima's smile widened. Competition for business among the Court's women, due to the higher wages that their status brought, was fierce so any helping hand would be much appreciated.

"Blessings on you Aiyshe!" she said. "And I will make sure that on the next visit to your courtyard you will receive a return for your patronage!" Aiyshe smiled thinly.

"I seek nothing in return Fatima, for a good deed offered is esteemed by Allah, praise be to His name." Fatima nodded.

"Yes, praise be to His name," she replied but then she tilted her head sideways as a thought struck her. "But how are you to speak to your sister when the inner courtyard of the Sultan's Court is closed to all who have no reason to be there?" The thin smile appeared again on Aiyshe's face.

"You have seen and spoken to my sister before on your visits to the courtyard?"

"Yes, as I have seen and spoken to many women of the Sultan's court."

"Then the answer is simple, I will return briefly to my Mistresses' oda to write a message to Ruhisar that you can give to her tomorrow."

Back in the oda, Aiyshe quickly wrote out the message in her native Armenian language. In it she outlined the scandal that had occurred and advised her sister to destroy the message after reading it; she also made reference to Fatima and suggested that Ruhisar give her patronage to the woman in favour for her acting as messenger.

Later, alone in her small room she sat and pondered on the possible results which might occur from her actions. The upstart would be removed from the oda and be severely punished and her fickle Mistress would lose much face as well as the position of favoured Ikbal to the Sultan. She nodded. It would be sweet justice for the way she had been treated.

Erin was taken by one of Kosem's eunuchs to a small two room apartment annexed to the Valide Sultan's suite that she was to share with one of the senior odalisques, Handeru, who had been in Kosem's service for over five years. The young woman, who was perhaps three or four years older than Erin welcomed her graciously.

"I am Handeru," she said pleasantly, "How are you called?" Erin smiled back.

"I am . . . was, Erin, but am now named Cyra."

"Er-in," the dark haired young woman stretched the strange name out. "That is a beautiful name where does it come from?" Erin who was now Cyra, smiled wanly.

"It comes from the land of my birth, Ireland."

"Ire-land? Is it a far land?" Erin nodded.

"Very far . . . but still dear to my heart." This time Handeru nodded.

"My land is also a far land; but Lebanon does not live in my mind or heart for I was taken before the age of six." Erin shook her head sadly.

"But you are content?" Handeru smiled.

"Yes, I am content. My life is pleasant and my Mistress, though sometimes harsh, treats me fairly."

"I am glad you are content," Erin, who was missing her 'sisters' greatly - and Alice in particular for her cool head and calming influence - said quietly, "but content will never enter my heart while I am here." Handeru noted the sadness in Erin's voice and tried to offer some comfort.

"I hear what you say," she said softly, "but know you this . . . time will dull the pain." Erin tried to force a smile but the young woman's words struck a chord in her and a lump rose in her throat and tears began to well in her eyes. Handeru, who had been instructed by Kosem to gain the newcomers confidence and to report back immediately if Cyra missed her next 'moon', was touched by the display of emotion and decided that she would offer what support she could. She changed the topic of conversation.

"My Mistress tells me that you have been honoured by the Sultan. Is this so?" Erin nodded.

"I have shared the Sultan's bed," she said truthfully. Handeru nodded. She herself did not possess the physical beauty demanded for gedikli training and had gained her position in the Valide Sultan's retinue by diligence, a sunny disposition and a total lack of jealousy regarding the advancement of others. She smiled brightly.

"Your beauty is there for all to see," she said simply. "And is it also true," she continued, "that this honour was given when you are not gedikli?"

"Yes, I was trained in language, dance, music and the erotic arts, but did not attain sufficient skills in the last art to move on to the Sultan's Court." Handeru shook her head in wonder.

"It has never been known in all the time that I have been at the palace that such a thing has happened!" Erin shrugged.

"The Sultan's moods are as unpredictable as the wind and he has the power to defy convention if he so desires." Handeru nodded.

"True, he is known to do so . . . and my Mistress is far from pleased!" she said with a little laugh.

Four days slowly drifted by and gradually Erin's sombre moods lightened. She still missed her 'sisters' greatly and they were forever in her thoughts, as was the fate of James, Helen and her boys; but she realised that there was nothing she could do from within the confines of her golden cage.

Her life as one of Kosem's many slaves, odalisques and ladies in waiting was, if not particularly pleasant, then one of little stress. Sometimes she was called upon to dance, play the lyre or recite poetry. Sometimes she helped the ladies in waiting to dress or bathe the Mistress, or assist slaves or odalisques in one of the many household duties that included preparing food. She did whatever was asked of her and because it helped to keep dark thoughts at bay, she was glad of it. And then six days after her arrival, she was summoned to the Valide Sultan's private reception room.

Kosem had been informed by Handeru that her companion had seen her 'moon' that morning and the Valide Sultan was pleased that her son's breach of protocol had not led to an irksome situation that would have called for action.

She had spoken sharply to Murad, reminding him that as the Valide Sultan she had to be informed immediately when he passed a silk handkerchief. "Tradition decrees that I must be given due time to prepare the girl for the honour," she had said firmly. He had nodded and had complied with her demand when again he had chosen the one called Firousi.

Erin stood respectfully with head bowed in front of the seated Kosem. "Handeru tells me that your union with my son is not destined to bear fruit," the Valide Sultan said. Erin nodded.

"That is so Highness." Kosem studied the girl for a few moments. *My son will not test my temper by calling for her again*, she thought, but then, knowing of his nature and the way that alcohol affected his moods, she reconsidered. Perhaps she could not count on it. *We have problems enough with the little respect that the Viziers and indeed, the Grand Vizier, have for him and flouting a hundred years of protocol will not be looked upon kindly,* she ruminated as she looked at the girl. *No*, she concluded, *it is best that she is moved on to where she is out of sight and out of mind.*

"I have decided that it is best to place you elsewhere," she said. Erin took a deep breath of relief. Away from the oda of Besma she would surely not risk a second summons to the Sultan's bed; a summons that if it came could only lead to one result.

"As you say Highness," she said meekly. Kosem nodded.

"Yes, you will be moved to the far side of the palace and placed in the *Kafes* in the retinue of Prince Ibrahim."

James' eyes streamed from the greasy grey-black smoke that a playful offshore sea breeze caused to swirl then dip and billow - and carry with it the smell of burning pine needles, amber resin and roasting flesh.

Ezra had led a detail of some twenty men to cut down a large number of trees from the stand where the raiding force had hidden the night before the attack on the fort – and now those trees, that had become three huge funeral pyres built on a level patch of ground outside the fort's walls, were serving to cleanse the area of the carnage that had resulted from the battle.

As he stood and watched the flames consume flesh blood and bone James absent-mindedly ran the fingers of his right hand across the breast of his shirt, tracing the curved line of his wound. The stitched slash had not been over deep and it did not cause him any great pain; but it could so easily have been so. He could have ended up in one of those pyres rather than watching them consume the last traces of what scant hours before had been living, breathing, life exulting men.

In a way, he thought, *I do lie there, for the old James, the callow, innocent James, is as dead as those poor souls.* His thoughts were then cut off by a heavy hand on his shoulder. "Morbid musings on life and death are for priests and poets," Ezra said brightly. James turned and smiled thinly.

"Yes, he said, and I have no fancy way with words and no use for priests." Erza grinned.

"Spoken like a true pirate!" he roared; then: "Come, we must make haste or the Admiral will leave us behind with the ashes."

Back on board the Admiral's vessel James watched as ashore on the high hill where the now lifeless fort stood, dense black plumes of smoke rose in slow lazy spirals towards the blue cloudless heavens.

He turned away to see the rest of the little armada begin to peel off for the journey back to Algiers, while the Admiral's vessel began to swing slowly towards the east; the east and the city of Constantinople where his heart yearned to be.

29

Anna's position in the Sultan's Court had been magically transformed from one of little consequence to one of importance and the Sultan's fourth selection of the new gedikli raised her profile even further. Now even Sarina, the Housekeeper of the

Harem, treated her with something approaching respect.

It was respect that was not returned as Anna remembered only too well the way that the Kahya had kept her from dancing for the Sultan and also the look on the woman's face when she had finally been selected. Now when the Housekeeper spoke to her she allowed a haughty edge to colour her replies.

"I am bored," Anna, who was now Firousi, said as she examined her hands after finishing painting her fingernails. Amara, who, like her, was seated on plump silk cushions beside the tinkling fountain smiled.

"Your new position as favoured of the Sultan seems to lead quickly to boredom with less exciting times!" she said archly. Anna blew daintily on her nails and shrugged.

"I am no longer one among many gediklis," she said casually. Amara nodded.

"No, even Shanez, who has been thrice honoured, must now bow to that fact when she sees the gifts that the Sultan has bestowed on you." Anna smiled thinly and fingered the necklace of matching emeralds that hung around her neck. As Amara spoke Shanez's name she suddenly brought to mind something that she had heard earlier in the day that had come from Shanez herself.

"Did you hear the gossip that is tripping round the Court?" Anna frowned lightly.

"Gossip, what gossip?"

"Shanez was in conversation with Ruhisar yesterday and she was told that Nubana now sleeps with one of her odalisques, Hafise!" Anna's eyes opened wider but then she shook her head.

"Gossip is gossip," she replied, "and does not always signal truth." Now Amara shook her head.

"This time it does," she said firmly. "One of Nubana's eunuchs saw the odalisque sneaking from the Mistresses' bedchamber before dawn." Anna had heard that because they hardly, if ever, were honoured by the Sultan, some of the women in the Court indulged in such practices. Indeed, she had heard also that the Sultan had come to hear of it and in his rage had decreed that no phallic shaped fruit or items were to be allowed into the Court.

That though was one thing; but this, this news concerning Murad's favoured Ikbal was another matter entirely!

"And how did Ruhisar come by this information?" Anna asked casually, as again she blew on her fingernails.

"Ruhisar's sister, Aiyshe, is an odalisque in Nubana's oda, the eunuch concerned told her what he had witnessed and Aiyshe then sent message to Ruhisar through one of the women merchants who visited the Court yesterday." As she finished speaking Amara did not notice the gleam in her friend Firousi's turquoise eyes, nor the way her lips twitched upwards to give birth to a fleeting smile.

"We must hope," Anna said sincerely, "that such news does not somehow reach the Sultan's ears."

The fifth honour came three days later. She spent another half hour in the Valide Sultan's private apartments where, as she sipped on the usual glass of cherry sherbet, she listened with half an ear to Kosem's instructions and words of advice. For her part the Valide Sultan was becoming a little worried. Murad had sent for the tiny golden haired one five times now and the girl's elevation at Court had obviously affected her attitude.

The glimpse of hidden depths that she had spotted weeks ago, was now much closer to the surface and with it she noticed – in the girl's tone of voice and bodily stance – a lessening in the level of respect that was demanded of all when in the company of the Valide Sultan. *You now bear close watching; very close watching*, Kosem mused as the girl took her leave.

It was late at night when Anna ran her fingers through the matted hair on the Sultan's chest then playfully squeezed a nipple. Murad growled, a heavy scowl clouded his features and she was briefly worried that perhaps she had gone too far. She raised her head off the pillow and said meekly, but with an impish smile on her face: "Please do not have me whipped my Lord! I am but a silly girl who does not know her place." His scowl faded and when he spoke his voice carried an edge of mock outrage.

"Whipped?" he said, "I have personally removed the heads of many who have offended me less!" She noted the tone and decided the time was right.

"I would never knowingly offend my Lord . . . even though others might." He lowered his head and his eyes narrowed as her words registered.

"Others, what others would knowingly offend me?" She steepled her fingers together and bowed her head respectfully.

"There is gossip, in your Court my Lord . . ." His eyes narrowed further.

"Speak!" he barked. And she did, making sure that she placed emphasis on the part that Shanez had played. Enraged he threw back the cream silk sheet and leaped out of bed. "I am Sultan," he roared, his face turning darker and the crimson thread veins across his nose and cheeks seeming to pulse with the words. She pulled the sheet up to her breasts and thought it prudent to remain silent as he paced the bed chamber like a prowling lion for a full minute muttering to him self.

The prowling stopped and as his blood engorged face returned to something like normal; she chanced to speak. "My Lord is angry with me?" she said meekly. He shook his head as if to clear his mind of savage thoughts.

"Angry with you?" he muttered. Anna nodded.

"Is my Lord angry with me for being the bearer of such news?" He shook his head and when he spoke there was ice in his words.

"My anger will be directed at those who have offended me, of that you may be assured."

"And so it should be Lord," she said softly, as he threw on his nightgown and strode from the bedchamber slamming the door in his wake.

Outside, he passed quickly through the apartment and entered the reception room where his two chief eunuchs sat dozing in chairs. "Up!" he ordered, causing the two men to leap to their feet in alarm - alarm which rapidly increased when they saw the look on his face.

"In two hours you will make your way to the oda of Nubana," he growled. "There you will use your Sultan's name to gain admittance to her apartments and in stealth enter the Ikbal's bedchamber. Should you find that she is not alone in her bed you will garrotte her and her companion immediately." The eunuchs exchanged quick glances as if to make sure they heard him right.

"If the deed is done you will dispose of the bodies in the Bosporus in weighted sacks." His orders given, he spun on his heel and made his way back to his bed.

In the ante room leading to the reception room in Nubana's apartments, a snoring Razi Abu was roused from sleep by an insistent knocking. Grumbling loudly he rubbed the sleep from his eyes, moved over to the locked door and slid the small viewing hatch open. As soon as he recognised the two faces he became instantly wide awake and quickly slid the door's bolt back.

He was a lowly servant to the Sultan's favoured Ikbal and the eunuchs who strode through the open doorway were known throughout the palace for their fanatical dedication to the Sultan; dedication that it was strongly rumoured had led to the disappearance of others who had annoyed his Highness.

"How may I help you?" Razi Abu stuttered. For answer, one of the eunuchs swept him aside with a bare muscled arm, while the other said simply: "The Ikbal's sleeping chamber." Razi Abu swallowed nervously and was almost on the point of questioning them as to why they wanted the information, when he decided that it would not be a wise course of action. "Follow me and I will lead you to it," he said.

Outside the door to the bedchamber he stood in an agony of indecision. They were obviously here to carry out some bloody deed on the Sultan's orders - and when the deed was done would the only witness to that deed be silenced?" He didn't wait to find out . . . as soon as they slipped in through the door he turned and hurried from the apartment.

Inside the darkened chamber the two men padded over to the raised bed that sat in deep shadow beneath a dark silk canopy. And yes, there were two bodies, lying close together. One of the eunuchs raised an arm and directed the other to move around to the other side of the bed. When they were both in position the first eunuch nodded lightly, then together, they took strong silken cords from their pockets and advanced on their sleeping victims.

Murad's senior eunuchs entered the Court early next morning and were seen in conversation with Sarina for a short time before the Kahya summoned Shanez and Ruhisar and the two odalisques were escorted from the common room. Anna, from her seat on one of the Ottoman divans where she was listening to Amara relating a folk tale from her native land, watched with a faint smile on her lips. Two hours passed before the common room door was re-opened and in much distress the two weeping odalisques were brought back. Sarina moved swiftly to their side as all conversation in the room stopped dead. "We have been whipped!" Ruhisar wailed as her legs began to give way and the Kahya stepped forward to guide her to a divan. Shanez, also in a state of near collapse, staggered over to the divan and lowered herself slowly onto the seat's satin cushions.

Anna, who was stood a distance away, smiled, then moved closer as the two women's upper garments were removed to reveal, on each of their backs, a dozen angry criss-crossing red stripes many of which were weeping blood. She stood silently on the fringe looking on as the babble of voices rose around the two injured women. She smiled again, then moved much closer until she stood less than three feet away from Shanez, who through tear filled eyes, noted the other's cold and steady gaze. Anna held her stare for long moments then nodded slowly and deliberately, before turning and casually walking away.

Kosem waved aside the doorkeeper and strode purposely into the Sultan's apartments. She had received news of Nubana's disappearance and that of one of her ladies in waiting and she was looking for answers. One of the Ikbal's eunuchs who had been stationed at the entrance to the oda had, after a search, been brought forward. He had prostrated himself in front of the Valide Sultan and stammered out the story. There was nothing he could have done . . . He was a lowly servant . . . The Sultan's chief eunuchs - who obviously carried orders directly from the Sultan -

had left him no option but to allow them admittance.

Murad's face showed no sign of emotion as his mother demanded to know what had happened to Kosem. He shrugged. "I am Sultan," he said calmly.

"And I am Valide Sultan," she replied coldly. "And all odalisques, gediklis and Ikbals are my responsibility!" He nodded acceptance of her words, but then continued firmly.

"And as Sultan," he said, "I will not tolerate my name being bandied about my Court accompanied by sniggers and laughter. Nor will I tolerate a woman of my Court visiting any but the Sultan's bed." Kosem was taken aback by his words and in a quieter tone of voice asked him to tell her exactly what had taken place.

He told her and when he admitted that he had had Nubana and her hand maiden strangled and thrown into the Bosporus she kept her temper in check. Nubana had been a valuable pair of ears and eyes and she would have much preferred that the Ikbal's sexual adventures had been kept secret; but what was done was done. He finished speaking and she took her leave.

Back in her apartments she went over their conversation. He had told her that the tiny golden haired one, Firousi, had brought the Court gossip to his attention (and why did that not surprise her!) and that on her words he had the gediklis Ruhisar and Shanez – who Firousi said had originated and spread the gossip – interrogated and then punished.

She had asked him how the two women had come by their gossip and he explained how, under threat of execution, Ruhisar had admitted that Aiyshe, her sister who was in the oda of Nubana, had sent her the details by note.

She was still much annoyed by the loss of her main spy in the Court, but she also understood why Murad had taken such drastic measures. It was imperative that the Sultan maintain total control and when the news of Nubana's disappearance – and the obvious penalty she had paid for her dalliances – reached everyone's ears, she knew that his authority would be reinforced.

That said there were loose tongues that needed to be tightened. The girl Firousi, for one, as the tiny golden haired one was too often in the Sultan's bed and obviously too ready with a word in his ear that might lead to her own advancement. Yes, she thought, *I will attend to that one soon; but first there is another pressing matter that must be dealt with...*

Ruhisar fell to her knees and prostrated herself in front of the Valide Sultan. "Highness," she cried, "my actions were born of a desire to see that the Sultan did not suffer insult." Kosem's eyes narrowed.

"Then why did you not openly bring your news to my attention?" Aiyshe clasped her hands in front of her breast.

"Highness," she said in quick answer, "the news was not really mine to pass on, it came from Razi Abu . . ."

"Razi Abu, the eunuch who stood guard outside the entrance to the oda?" Sensing a chance to move the blame away from her self, Aiyshe dared to raise her head.

"Yes Highness!" she said eagerly, "It was he who saw the odalisque coming from the Mistress' bedchamber!" Kosem nodded and turned to one of her eunuchs.

"Bring the eunuch Razi Abu to me now and do not tell him why his presence is demanded."

Kneeling beside the already prostrate Aiyshe, Razi Abu trembled as the Valide Sultan looked down and fixed him with a withering stare.

"You are the one who saw the odalisque leaving the Mistress' bed chamber?"

"Yes Highness," he croaked from a suddenly dry mouth.

"Then why did you not come to me with what you saw?" He swallowed again.

"Highness, I am but a lowly eunuch, I could not see myself approaching the mighty Valide Sultan . . ." Kosem shook her head slowly and signalled to two huge muscular eunuchs who stood with arms folded against a wall. "Remove these two from my sight," she said tiredly. As the eunuchs stepped forward, Aiyshe and Razi Abu, with looks of relief on their faces, climbed quickly to their feet and were about to offer thanks to the Valide Sultan, when she added coolly: "and see that their flapping tongues are ripped out."

Sarina bowed her head as she was ushered into the Valide Sultan's presence.

"You wish to speak with me Highness?" she said. Kosem smiled thinly and signalled the Kahya, who had proved to be a very useful pair of eyes and ears in the Sultan's Court – although certainly not as useful as Nubana had been with her direct access to Murad – to take a seat by her side. "You are aware of the fate of Nubana," she stated flatly as soon as Sarina was seated.

"Yes Highness, as is the whole palace!" Kosem's face hardened.

"And are you aware how the Sultan came to hear of Nubana's folly?" Sarina shrugged lightly.

"It would seem that he came to hear some gossip Highness."

"Yes, and do you know from whose lips that gossip found its way to his ears?" The Kahya shook her head. "It came from the golden haired one, Firousi," Kosem added sourly. Sarina nodded slowly.

"Ah, yes, the one with the angel face and the heart of ice."

"Yes Firousi, the one who has become too favoured in the Sultan's bed and now aspires to be Ikbal in place of Nubana."

"It is so Highness, but the Sultan is the Sultan and she is his choice."

"And I am the Valide Sultan," Kosem spat. "And I will not allow her scheming to bear fruit!"

"That would please me greatly Highness, for the girl shows no respect," Sarina said softly.

"Then between us we must put a permanent stop to her scheming," the Valide Sultan replied firmly as she took a small brown glass bottle from a pocket and handed it to the smiling Kahya.

Anna had been given her own apartment by the besotted Sultan, who also gave her a young serving girl to use as she chose

– and on the day that she moved her belongings into the apartment she was visited by Amara who shook her head in wonder. "Your very own apartment!" she said in greeting as she passed through the door. Anna's smile teetered on the edge of turning into a smirk.

"It will suffice," she said coolly, "until the Sultan makes me Ikbal and then I will move to one that is more fitting." Amara shook her head again.

"And your very own servant girl!" She exclaimed glancing down at the dark skinned, raven haired girl who knelt attentively with head bowed at Firousi's feet. Anna smiled again.

"And when I am Ikbal I will request that you join my new oda to become my senior lady in waiting." Amara beamed. She had given up on ever being summoned to the Sultan's bed herself and was now content to bask in the reflected glow that came with being the best (and perhaps, only) friend to the Sultan's new favourite.

They spent a pleasant hour chatting, before Amara excused herself and Anna dismissed her servant with instructions for her to return from her dormitory early next morning to prepare her breakfast.

Alone, she casually wandered through the four large rooms that made up her new living accommodation running a red nailed hand lightly over the beautiful furniture, the black silken sheets that covered the canopied bed and the gold taps that fed the sunken pink marble bath. "Yes," she murmured, "It will suffice . . . for now."

Her rapid rise in the Sultan's Court had given her much pleasure but the next phase would bring even more satisfaction. Once she managed to conceive and present him with a son, he would make her Kadin and then she would have true power.

She made her way out onto the little balcony to breathe in the late evening air and her mind went back to the other little balcony that she had shared with her 'sisters' months ago. They were very different to her. They had refused to accept their fate; had held on to dreams of rescue, of returning to the land of their birth! She snorted lightly. Fools! Rescue would offer them nothing but a return to a life of grind and poverty!

She shook her head at their folly; before a tender feeling briefly washed over her. They had been kind to her, had gone out of their way to comfort her when she needed it. She nodded slowly. *Yes*, she thought, *we were sisters and friends, but I am now on my own and I have no further need of sisterly love.*

She sat on the balcony for several minutes and allowed her thoughts to wander at will. Thoughts of dozens of servants living solely to fulfil her every wish; thoughts of cascading diamonds, emeralds, rubies; and thoughts of mountains of beautiful clothes, tripped through her head - and then suddenly, from somewhere - a dark interloper. She thought of Nubana and the part that she had played in her death. *It was not my fault* she told herself. *I only wanted her to lose the Sultan's favour.* The fate of the unknown hand maiden, Hafise, was also unfortunate . . . but it did not really have any impact on her mind.

A sudden insistent knocking on the apartment door brought her back to the here and now. She rose and made her way back inside, opened the door and was greatly surprised to find a softly smiling Sarina standing there with a bottle of wine in her hand.

"A present," the Kahya said pleasantly, "to welcome you to your new status." Anna's eyes narrowed slightly. This was the last thing she might have expected - a friendly visit from a woman who had never shown any inclination towards friendliness! And then the reason for the visit suddenly became clear to her. *She is worried that I am becoming powerful in the Sultan's Court and she seeks to curry favour!* Anna smiled thinly and waved the Kahya in through the door. "An unexpected visit," she said coolly.

"We have not had occasion to share company together before and I thought the time was now ripe," Sarina said pleasantly holding up the bottle of wine. *No*, Anna thought as she led the Kahya to a chair. *You have not sought my company; but now you find that your future well-being might depend on my goodwill*. She took the bottle from Sarina's hand and placed it on a low gilded table that separated their two chairs before leaving the room briefly and then returning with two crystal goblets. "Your new apartment is to your liking Firousi?" the Kahya said.

"It will suffice," Anna replied injecting a deliberate note of boredom into her words. Sarina noted the tone and as she lifted the bottle and filled the two goblets thought: *Yes, you continue to play the high and mighty fool while we drink to your good fortune*.

For a few minutes they went through the charade; the Kahya feigning pleasure in the spectacular rise in status of one of her charges; Firousi smiling thinly and thinking *your honeyed words will gain you nothing.*

Their glasses were half emptied when Sarina suddenly waved a hand in front of her face. "My, she said taking in a deep breath, "I find the drink is quite strong; could you perhaps add some water to my glass?" Anna rose, took up the Kahya's goblet and left the room for half a minute . . . half a minute that was long enough for Sarina to remove the little brown glass bottle from her dress and pour the colourless liquid into her companion's drink.

Anna returned to her seat and passed the now full glass to the Kahya, who flashed the girl a genuine smile. "Thank you Firousi," she said warmly as she raised her glass and over the rim saw her victim follow suit.

The Valide Sultan had assured her that the liquid was odourless and tasteless and Sarina watched the girl's face closely as she took a generous swallow. There was no hint of suspicion and the Kahya nodded slowly and smiled.

Anna put down her goblet and a puzzled frown creased her brow as she saw the wide smile on Sarina's face and the sparkle in her eyes. "You are amused by something? Perhaps you will share your humour with me?" The Kahya nodded.

"Yes," she said coldly, "I will share with pleasure. You are a foolish child who thought that your beauty, body and naked ambition would lead you to high office!" Anna rose swiftly to her feet.

"You dare to speak so to the Sultan's favourite!" she spat. "I will ensure that . . ." Her tight lipped words were suddenly cut off, her head tilted backwards, her mouth gaped and a strangled cry of agony rose from her throat as a terrible searing pain doubled her up. Her hands clutched her stomach, her fingers hooked into claws, her legs folded and she pitched to her knees in front of the Kahya who took a pace back and looked down blank faced at the girl's long drawn out death throes.

Later with the half empty re-corked wine bottle and the two goblets wrapped in a midnight blue silk scarf, Sarina left the apartment and closed the door quietly behind her.

30

The Valide Sultan's oda was awash with the gossip. "It is so," Handera said to Erin. "Nubana has been murdered and disposed of in the Bosporus along with one of her hand maidens, a girl that you know!" Erin frowned.

"A girl that I know?" she said.

"Yes, one called Hafise!" Erin, puzzled, shook her head.

"Hafise? I do not know anyone of that name."

"She was not so named until recently. Before that her name was Alice." The name struck her like a hammer blow.

"Alice! Alice is dead!" Erin wailed as her hand flew to her mouth to stifle a gasp and her legs threatened to give way. Handeru moved forward quickly to support her stricken friend. "Yes Cyra, it is so. I am sorry to be the one to bring you tidings that cause so such pain." Erin shook her head, still not believing the terrible news.

"But how . . . Why?"

"Word reached the Sultan that his favoured Ikbal was sleeping with one of her handmaidens and this so enraged him that he had them both strangled in their bed."

Alice! Lovely wise Alice! My dear sister who has shared so much with me! The words burned their way across Erin's mind. And she was still numb with shock, when a day later she was moved to the *Kafes*, a prison within a prison.

The large two storey apartment building that she found herself in contained over one hundred rooms and although it was as luxuriously furnished as any other part of the palace it retained an air of brooding seclusion, due in no small part to the huge locked and guarded door that separated it from the rest of the palace complex and thus ensured that those inside were - unless permission was gained from outside - kept virtual prisoners.

Dull routine was really only held at bay by the one day at

the end of the month when the Hazendar Usta arrived with her leather bound ledger and little blue velvet bag and the 'prisoners' made their way out into the spacious landscaped tree lined courtyard with its fragrant flower beds and little benches, to examine, and perhaps if their meagre wages allowed, buy the wares of visiting women merchants.

Prince Ibrahim's retinue contained three dozen sterile concubines, a dozen eunuchs and some sixty general slaves who were responsible for the Prince and his concubines' comforts as well as for all the general duties that went towards the apartment's smooth running and upkeep. She became one of these general slaves, under the direct instruction of Hosneva, a plump matronly late middle aged woman with silver streaks in her black hair, who had originally been in the retinue of Ibrahim's father, Ahmed I.

Hosneva was intrigued by the arrival of the new slave girl and lost no time in asking her where she had come from and why. When Erin told her that she had been trained towards the station of gedikli and had shared the Sultan's bed, she was astounded. "Why then," she asked, "if you were so honoured are you now reduced to a lowly position in the *Kafes*?" Erin smiled thinly.

"I did not attain gedikli status and when the Valide Sultan discovered I had still been summoned she was not pleased." Hosneva nodded.

"Ah, yes," she said. "Her Highness has always taken great pride in maintaining protocol and tradition and is keen to ensure that the Grand Vizier and Viziers have no further reasons to feel aggrieved in these much troubled times."

Her duties in the *Kafes* were not onerous and she soon fell into a routine that helped the days drift by. She also, through Hosneva's benign patronage - for the Housekeeper held her in some esteem because of her training and her visit to the Sultan's bed - became something of a celebrity among the general slaves who enjoyed listening to her lyre playing.

Ten days after her arrival she came face to face for the first time with Ibrahim the Mad.

Hosneva flung open the double doors to the bath chamber and at her back Erin, who was pushing a wheeled serving trolley piled with honeyed cakes and sweetmeats, came to a startled stop as she took in the scene that unfolded in front of her.

The large room was full of what seemed a multitude of obscenely bloated naked women who were either lounging on plump cushions or splashing about in an enormous forty foot long and twenty foot wide rectangular sunken marble bath . . . or were being chased around its perimeter by a huge, grinning, naked man with an erection.

Stunned, she watched as the shaggy haired heavily bearded man caught hold of one of the fat fleeing women, bent her roughly forward and plunged his member into her, before, after a few sharp thrusts, withdrawing and chasing after another.

Hosneva saw the look on Erin's face. "It is play time for the Prince," she said simply as the man caught another of the fat women, repeated his earlier actions and then with a roar leapt into the bath creating a wave that threatened to drown a number of the laughing, shrieking women.

"It is an affront to decency!" Erin said, appalled at the sight. Hosneva shrugged.

"The Prince is a prisoner and his captivity is eased by such pleasures." Erin looked directly at the woman and shook her head.

"But surely, even by the standards of your country where men of power have many wives such behaviour is disgraceful!" Hosneva nodded lightly.

"Yes, that is so, but Royal Princes, oft times are a law unto themselves." Erin was about to comment further when her words were chopped off by the arrival of the man, who had waded through the chest deep water to the edge of the bath and with an effort heaved him self out to tower not four feet from her side. Hugely embarrassed, she raised her eyes quickly away from his still erect member to take in the rest of his form.

Unlike his brother, his body was soft and podgy and in comparison to Murad's, relatively hairless. He was slack jawed and framed by an unkempt beard, his mouth hung slightly open with the fleshy bottom lip hanging loosely and exposing yellowed lower teeth. His eyes, which were a watery grey colour and curiously without depth, were set close together either side of a long narrow nose that ended with a bulbous tip and she got the impression that behind those dull orbs lay a stunted mind that had never given birth to a noble thought.

Her brief examination of the man was then interrupted by the approach to the side of the bath by one of the hugely bloated women who after a struggle, heaved herself up out of the water and onto the tiled floor where she momentarily flopped about like a beached whale.

Erin gaped at the wobbling mountain of flesh – that rendered the rest of the women almost *slim* by comparison – as the woman struggled to her feet and scuttled over to the serving trolley where she snatched up a handful of the little honey cakes and crammed them into her mouth. Ibrahim roared with laughter at the sight of thick dribbles of honey carrying pastry flakes that covered her chin and dripped down over it onto the rolls of fat that encircled her neck.

"Yes Sheker Pare!" he yelled in a reedy voice that seemed at odds with his huge size; "Stuff them all into your mouth; we will send for more!" At his words and the sight of the cakes rapidly disappearing, the women who lounged at the side of the bath struggled to their feet and converged on the trolley - and on a nervous Erin whose hands still gripped the handles.

"Come," Hosneva said calmly, "One trolley will not suffice today."

Back in the common room Hosneva sent two of the servants to the kitchens with the trolley with orders to pile it as high as possible and to do the same with a second one as well. When they had gone Erin turned to Hosneva. "Mistress," she said, "Those women; I have never seen such!" Hosneva smiled.

"The Prince is obsessed with fat women and the fatter they are, the better. The enormous one, Sheker Pare, was brought from Armenia and is his favourite."

"*Sheker Pare* Mistress? It means 'piece of sugar' does it not?" Hosneva nodded.

"Your grasp of language does you credit child; even though in Sheker Pare's case, 'Mountain of Sugar' would certainly be much more fitting!"

The slave girls returned with the loaded trolleys and Hosneva - to Erin's relief; for she had been a little unnerved by the feeding frenzy, sent them into the baths instead.

Ezra entered the Admiral's cabin and stood loosely to attention as Ali Bichnin cleared away some papers from his desk before nodding in the boson's direction.

"We will enter the Bosporus tomorrow Admiral and the men have charged me to make a request." The Admiral's lips twitched into the beginnings of a smile - he knew what was coming.

"A request boson, and what might that be?" Ezra returned the smile.

"They have fought well and ask that half of their wages be advanced now and the rest on our return to Algiers."

"Aye, they fought well; but do they know that Constantinople under the Sultan's laws forbidding alcohol and other vices is not as Algiers where any manner of excess is to be found?" Ezra nodded.

"Aye Admiral, they are aware, but men of the sea will always find ways to indulge their vices."

"Yes, that is so boson. Very well; but you must impress upon them that our stay in Constantinople will be a short one and that any who go missing for days on end will find themselves stranded." Ezra grinned.

"Many thanks Admiral. The men will sing your name in praise of your generous nature!" Ali Bichnin growled.

"Be gone!" he roared "And take your flowery words with you!" Ezra grinned again, turned on his heel, then stopped and turned back to face the Admiral.

"James Pallow," he said. The Admiral cocked his head.

"Yes, what of him?"

"He is your slave, is he not? And as such is not entitled to payment . . ."

"I did not buy the man," Ali Bichnin said, "So treat him as any other who fought."

The Admiral's vessel inched its way into the busy harbour and as he stood on the deck James' eyes were fixed on the enormous palace that dominated the skyline and in particular on a soaring tower within the walls that pricked the early morning clear blue sky like the index finger of the prophet pointing the way to paradise. "It is the *Adalet Kulesi*, the Tower of Justice," Ezra, who stood by his side, said, when James asked.

"And will I find justice within those walls? Or is justice here reserved for the followers of Islam only?" James muttered softly. Ezra shrugged.

"The chances of you rescuing her are remote my friend for no whole man is allowed within the confines of the harem." James shook his head firmly.

"If it is humanly possible I will find a way . . . I must."

An hour later the vessel bobbed gently at anchor with only a skeleton crew above deck and its miserable oar slaves shackled below; while most of the rest of the crew had rapidly melted into the dockside crowds in search of whatever vices they could find.

James sat next to Ezra and opposite the Admiral and the Sultan's Chief Eunuch, the Kizlar Agha, who on hearing of the Admiral's arrival had insisted on accompanying them to the palace. Fifty feet in front of the horse drawn carriage four of Ali Bichnin's longest serving renegadoes formed an escort around the Sultan's one time trusted General, a heavily foot shackled Jafar Ben Ali.

The Admiral gave the order and the little cavalcade set out on the short journey that would bring payment of gold to him and what was sure to be a cruel and perhaps lingering payment of another kind to the prisoner. "He does not look like a man striding to his death," Ezra said as he noticed the general's proud bearing. James agreed.

"He displays courage," he said quietly. The Kizlar Agha turned in his seat to briefly study the General's straight back.

"He will need to draw deeply on that courage I fear, for our dear Sultan is famed for the varied ways by which he despatches those who have, in his own mind, wronged him."

Within minutes they approached the *Byzantine Mese*, the avenue that led to the massive Imperial Gate with its towering central arch flanked by two smaller arches. There, the two sentries moved sharply to swing open the huge double doors, before standing back stiffly to attention as the carriage trundled slowly through.

They passed through the First Courtyard; through the crenelated *Gate of Salutation* that guarded the Second Courtyard and finally through another gate where the Kizlar Agha climbed down from the carriage and signalled for the others to do the same. "We are now to enter the Inner Council Hall," he said. "You will remove any arms before we enter."

James had quietly marvelled at the scale and grandeur that had revealed itself during their passage through the inner courtyards; but now he stood stunned by the sheer opulence that surrounded him in the Inner Council Hall with its huge raised canopied and jewel encrusted golden throne. *I am in another world*, he thought with a mental shake of his head. *One that signals power beyond my ken!* He took a deep breath and pushed back his shoulders. "She is here somewhere," he said quietly under his breath. "And I will find her."

The Chief Eunuch told them to wait before disappearing through a door behind the ornate throne. "He has gone to fetch the Sultan," the Admiral said looking directly at the shackled General, who glared defiantly back.

"I am ready," Jafar Ben Ali answered coolly. "Allah has set aside a place of honour for me." Ali Bichnin shrugged and turned to James, Ezra and his renegadoes.

"The Sultan will appear shortly," he said, "and when he does make sure that you quickly fall to your knees and bow your heads."

Five minutes dragged by before the door re-opened and the Kizlar Agha swept back into the room followed by what looked to James, a bearded giant - and close behind him two heavily muscled shaven headed black men. "To your knees!" the Chief Eunuch shouted and almost as one, seven men obeyed; while the eighth remained defiantly on his feet. The Sultan's eyes latched onto the lone figure and his mouth twisted into a snarl. "So," he spat, "The dog is brought back to heel!" The General held eye contact and smiled thinly.

"Brought back, yes, but to heel never," he said with iron conviction. James felt a sudden surge of respect for the man; a man who knew that his life would soon be snuffed out - and almost certainly snuffed out in a most painful and horrible fashion.

Murad's eyes narrowed for a second but then his clouded features relaxed and he shrugged. "Brave words," he said pleasantly before signalling for the kneeling men to rise. "Take the Admiral's men and see that they are fed well, before returning with them in one hour," he said to the Kizlar Agha, who bowed. "And you," the Sultan continued, speaking to the two large black men, "remove our honoured guest and prepare him as ordered, before bringing him back in one hour."

When the others had gone the Sultan turned to the Admiral and his features suddenly clouded. "Did I not ask for you to bring to me all the leaders of the revolt Admiral?" he said through pinched lips. Ali Bichnin nodded.

"You did Highness; but the battle was most bloody and dire," he replied, before adding: "and caused me the loss of many good men. Indeed, we were a little fortunate to secure our main target the General alive..." Murad scowled lightly then shook his head. He had been looking forward to lengthy and extended retribution.

"Very well," he said, "What is done is done and but for that one failing you have carried out your mission and I will honour my pledge to pay you in full." Ali Bichnin smiled.

"Your Highness is most magnanimous," he said smoothly. Murad nodded.

"A fact well known Admiral," he said before suggesting that they now adjourn to an outer palace reception room for lunch and brandy aperitifs.

Well fed on delicious cooked meats and exotic fruits and watered on cherry flavoured sherbet, James, Ezra and the renegado escort arrived back at the Inner Council Hall within the hour, to stand and wonder what would come next. They didn't have long to wait, as less than two minutes later the door behind the ornate throne opened and the Sultan and the Admiral entered, followed after two more minutes by the black eunuchs who between them were carrying a long wooden trestle bearing a naked General.

They had forced two five foot long planks of wood under each of his armpits and tightly bound his arms and legs to them with thick leather thongs. He had been placed on his side and the lower plank had been firmly nailed to the trestle stopping him from moving. Murad took his seat on the throne and the trestle was placed just in front of him.

"You are comfortable?" the Sultan asked pleasantly. Jafar Ben Ali's mouth opened and Murad leaned forward to catch his response, but instead of words the General spat. The saliva, aimed at the Sultan's face, fell short and landed instead on Murad's chest. He casually removed a silk handkerchief from a pocket and slowly wiped the front of his garment. It seemed that he was determined to remain totally in control of his temper; perhaps to better appreciate what was to follow. He turned on the throne and with a smile on his lips, signalled one of the eunuchs to leave the room.

James and the others stood quietly and waited while the Sultan dabbed lightly at his tunic with the handkerchief and hummed a tune to him self. The door opened again and the eunuch entered . . . carrying a four foot long double handled, cruelly toothed saw. He moved over to the bound General and at a nod from the Sultan slid it between Jafar Ben Ali's legs above his shackled feet. The second eunuch then moved to take up the other handle.

James' stomach lurched as he saw what was going to happen. *No!* His mind screamed; *surely no one could even contemplate such barbarity!* The eunuchs looked towards the Sultan who nodded lightly and the saw slid up the General's legs and rested against his scrotum. As the cold metal made contact Jafar Ben Ali gasped, his eyes began to roll in his head and the watchers heard a wet plopping sound as his bowels suddenly emptied. Murad smiled.

The eunuchs looked again in the Sultan's direction and received a nod, followed by the single soft word, "slowly".

As the first scream filled the audience room James' eyes flew shut. And when it was followed by another long drawn out howl of agony he clamped his hands over his ears. The vicious saw blade, lubricated by blood and faeces tore its way through the writhing body and as the blade finally met breastbone the last scream cannoned off the walls of the chamber.

As its echo died he slowly opened his eyes, but made sure he did not focus them on the trestle and the gory remains of what had so recently been a man. Instead the Sultan's blood engorged grinning face filled his vision causing a shudder of revulsion and rising hot vomit threaten to spew from his mouth.

He swallowed hard to force back the gag reaction and glanced sideways at the other witnesses to the barbaric act. To a man their faces were ashen copies of what he felt his own face must look like. They were men who had almost certainly ravaged and killed - and taken pleasure in it - but this, this abomination, had shaken them to the core.

He swallowed again as Murad spoke. "Take it away," he said to the eunuchs, casually waving a hand in the direction of the bloody remains. "And bring water and cloths to clean up the mess."

Less than an hour later with the Admiral still inside, James, Ezra and the escort from the Admiral's vessel stood outside the palace gate where a carriage waited to take them back to the harbour. "No," James said firmly as Ezra held out a hand to help him into the vehicle. "I have need of a long walk with clean air in my face and in my lungs." Ezra nodded, he understood James' need and as he looked into the other's eyes he suspected that they might not meet again for some time. "Take care," he said quietly. "And may your God go with you." James nodded.

"And you also," he replied as the carriage set out on its journey to the harbour.

As he stood beneath the mighty walls of the enormous palace with its huge guarded gate, his heart sank. Ezra was surely right he thought; how could he a mere lone man accomplish the impossible? He shook his head and took a deep breath. "I will do it," he said firmly, "because I must!"

He made his way back down a busy side street and found a

small pavement café where he ordered a glass of sherbet and some oat cakes and gloomily sat watching life go by.

He had made his mind up to stay in the city for as long as his pay from the attack on the fort held out; so now he needed to find somewhere to lay his head. As he sipped his sherbet and nibbled at one of the oat cakes a short grizzled and bald middle aged man dressed in a loose white gown emerged from the café and began to sweep away dust from around the tables.

Something about the man caught James' attention. He looked closely and saw it - the man was European! His skin was burnt to a mahogany colour, but his eyes were dark blue and his features were certainly not Moorish. As the man approached James caught his eye.

"You are European?" he said in English.

"Dutch," the man replied in the same language. James grinned.

Koos Muhren and his wife Ingrid had been taken nine years earlier while on their way back to Holland from London - where they had lived for over six years. Koos had been employed by a small shipping company before it went out of business leaving them with very little savings. Despondent, they had decided to return home, where, although they had no close family, they thought there was a better chance of starting again. Instead, they had ended up in a Turkish slave market where they were sold as a couple to a Jewish merchant who had fingers in various pies; one of which was a number of small cafes.

Their purchaser was a fair man and when he discovered that Ingrid was an excellent cook he had installed them in one of his establishments. They had worked long and hard hours and eventually, after three years they had been rewarded with a small share in the café. The money was not enough to make them comfortable, but it was enough for them to get by, with a little set aside.

James learned all this within half an hour of meeting Koos. He had also asked his new friend if there was anywhere close by where he might rent a room and was delighted when he was offered one above the café at a very reasonable rate.

Ingrid was a plump rosy cheeked woman who seemed to be

permanently welded to a pristine white apron. She had never had children of her own and within a week of his arrival she doted on him like a son. And for his part James laid bare his reason for being in the city.

His surrogate mother was moved to tears by his sad tale and by his melancholy mood . . . and one morning she suggested a way by which he might be re-united with his lost love.

31

James listened with a growing sense of hope as Ingrid outlined a possible plan. She was friendly with a regular customer, the wife of a merchant who dealt in hand made jewellery and fine fabrics. This merchant had secured a position whereby, with other selected merchants, he offered his wares for sale within the palace walls. His wife was allowed to enter the female only sanctuary at the end of each month when the palace women were paid and it would be possible, Ingrid said, for a message to be passed during the next visit in a week's time.

"But would this woman do it?" James asked. Ingrid nodded.

"Leila will do it if sweetened by payment."

James spent a night of fevered excitement, tossing and turning in his bed. It could work couldn't it? Yes, but it depended on crucial factors: would Erin be allowed out or even choose to go out into one of the courtyards on the day? And would Leila recognise Erin amongst perhaps hundreds of other women if her most distinguishing feature - her hair - was covered up?

Leila sat at the table in the little kitchen and listened while Ingrid explained James' dilemma. She listened and sat opposite, James searched her face for a favourable sign. Finally, she nodded.

"It can be done," she said. "But you do not know where the girl is. She could be in any of a number of places. She may be in the Sultan's Court, or in the oda of one of the Sultan's two Ikbals. She may be in the retinue of the Valide Sultan or even in the *Kafes* where Prince Ibrahim languishes.

James looked on blankly as Leila spoke. "There may be problems in finding the girl," Ingrid said before outlining Leila's concerns. "The merchant women have to visit a number of courtyards and their visits take place over a number of days at the end of the month. If the girl can not be found you will have to wait another month before she can try again." James nodded. There could be obstacles; no, there *would* be obstacles, but that did not matter – there was hope in what before had seemed to be a hopeless situation!

The day approached and James wrote out his note. He told her to be brave and that the teeth of time would grind his bones to dust before, having found her, he would now abandon her. He also told her to return to the same place on Leila's next visit when he would send another message. He passed Leila the note and once again Ingrid described Erin's appearance: her height, flaming red hair, green eyes and the band of freckles across her nose.

"All you can do now is sit and wait," Ingrid said as Leila left the café.

The first day of the women merchant's visit to the palace drew to a close and in an agony of anticipation James sat outside the café scanning the street for a sign of Leila's approach. Finally he saw her and he leapt to his feet to stand with sweating palms as she neared. He searched her face and saw her shake her head slowly.

"We visited the oda of Besma," Leila said to Ingrid. "But there was no sign of the red headed one. We also visited the oda of Nubana, with the same result." She also told Ingrid of the news from Nubana's oda that the Ikbal and one of her ladies in waiting had been strangled on the orders of the Sultan! "Tomorrow," she continued, "we will visit the Sultan's Court and the day after, the Valide Sultan's large retinue, which are our most profitable visits." Ingrid smiled lightly at Leila's last words as her friend was well known for her love of a good profit. "If we have no success," Leila concluded, "the *Kafes* is our final visit until next month."

Ingrid translated Leila's words (leaving out the news of the Ikbal's death, which was not relevant) and a downcast James nodded his understanding.

The next day brought the same result, as did the next and

on the fourth day, unable to stand the tension of sitting at the café, he followed Leila to the Imperial Gate where he stood out of sight while she joined about a dozen other white linen clad merchant women with their carts of wares who were waiting for permission to enter. He stayed until the gate was opened and the women disappeared inside before wandering off aimlessly through the nearby streets to kill a little time.

Erin lined up with the others waiting for the Haznedar Usta to dispense coins from her velvet bag. She wasn't really concentrating on the proceedings as her mind was still reeling from the news that had found its way into the *Kafes.* She had heard that Firousi the tiny golden haired favoured gedikli of the Sultan had been poisoned. *Surely not!* She had thought; but then *tiny golden haired?* Her mind in turmoil, she had asked Hosneva to find out if her fears were warranted. They were.

The line shortened and soon it was her turn to sign the leather bound ledger. She curtsied to the Haznedar Usta, took her coins and then remembered just in time to curtsey again, before beginning to make her way back to the common room when she was stopped by Hosneva. "You do not wish to go into the courtyard Cyra?" Hosneva said.

"No Mistress my mood does not allow it," she answered quietly. Hosneva shook her head slowly.

"I understand your mood child; but what is done is done and life for you continues." Erin forced a thin smile.

"Yes Mistress my life continues; but I have lost everything I hold dear . . ."

"The pain will ease child."

"How can you say that, Mistress?" Erin said with a trace of anger in her voice. Hosneva ignored the tone and when she answered her own voice was without emotion.

"Many years ago Cyra, when I was not much younger than you a Tartar band raided my village. They killed my father and three younger brothers, they raped my mother before slitting her throat and then eight of them took turns with me before I was dragged naked to the market place and sold. I too have felt pain child." Erin lowered her head briefly then raised it again.

"Apologies Mistress," she said softly. "Perhaps with age this child will not act so selfishly." The older woman placed a hand on Erin's shoulder and smiled.

"Apologies are not necessary Cyra, all wounds to the heart inflicted on the young cut deeper than those inflicted on the old. Now," she said firmly, "away with you to the courtyard to spend your coin!"

With a brief backward glance and a little nod of the head in appreciation, Erin made her way into the spacious high walled enclosed courtyard with its guarded exit gate, where she joined a crowd of browsing women and eunuchs. She did not really want to buy anything but Hosneva's motherly words and her insistence that she 'spend her coin' forced her to at least look at the wares displayed on the dozen or so permanent trestle tables manned by merchant women dressed in long loose white linen shifts and matching white linen head scarves. She idly picked up then put down a pair of brocade slippers stitched with gold thread and beaded with pearls. She moved to another table and ran her hands over a bolt of sky blue silk shot with silver thread. "E-rin?" the oddly pronounced word took a long second to register. She looked up, surprise on her face.

"My name," she said. "You speak my name!" The middle aged woman smiled.

"Yes, and I carry a message from one who waits," she said, handing Erin a small folded piece of paper. Erin looked blankly at the piece of paper in her open palm and shook her head.

"A message?" was all that she could say.

"Yes, read it somewhere safe and write your reply. We will leave the courtyard in one hour."

Sat in a quiet corner of the common room she unfolded the piece of paper and her heart lurched and her stomach turned somersaults as she realised who the short message was from.

She read it over three times and would have read it a fourth, but for the tears of joy that blurred her vision. *He was alive! He was free!* She clasped the message to her breast, rose and made her way quickly to her room where she penned a response before flying back down the stairs and out of the double doors leading to the courtyard. There, she checked her pace, took a slow deep breath and casually strolled over to the stall behind which the bearer of wonderful news stood.

She picked up an amber necklace and briefly held it to her throat before putting it down carefully and checking to see if anyone was looking in her direction. Nobody was paying her any attention, so she quickly passed the folded piece of paper to the woman who tucked it into a pocket and nodded.

Leila's face registered shock as the grinning infidel took the message from her hand, read it quickly, then threw his arms around her and hugged her to his broad chest. "I am a married woman!" she squeaked. James released her and apologised and she tried to look affronted, but her stern look faded and was then replaced by a smile. "You are pleased?" she asked. He fairly bounced up and down in his excitement.

"You have given me hope!" he shouted.

"He is pleased," Ingrid said in translation.

He paid Leila a bonus for bringing him such joy and asked her if she would take another message on her next visit. She said that she would, before reminding him that the price he had paid was for the first message only.

Later lay on the bed in his room his elation cooled a little. It was wonderful to learn that she was safe and well and the loving words in her reply almost brought tears to his eyes - but what now? Were they fated to send messages back and forth until they both grew old and weary? NO! There had to be a way! An hour later as he lay staring up at the cracks in the plastered ceiling above his head the germ of an idea began to form.

As the days went by Hosneva noticed a welcome change in Cyra. *She has taken heed*, she thought, and was pleased that her wise words had been well received. For her part, Erin determined that she would push all sad and bad thoughts to the back of her mind. During quiet times, mainly when she lay in her bed, her 'sisters' faces did swim into view and she allowed herself to grieve and shed a tear for young lives so cruelly snuffed out. "I will never forget you," she would whisper firmly before shutting the door of her mind to sorrow and trying to concentrate on a brighter future.

Leila shook her head. "There is much risk," she said flatly. James noted the tone of her voice and turned to face Ingrid.

"It can be done; I know it can!" he said.

He had explained his plan to Ingrid that morning. Told her that if Leila was to take a hidden spare linen shift and head scarf in with her wares, she could pass it with a note from him to Erin telling her to don the clothes (making sure to hide her hair under the scarf) and when the women began to make their way out, she would casually follow at the rear of the little party where none of the women would notice her. When they approached the gate she would move close to the other women, keep her head down and follow them out of the gate. Once outside the women would not congregate as they did on waiting to enter, they would rather split up and go their separate ways.

"She if afraid that she will be discovered," Ingrid said. James shook his head.

"She can move to the head of the women and be out of the gate before Erin even approaches it, he countered. Ingrid translated James' words, but again Leila was not convinced.

"And if she is caught, how will she explain her clothes?" she said.

"She will say that she made them up from inside the palace somewhere," James replied when Ingrid had relayed Leila's concerns. Again Leila's face showed doubt. "Tell her," he said with a last throw of the dice, "that I will give her ten times the money that I have given her before if she will agree." Ingrid translated. Leila paused for several seconds before she said: "Twenty times." James saw the slow smile blossom on Ingrid's face and expelled a long breath in sweet relief.

The day finally arrived and James decided that he could not risk standing outside the Imperial Gate to see if his plan had borne fruit. *I would betray my emotions, as I am sure would she*, he thought. *So it is best that I remain waiting here at the café well away from curious gazes.*

He carefully wrote down instructions and begged her to follow them to the letter. That done, he added a request for her to destroy the note when she had read it and finally said that if things did not work out she must say that she herself had made the linen clothes and that she had no help from anyone else. He handed the note to Leila, telling her as he did so the final wording and taking the chance again to reassure her that she would not be at risk.

Erin joined the crowd out in the landscaped courtyard and as soon as she saw that Leila was not busy she made her way over. The merchant, spotting her approach reached under the stall and from a shelf took out a small roll of dark green silk; she then named a price and held out a hand. Confused, Erin reached into a pocket, took out some coins and gave then to her. "The colour will suit you, and if not, please return before we leave in two hours and I will exchange it," Leila said casually as she handed the silk over and nodded towards the entrance door.

Back in her room Erin unrolled the silk, and puzzled, saw that there was a white linen garment and head scarf together with a folded piece of paper wrapped in it.

Her heart pounding in her chest, she snatched up the message and her eyes began to widen as she read. Seconds later she stepped out of her dress and donned the white garment. She then slipped her own dress back on over it to make sure that the hidden garment did not show.

Satisfied, she tied the headscarf around her head and firmly tucked in her rebellious hair that, as ever, threatened to run wild. She removed the scarf, patted her hair into some kind of order and took several deep breaths.

The crowds had thinned to almost nothing when she strolled back out into the courtyard and made a casual circuit of the stalls. She glanced across at the small barred and locked exit gate built into the stone walls and noticed that the single guard was stood loosely to attention with a bored look on his face.

Please, please, please remain so! She thought as she strolled over to sit on a bench beneath a blossoming cherry tree that was out of the guard's eye line.

There was almost no-one other than the merchant women in the courtyard now and they had all begun to pack away their wares into the little hand carts. She risked a glance across at Leila, who quickly lowered her head and carried on packing away her own goods. She *is as afraid as I am,* Erin thought. Two minutes later the guard stretched, yawned, and taking a thick key from a pocket, unlocked the gate and swung it open.

Erin got to her feet as the merchant women began to move. She strode quickly behind the tree, took the scarf from a pocket, wound it tightly around her head, tore off her dress, wrapped it into a tight ball and slipped it under an armpit - before stepping out to join the end of the line of women who, with their backs to her, were moving over to the gate.

Do not look at him and keep your green eyes lowered, she told herself as she lifted a quick hand to her head to make sure that none of her unruly hair was showing.

The line of women began to pass through the gate and she fixed her eyes firmly on the broad lower back of the woman in front. Seconds that seemed to stretch forever passed and then she jumped in shock as there was a heavy clang behind her that was followed by – what until that very instant had been a doom laden sound – the sound of a turning key. *Thank you God!* She murmured, before adding mentally: *But there are still courtyard gates to pass through and there is still the main gate.*

The line of women passed down a narrow roofed and colonnaded passage that opened out onto a large courtyard at the end of which there was another gate. She was relieved to see that it stood open.

They passed through into another landscaped courtyard and although the huge crenelated gate with its two pointed towers at the far end stood open, there were two guards. But again to her relief, they stood facing towards the palace entrance.

The little line of women passed through what she recalled from her entrance all those many months ago, was the *Gate of Salutation* and then they were in the First Courtyard at the end of which stood the gateway to freedom - that was shut!

Heart thumping and knees suddenly weak, Erin kept her head low as the procession of women with their little handcarts crossed the courtyard and approached the two guards who stood idly by the gate *Please . . . Please . . . Please*, she muttered fervently again under her breath as the distance slowly, oh so slowly closed.

The guards stepped out and with hardly a glance at the women, swung the heavy doors open . . . and for the first time in all those miserable months, she caught sight of normal life outside the confines of the palace grounds. And then, it was done! She stood outside in the street among a host of early evening city dwellers going about their business.

The group of women melted into the crowds and she was left with a pale faced Leila who was anxious to move away from the gate. "Come," the merchant ordered, as she placed a hand on the young woman's arm and quickly led her off in the direction of a side street.

Erin's head was whirling. She was free! And all that mattered now was that she was on her way to him - after that she didn't dare to think what their future might hold.

"Is he near?" she said breathlessly. Leila managed a smile.

"He is not far, come, it is but two minutes walk."

James had not moved from the little first floor window, where his moods had swung wildly between longed for hope and dreaded disappointment over the last two agonisingly long hours.

His back suddenly stiffened as he caught sight of Leila pulling her little handcart. Was she alone? He craned his neck, and there! There at Leila's side a small figure with head bowed! And from beneath the figure's head scarf a stray tress of fiery hair! He raced for the door, pounded down the rickety stairs and out into the street and came to a skidding stop.

From thirty feet away she saw the brawny deeply tanned figure with close cropped fair hair and heavily stubbled chin staring back at her. It was . . . wasn't it? But this figure was that of a man, surely not the boy she had come to love? Then he smiled.

Her heart leaped up into her mouth and hot tears welled up

in her eyes as she raced across the space that separated them and flung her self into his arms. "Oh James!" she repeated over and over again, and in reply a deep shuddering breath and a little strangled sob. He slowly removed her arms from around his neck and still not trusting his voice, held her gently at arms length, smiled and nodded slowly, before moving over to the waiting woman. After brief exchanged words he pressed some gold coins into her hand and then turned and made his way back to her side.

"Come," he said, his voice shaking a little with emotion as he took her hand in his and led her back up the stairs to his room. He closed the door on the world and this time didn't wait for her to fly into his arms.

Much later, when her 'gift' had been bestowed and his eyes closed, she lay with her head resting on his shoulder and with a finger gently traced the livid scar that crossed his chest. She would not ask him about it. He would tell her when he decided to.

Darkness had fallen when they made love again and this time, unlike the first frantic life affirming time, it was gentle and deeply, deeply beautiful. And then they talked. She told him what had befallen her and of the deaths of Alice and Anna - and in the darkness he had nodded sadly as he read her pain.

She cried when he told her about the dreadful fate of young Jonathan and was greatly saddened to hear of the deaths of Samuel and the others. He told her how he had descended into barbarism and why, and she kissed him and told him that it was a good man who could lay bare his soul as he had done. And finally he had told her who was the true architect of their misery and this time her anger burned and he had promised that somehow, some way, they would see that justice be served.

In the early hours, well east of midnight, he awoke with a start from a blood drenched dream. He opened his eyes and inches from his face he beheld a soft moon lit vision. A wild tangle of hair framing a heart shaped face; a tiny frown crease between arched eyebrows; a little band of freckles that marched across a button nose and long curled lashes that guarded the portals to a soul - the twin emerald orbs that held him an oh so willing captive.

He was a simple fisherman and did not have the words of a poet to describe the sight but if he had suddenly discovered those words, they would perhaps have included *ethereal* and *achingly beautiful.*

He raised his head from the pillow, leaned forward, and placed the softest of kisses on the tip of her nose - and experienced a sudden stirring in his groin. He fought and mastered it and slowly, reluctantly, turned onto his back.

Later in the pre-dawn early gloom she awoke and saw again the livid white scar that began by his left armpit, crossed a heavily muscled breast, leapt the valley in between to emerge and cross his right breast, before finishing close to his right armpit. She lifted her left arm with the intention of placing a hand gently over his heart, but sleep heavy, the hand landed with much more force than she had meant and a long fingernail caused a sharp intake of breath and a soft moan to issue from his lips. She whispered a soft "sorry my love" into his ear and "shushed" him back to sleep.

The sun rose over the crowded roof tops and soft golden light flooded their little room bringing with it the shared waking knowledge that two individual lives were now forever one. They lay close together in bed; she feeling safe and secure in his muscular arms, he quietly revelling in his new role of protector. She nuzzled his ear, a deep growl emerged from his throat and she squeaked in mock terror as he rolled onto her.

A half hour later and feeling the pangs of hunger after their love making they rose, dressed and made their way down the stairs and outside where he took her to a stall and bought a loaf of bread, some cheese and two large red apples which they took back to his room. Their breakfast over, they then discussed what they were going to do next. "We must get back to Algiers," he said firmly. She asked him why. "Because," he said, I must speak with the pirate Morat Rais." She frowned lightly.

"Why must you speak with him when he is the scoundrel who was responsible for our abduction?"

"Because, my love, he holds the key to Walter Coppinger's downfall!" She looked puzzled.

"But why would he offer any help?"

"Morat Rais owes me his life my love. And when we get

back to Algiers I will remind him of that debt."

"And then what?"

"I will ask him to come with me to the English Consul where he can attest in a written statement to Coppinger's guilt in setting up the raid."

"But why," she said, "would he admit to his own part in the kidnap?" James smiled.

"The old rogue has half a mind to seek an amnesty and return to his roots in Scotland where he will be able to live out his life in peace and his aid in bringing Coppinger to justice would stand him in good stead with the authorities!" She blinked.

"He has told you this!" He shook his head.

"No, it is not common knowledge; but I have been told by a friend, a trusted Cornish member of Admiral Bichnin's crew who was told in passing by the Admiral himself." She nodded.

"Then we must make haste," she said brightly, I do not wish to spend a minute more than needs be in this city of bitter memories."

They made their way down to the harbour where James made a number of enquiries before finding a vessel that was due to sail for Algiers the next day. He haggled with the master and it took almost the last of his purse before a deal was struck.

The journey was without incident and a month later the little vessel breached the gap in the mole and sailed into the harbour in Algiers. As they stood by the vessel's rail James' mind slid back that other time he had seen the gap in the mole; the time when he and his fellow prisoners had prayed for a fair wind; a wind that had arrived and ultimately carried his countrymen to their watery graves. She sensed his melancholy attitude.

"We reach the end of the first part of our journey back to the land of our birth my love!" she said with forced brightness. He turned to face her and smiled sadly.

"Yes . . . and thank you," he replied softly, knowing that she had noticed his solemn mood.

As soon as the vessel was moored they made their way onto the busy dock side where before they had taken a dozen paces he suddenly halted. "James?" she said, noting his hesitation. His shoulders rose and dropped.

"The city is large and I do not know where we might find our captain; or even if he is here and not out plying his infernal trade." She nodded then turned to face the mole and the dozen vessels that were tied up there. "The third one," she said pointing, I am sure that is the one that we were brought from Baltimore on." He followed her finger.

"Are you sure?" She nodded slowly.

"Yes . . . Yes, it is the same vessel!"

"Wait here," he said indicating a rough bench. "While I go and see if there is anyone aboard."

Erin sat on the wooden bench and watched as he made his way over to the track that led to the landward edge of the mole and from there up onto the broad stone breakwater itself. He reached the third vessel and she saw him tilt his head back and shout something. Half a minute later she saw a figure emerge on deck and apparently enter into a brief conversation with James. Two minutes more and James began to make his way back to her side.

He is at his palace," he said, "and the vessel's watchman has given me directions. It is a goodly stroll my love so it is well that we have a fine day for it!"

An hour later they entered a tree lined approach road that led to a substantial white walled building with a central blue domed cupola. "A grand home," James said with a nod, "But not as grand as that of the Admiral, which I think is not far from here itself." At mention of the Admiral Erin frowned lightly.

"I have spent time in his company James and he is a man of some breeding, but you told me that he regarded you as his slave. Will he not lay claim to you again if he finds that you have returned?" He shrugged.

"It is possible my love, but he holds me in some regard apparently and I am hopeful that he will look kindly on our plight. And if not, as long as we are together, we will somehow prevail."

James recognised the guard on the entrance door to the palace immediately as one of the captain's crewmen who took part in the attack at the fort and was himself recognised. They exchanged greetings and the man unlocked the door and ushered them through into the landscaped gardens, before locking the door behind him and signalling for them to follow.

Within two minutes they were sat in a cool reception room while the guard went off to carry news of their arrival to his master. Ten minutes more and the man returned to lead them to the captain's apartments.

"Ah, the insolent slave!" Morat said as they were led into his presence. "And, if my eyes do not deceive me, the fiery one who by rights should now grace the Sultan's bedchamber!" he added with a rich laugh. James nodded.

"The same captain; and now we are come to beg favour." Morat's heavy brow ceased into a frown and he said:

"Favour; what favour?"

"A favour due, captain, for a service freely given."

"Ah, yes, you speak of the hand that severed a hand that would have blown a pretty hole in my head . . ." James nodded.

"We would ask that you come with us to the English Consul to attest in writing to the part in our kidnap played by Walter Coppinger." Morat snorted.

"And why pray should I incriminate myself by so doing?"

"Perhaps by so doing you would pave the way to gaining a future pardon?" Morat's eyes narrowed and he scratched his chin reflectively.

"It is true," he said quietly, "that I have thought it perhaps time for me to move away from current employment and to shed the name of Morat Rais for my birth name of Robert Fleck . . ."

"Then," James said forcefully; "what better way to achieve that goal than by being the person who delivers to the authorities the one who was the true force behind the kidnap of over one hundred villagers!"

Morat continued to scratch his chin. *Yes,* he thought, *I owe him my life but If I grant his request I incriminate myself; but then I am far removed from English justice and should my testimony include a plea for pardon I can wait here in safety for a response. If the response is favourable I can then decide if I accept or not - and if the response is not favourable . . . then I remain Morat Rais, Scourge of Christendom.* He nodded slowly.

"Very well," he said casually. "I will repay the debt."

John Frizell was startled when the door to his little office was flung back and the hulking figure of Morat Rais strode through closely followed by a man and a young woman.

"Captain . . ." he managed, before Morat waved a dismissive hand.

"I have come," the Captain boomed, "to make use of your consular offices." Frizell nodded dumbly. "You will write down my statement regarding the capture of the Baltimore slaves. You will also write down a separate request from me to the English authorities for their consideration towards granting me amnesty. I will sign both statements." He then paused for a second or two before adding: "And should you reveal anything regarding my own request to any other living person I will return and slit your throat." Frizell swallowed hard.

An hour later the Consul had taken the Captain's statement regarding his plea for amnesty. The testament was signed by Morat Rais (in the name of Robert Fleck) and countersigned by Frizell, before the Consul applied the Consular Seal and addressed it to the First Lord of the Admiralty, the Earl of Portland. The second document outlining the Captain's dealings with Walter Coppinger that led to that fateful June day in 1631 was also signed and sealed.

"Your plea for amnesty will need to be ratified by King Charles," Frizell said as he handed the document over to the Captain. "But the Earl of Portland will first need to give his support." Morat frowned and was about to say something; but Frizell continued quickly:

"The First Lord would, perhaps, prefer to see you swinging from a gibbet," he said coolly, looking over the top of his spectacles at the Captain. "But he will almost certainly give his backing, as the name Morat Rais is well known and feared and his decision to return to a law abiding life might very well encourage others – of a similar nature – to follow suit."

Frizell then handed the second document to James. "The Admiralty will not act on this document, you must present it to the Courts and it is for them to decide what action to take."

Minutes later they stood outside Frizell's office and James

held out his hand.

"I do not absolve you from all blame," he said, "but I understand that your part in that which has befallen us and the other Baltimore captives was one that was born of the times." The captain nodded as he took James' hand and shook it vigorously.

"And now," he said, "you will make haste to deliver my request and statement to England." James nodded but then felt a tug on his arm. He turned to Erin who said softly "George?"

"The boy George," James said; "Would you allow him to return with us?" The captain's face hardened slightly.

"The boy has embraced Islam and is well cared for . . . but," he added with a sly smile, "should your entreaties on my behalf bear fruit . . . then I will allow him to accompany me on my return."

"You give your word?"

"It is given." James felt another tug on his arm.

"His mother and brothers?" Before he could repeat the question Morat growled.

"There are a total of some 20,000 slaves in Algiers and the only details written down are the prices they have brought in the market. There is no way that the boy's family can be located. They could still be somewhere in the city or they could have been purchased by visiting merchants from anywhere along the coast. Now do not try my temper. Are you ready to depart?" James saw that it was useless to press the captain further and nodded.

"We are captain . . . should you grant us one more small boon."

"And what might that be?" The captain asked with a strong note of exasperation in his voice.

"We are lacking any means to pay for our voyage and our lodgings in London." Morat's salty oath brought a quick blush to Erin's cheeks but the belly laugh that followed brought a smile.

32

Their second long voyage together passed like the first, without incident, and after more than a month at sea the vessel nosed its way into the muddy brown water of the River Thames. They stood and watched at the vessel's rail; marvelling at the activity on or around the dozens of vessels moored at busy jetties along either bank, where regiments of dockside labourers swarmed like ants loading or unloading cargo from, or bound for, distant ports.

Their own vessel inched its way into a vacant berth on the north bank of the river and soon they made their way back onto dry land where they secured a hackney carriage to take them to the Admiralty building.

During the journey they both commented on the differences between Algiers, Constantinople and London. Where the Moorish cities presented remarkably clean and bright faces under pleasant blue skies, the London they were passing through was overcast and dull beneath a smoke hazed canopy. Its narrow crowded streets were awash with the stench of stagnant water and raw sewage and many of the sallow faced people they passed were dressed in nothing better than rags.

They arrived at the imposing Admiralty building and made their way up the steps and into a reception area where they presented themselves and were asked to state their business before being told to wait until someone would be available to see them. A full hour passed before they were escorted into a large office. "The First Lord is at present consulting with King Charles at the Palace of Westminster," the man behind the desk, who was wearing the uniform of an Admiral, said coolly remaining seated. "I am told that your presence is connected with a plea for pardon, is this so?" James nodded.

"It is sir, we come bearing a written plea authorised by the English Consul in Algiers."

"And this plea is in the name of that blackguard, Morat Rais, is it not."

"It is sir and we also come with written testimony from the same man naming the person responsible for the raid on Baltimore that led to over one hundred villagers – including ourselves," he said tersely, "being stolen and sold into slavery." The plump, red faced and middle aged Admiral's face took on an interested look.

"It was a most a grievous action and one that has angered the King greatly," he said as James took the sealed documents from a pocket and handed them across the desk. The Admiral took up the document addressed to the First Lord and breaking the seal, sat for a full two minutes reading it before nodding. "The man has caused great distress with his attacks against unarmed vessels and civilians," he muttered, as he placed the document down on the desk. "And you . . ." he waved a hand in James' and Erin's direction.

"James Pallow and Erin O'Connor," James responded.

"You are familiar with this rogue Mister Pallow?" James nodded.

"We have spent long weeks, even months, in the man's company," he said.

"And you will attest to his sincerity in seeking a pardon?"

"He is sincere in his wish to renounce Islam and take up again his birth name of Robert Fleck and retire to Scotland." The Admiral pursed his lips, drummed his fingers on the top of the desk and sat in quiet reflection for half a minute.

"The King will have the final say; but I am sure that he will look favourably on a course of action that, with the retirement of such a rogue, will render our seas and shores much safer," he said nodding firmly.

"And the other reason for our presence?" James asked. The Admiral shrugged.

"You refer to evidence given by Fleck regarding the raid on Baltimore?"

"I do sir; evidence that places the blame firmly on the instigator, Walter Coppinger." The Admiral picked up the sealed document then handed it back to James.

"This is a matter for the Irish Courts," he said firmly, "And must be placed before them." James shook his head.

"The man holds great sway with jury's in Cork and would likely escape punishment."

"Then you must present the document to Richard Boyle, Great Earl of Cork, who is Joint Lord Justice of Ireland. He will ensure that any proceedings taken will be fair and just."

"Will you provide us with a letter of introduction sir?" Erin asked. The Admiral rose from his seat.

"I will see to it this minute," he said holding out his hand.

Once more they sought out a vessel and within the week their hackney carriage was driving down a tree lined avenue that ended at the impressive porch of a large Elizabethan country manor house. "Justice waits within those walls," Erin said quietly as the carriage pulled up and James paid the driver and they dismounted.

Their knock to the door was answered by a liveried servant who directed them to a reception room where, after accepting James' letter of introduction he left them while he went in search of his master.

"The Earl will see you now," the servant said twenty minutes later. "Please follow me."

The tall thin elegantly dressed late middle aged man rose from his seat behind a desk and held out a hand in welcome, then directed them to take a seat before returning to his own chair behind the desk. "I have read with interest the letter from London and am intrigued with its suggestion that you have vital information relating to the dreadful events at Baltimore." James nodded.

"We do sir and it is Information that damns a man of some standing in Cork." The Earl's eyes opened wider.

"A man of Cork you say!"

"We do sir," James said firmly holding out Fleck's testament. The Earl took the document from James' hand, broke the seal and settled back in his chair to read while James and Erin looked on and were relieved to see the look on Boyle's face slowly change from one of interest to outrage.

"You attach credence to this document?" he asked sharply as he placed the testimony back on his desk.

"We do sir," Erin replied. "For we ourselves were taken captive on the day in question and have spent much time in the Captain's presence."

"And this captain," Boyle said, "he is seeking pardon?"

"He is sir," Erin replied. The Earl nodded.

"He is a scoundrel that has greatly tested his majesty's temper and an end to his pirateering would be most welcomed."

"He is sincere sir, and has even promised to return to England with one of the Baltimore captives, a young boy of our acquaintance." The Earl picked up the letter and briefly scanned it again.

"This Morat Rais, or Robert Fleck, describes in detail his dealings with Coppinger and the man's appearance, down to the fact that he wears a ruby ring on the third finger of his left hand."

"Proof if needed sir that he has entered into close contact with the man," James said. Boyle nodded.

"Indeed, and it is true that Coppinger has gained a reputation throughout Cork for sharp practices . . . but to condemn a whole village of men, women and children to a Moorish slave market!"

"He has tried and failed for years to oust the settlers," James said calmly, "and has employed all means fair and foul at his disposal. This last, was his most vile and the one that succeeded." The Earl smiled thinly.

"It may have succeeded in ousting the settlers Mr Pallow; but he has gained little from his victory . . ." James frowned.

"How so sir?"

"Because not long after he rebuilt the burned village from his own pocket, the pilchards upon which the fishers relied on stopped running. He now, so I believe, has an idle processing plant and many of the cottages lie empty with their occupants moving on to other employments."

"A small payment for a grievous sin," James said softly. "But the man still stands accused of the grievous sin."

"Then he must stand trial and if found guilty pay the penalty."

"And therein lies the problem sir;" James muttered shaking his head. "Will he be found guilty? For the man is known to exercise much power over juries." The Earl smiled thinly.

"There will be no chance for him to use his influence. He will be tried in Dublin by the Court of Star Chamber." Seeing that both James and Erin looked puzzled at his words, the Earl continued: "The Court of Star Chamber does not sit with a jury.

Coppinger will be prosecuted by a King's Council and will be given the chance to refute charges and to speak on his own behalf. If he is found guilty there will, unfortunately, be no death penalty – but he will face life, or long imprisonment, seizure of assets and property and possibly whipping and or mutilation."

James turned to Erin and she saw conflicting emotions on his face. She knew he, like her, would have preferred a life for a life in payment for Thomas and the other lives cruelly snatched away, but months ago they had despaired of Coppinger ever being brought to book at all. She smiled back at him and nodded slowly and was pleased to see him return her nod. The Earl then rose from his chair, held out a hand and said: "There will be a short delay before the trial can proceed, but with God's grace you will see justice done."

Two weeks later Walter Coppinger's face displayed a mixture of shock and outrage as three of the Sheriff's men forced their way passed one of his servants into his Bandon study and arrested him. He was manacled and bundled into an enclosed carriage and driven on the journey to Dublin.

They sat at the back of the courtroom as the judge, in his red and white robes with broad black sash, full bottomed powdered wig and stiff white cross collar – that represented the twin white tablets of the Ten Commandments – entered and took up his seat. Walter Coppinger, dressed head to toe in sober black, was then brought into the courtroom, where he stood defiantly in the raised dock as the charge was read out to him. A smirk slowly spread across his face and when asked to enter a plea he spat out the words, "*Non Culpabilis*!"

"He pleads not guilty," Erin said turning quickly to James - who smiled. He knew no Latin but would have been shocked if the blackguard would have pleaded anything else.

As Robert Fleck's detailed account of the prisoner's involvement was read out, the sneer on Coppinger's face slowly faded and by the time James had given his own account of Fleck's' words of condemnation, that face had turned an ashy grey.

"You refute the charge?" the King's Council asked suavely. Walter swallowed hard and his voice quavered a little as he replied.

"Of course," he said before his anger reasserted itself. "How can you," he almost shouted at the Judge, "accept the word of a murderous rogue who has forsaken his religion against that of a devout practising Christian?"

"Would you say that you are a man who holds grudges?" the King's Council said in an apparent change of direction. Coppinger frowned.

"I am a man of strong principles," he replied.

"Indeed, and those principles have led you to pursue all manner of people through the courts, have they not?"

"Yes, as I have said; I am a man of strong principles." The King's Council nodded.

"And have you not pursued various actions against the Baltimore settlers over the space of many years?"

"Yes; as was my right in law."

"Yes, and when your final recourse to the law failed after the settler's 21 year lease ran out on, what was it? Oh yes, the 20th of June in the year of Our Lord, 1630, you then decided to set in motion non legal action . . ." Coppinger gripped the edge of the dock firmly and his eyes blazed.

"I did not!" he yelled. The King's Council shrugged lightly.

"You have said earlier that you consider yourself to be a man of principle did you not?" Walter nodded. "A man of principle who considered him self wronged would take much satisfaction in seeing that wrong put to rights, would he not?"

"Of course, as would any man of honour . . ."

"He might even gain extra satisfaction if that wrong was righted at a significant juncture." Walter frowned and shrugged again as the King's Council moved closer to the dock and looked up at him. "Tell me, Mr Coppinger," he said softly, "What was the date of the attack on defenceless Baltimore?" The blood slowly drained from Walter's face as he looked down at the King's Council.

"No response, Mr Coppinger? Very well I will answer my own question. The brutal attack on Baltimore took place on June

20th, 1631 . . . EXACTLY one year to the day after the lease expired! A case of poetic retribution is it not, in the eyes of a strongly principled man who considered himself wronged!"

When the judge's verdict was given it arrived devoid of emotion. "I would, if given the power," he said flatly, "have delivered one word; *suspendatur* - let him hang. That power is denied to this court; therefore all your properties and assets are forfeited to the Crown. From those assets the sum of £500 is to be paid to James Pallow in part recompense for the death of his brother and you will suffer 50 lashes before you are taken to serve a total of 25 years in prison." Walter reeled, his hands again grasped the rim of the dock for support and were then torn loose as two court wardens dragged him down and led him away.

Erin turned to James. "The sentence is one of lingering death my love," she said softly. "For he is a man of years and surely will never again foul the blessed air or light of day with his evil presence. And now that justice is served," she added, "there is one other place where we must go to pay respects."

They stood on the little pebble beach looking out to sea for a minute then made their way over towards the necklace of almost newly thatched cottages where they stopped for a few seconds outside the door way of what was the Gaunt's.

She shook her head and they moved over to the furthest cottage, the one that held terrible memories for him. He stood outside the front door and she knew that a dark bloody scene was re-playing through his mind. She reached out and took his hand and he turned to face her with the faintest trace of a sad smile one his lips. She nodded and then side by side they made their way up to the village proper, where beneath the walls of the *Fort Of The Jewels* – two full years after their last visit – the stalls were laid out for the Midsummer Day Fair.

"It seems a lifetime ago," Erin said softly. He nodded.

"And we were both little more than children," he replied. They made their way passed the stalls and almost unconsciously found themselves at the gates of Tullagh Church and its little graveyard that faced out to sea.

Inside the cemetery they stood silently facing the graves of his parents and his brother. She squeezed his hand and as she did so a firm wind, carrying on it, perhaps, the faintest scent of jasmine and orange blossoms sprang from out of the east; and with it brought ghostly shades of pale faces. Dear, dear, gentle Alice; bewitched Anna; poor Jonathan; baby Mary; Helen and her darling boys and all those others who were ripped from their homes and carried away to a strange land where tortured dreams were all that remained of their own far off land . . . their land of lost content.

The wave of sadness slowly faded and as they stood hand in hand looking out over the bay and over Inisherkin Island to the hazy eastern horizon, she raised her free hand and pressing it against her swollen stomach, felt the first kicks of new life.

The Sack of Baltimore

Thomas Osborne Davis

The summer sun is falling soft o'er Carbery's hundred isles
The summer sun is gleaming still through Gabriel's rough defiles
Old Inisherkin's crumbled fane looks like a moulting bird,
And in a calm and sleepy swell the ocean tide is heard.
The hookers lie upon the beach; the children cease their play;
The gossips leave the little inn; the households kneel to pray;
And full of love, and peace, and rest - it's daily labour o'er -
Upon that cosy creek there lay the town of Baltimore.

A deeper rest, a starry trance, has come with midnight there;
No sound except that throbbing wave, in earth, or sea, or air.
The massive capes and ruined towers seem conscious of the calm;
The fibrous sod and stunted trees are breathing heavy balm.

So still the night, these two long barques round Dunashad that glide;
Might trust their oars - methinks not few - against the ebbing tide.
Oh! Some sweet mission of true love must urge them to the shore:
They bring some lover to his bride, who sighs in Baltimore!

All, asleep within each roof along that rocky street,
And these must be the lover's friends with gently gliding feet -
A stifled gasp! A dreamy noise! "The roof is in a flame!"
From out their beds, and to their doors, rush maid, and sire, and dame,
And meet upon the threshold stone the gleaming sabre's fall,
And o'er each black and bearded face the white or crimson shawl;
The yell of "Allah" breaks above the prayer, and shriek, and roar -
Oh! Blessed God! The Algerine is lord of Baltimore.
Then flung the youth his naked hand against the shearing

sword;
Then sprung the mother on the brand with which her son was gored;
Then sunk the gransire on the floor, his grand- babes clutching wild;
Then fled the maiden moaning faint, and nestled with the child,
But see, yon pirate strangled lies, and crushed with splashing heel,
While o'er him in an Irish hand, there sweeps his Syrian steel:
Though virtue sink, and courage fail, and miser's yield their store,
There's one hearth well avenged in the sack of Baltimore!

Mid-summer morn, in woodland nigh, the birds began to sing;
They see not how the milking maids – deserted in the spring!
Mid-summer day - this gallant rides from distant Bandon's town;
These hookers crossed from stormy Skull, that skiff from Affadown:
They only found the smoking walls, that neighbour's blood besprent,
And on the strewed and trampled beach awhile they wildly went;
Then dashed to sea, and passed Cape Cléire, and saw five leagues before
The pirate galleys vanishing that ravished Baltimore

Oh! Some must tug the galley's oar, and some must tend the steed;
This boy will bear a Sheik's chibouk, and that a Bey's jerreed.
Oh! Some are in the arsenals, by beauteous Dardanelles;
And some are in the caravan to Mecca's sandy dells.
The maid that Bandon gallant sought is chosen for the Dey:
She's safe - he's dead - she stabbed him in the Midst of his serai;
And when, to die a death of fire, that noble maid they bore,
She only smiled - O'Driscoll's child - she thought of Baltimore

'Tis two long years since sunk the town beneath that bloody band,
And all around its trampled hearths a larger concourse stands,

Where, high upon a gallows tree, a yelling wretch is seen -
'Tis Hackett of Dungarvan, he who steered the Algerine!
He fell amid a sudden shout, with scarce a passing prayer,
For he had slain the kith and kin of many a hundred there;
Some muttered of MacMurchadh, who brought the Norman o'er;
Some cursed him with Iscariot that day in Baltimore.

And Finally. . .

The sun has risen and set over 175,000 times since the events - actual and imagined - that are portrayed in this book took place. Those real life characters who appear in these pages may have faded into the mists of time, but their stories still resonate today in a world of religious and sectarian strife; in a world where greed, corruption and yes, slavery and piracy, still exist.

Baltimore's story was not, in the 1600's and 1700's a particularly uncommon one. During that period over 1,000,000 European men, women and children were stolen from their homes and sold in the slave markets of Algiers, Tunis and Morocco. Many were subsequently ransomed, many 'turned Turk' and embraced Islam and many more, like the victims from Baltimore, simply vanished from sight.

Now, almost 400 years after the event one can still come across numbers of blue eyed, fair haired Arab citizens of the cities of Algiers, Tunis and Morocco - throwbacks perhaps from the golden age of piracy?

Of the 107 men, women and children who were taken from Baltimore only two ever returned to tell their tale; a tale that has also been lost. Those two unknown people became, for the sake of this story, star crossed lovers Erin O'Conner and James Pallow.

The story you have just finished is one of 'faction'; that is to say that it is based on a mixture of fact, fiction and supposition.

MORAT RAIS who raided Baltimore was in fact a Dutch pirate,

Jan Janszoon. He converted to Islam in 1620. His fate has not been recorded. The only vague reference to it was that his end "was very bad".

MURAD IV who had banned alcohol died on February 9, 1640 from cirrhosis of the liver after a seizure brought on when witnessing an eclipse of the moon.

KOSEM Was an ethnic Greek, originally called Anastasia. As the Valide Sultan she was the power behind the throne for much of the reigns of her sons. She was murdered in 1651 on the orders of Turhan Sultana, mother of Mehmed IV, Kosem's grandson.

IBRAHIM I known as 'Ibrahim the Mad' became Sultan on the death of Murad IV. His reign was marked by a rapid decline in the power of the Empire. Notoriously unstable, he once had all 280 women in the harem sown into weighted sacks and thrown into the sea because he heard a rumour that his harem had been compromised by a man. He was deposed in a coup by the Grand Mufti and was strangled in 1648

ALI BICHNIN is recorded in history under a bewildering number of names, including Ali Bitshnin, Ally Pichelin, Ali Piccinino and Ali Pegelin. An Italian national, he died in 1645 of a mystery illness. It was popularly believed in Algiers that he was poisoned by agents of Ibrahim I.

WALTER COPPINGER was by all accounts a villain of the first order. He was never charged with being implicated in the abduction, but many threads lead to the conclusion that he was the prime mover. He regained control of Baltimore but it did him little good as the pilchard run suddenly stopped. Actions attributed to him in this work are a mixture of fact, supposition and fiction.

JAMES HACKETT was hung for his part in the abduction of the Baltimore villagers.

LIST OF BALTIMORE VICTIMS

William Mould and a Boy
Alexander Pumery and Wife
John Ryder, Wife and two Children
Robert Hunt and Wife
Abram Roberts, Wife and three Children

Corent Croffine, Wife, Daughter and Three Men
John Harris, Wife, Mother, three Children and Maid
Dermot Meregey, two Children and Maid
Richard Meade, Wife and three Children
Richard Lorye, Wife, Sister and four Children
Stephen Brodderbroke, Wife (pregnant) and two Children
Ould Haunkin, Wife and Daughter
Evans, Wife, Boy, Cook, Maid
Bessie Flood and Son
William Arnold, Wife and three Children
Michaell Amble, wife and Son
Stephen Pierse, Wife, Mother and two Children
William Symons, wife and two children
Christopher Norwey, Wife and Child
Sampson Rogers and Son
Besse Peeter and Daughter
Thomas Payne, Wife and two Children
Richard Watts, Wife and two Children
John Amble
Edward Cherrye
Robert Chimor, Wife and four Children
Timothy Corlew and Wife
John Slyman, Wife and two Children
Morris Power and Wife
William Gunter, Wife, Maid and seven Sons

REFERENCE SOURCES:
The Stolen Village by Des Ekin (The O'Brien Press Ltd)
Pirate Utopias by Peter Lamborn Wilson (Autonomedia)
White Gold by Giles Milton (Hodder & Stoughton)
Pirates of Barbary by Adrian Tinniswood (Vintage)
Kadin by Bertrice Small (Avon Books)

38783021R00153

Made in the USA
Charleston, SC
15 February 2015